The Secret Diaries of Abigail Titmuss

'When Abi poses for a set of pictures she feels sexy and is having a tremendous time. Readers sense this. Men are fascinated by real women with real bodies and real sexual appetites. The last Abi cover we put out sold astonishingly well. There is no one who shifts men's magazines like Titmuss.'

Phil Hilton, former editor of *Nuts* magazine.

'Abi exists as this strange sexualised cartoon of minor celebrity because that's what people, or enough people, want. Yet to read some of her critics – most of them women – you would think that she was the embodiment of every vice and indecency known to man.'

Andrew Anthony, *Observer Magazine*.

D1100370

The Secret Diaries of Abigail Titmuss

Abi Titmuss

With Lucie Cave

headline
review

Copyright © 2008 Abi Titmuss with Lucie Cave

The right of Abi Titmuss with Lucie Cave to be identified as the Authors of the Work has been asserted by them in accordance with the Copyright, Designs and Patents Act 1988.

First published in 2008 by
HEADLINE REVIEW
An imprint of HEADLINE PUBLISHING GROUP

1

Cataloguing in Publication Data is available from the British Library

978 0 7553 1790 5

Typeset in Garamond MT by Palimpsest Book Production Limited, Grangemouth, Stirlingshire

Printed and bound in Great Britain by
Clays Ltd, St Ives plc

Headline's policy is to use papers that are natural, renewable and recyclable products and made from wood grown in sustainable forests. The logging and manufacturing processes are expected to conform to the environmental regulations of the country of origin.

HEADLINE PUBLISHING GROUP
An Hachette Livre UK Company
338 Euston Road
London NW1 3BH

www.headline.co.uk
www.hachettelivre.co.uk

'If I'd observed all the rules, I'd never have got anywhere.'

Marilyn Monroe

Prologue

5am July 2004, Hackney. It's a warm summer morning – the birds are singing, the shopkeepers are already whistling and the traffic is beginning its daily build-up. A black cab approaches. I wait for a white van to pass me (with its obligatory toot) – then, in one swift move rip off my robe and throw it to the ground, pick up my brief-case and stick out my arm to hail the cab.

The driver pulls over trying desperately to avert his eyes.
The reason he's too scared to look at me is that I am completely, utterly naked. Even the pigeons are staring at me.

N.A.K.E.D.

(Well, except for a gorgeous pair of black Jimmy Choo's).

I forgot to mention that I am having the time of my life, although I am wondering how, in the name of arse (*my* arse), did I get here?

Let me take you on a journey. I must warn you, it's not for the faint-hearted and you might not like every step, but I hope that you will still enjoy reading it (even if you secretly don't want to).

One thing I do promise is that there will be plenty of surprises.

10th December 1998

We only had ten quid each to spend tonight, but I didn't want to go to some old spit-and-sawdust pub. I wanted to go somewhere nice, let our hair down and maybe meet some interesting men. After all, we deserved it after the hard week we'd had. We have celebrity magazines on the ward and I flick through them sometimes to try and spot nice places to go out. Whatever they hailed as the latest celebrity hotspot. None of the other nurses would bother, they'd be happy to hang out in the pub. So it was down to me to do the groundwork.

It wasn't that I wanted to meet any celebrities – I just had a desire to explore life and be a bit adventurous. And quite frankly if I spend any more time playing darts in the hospital social club, I'm going to start looking like Eric Bristow.

There are three of us that are best friends – Marisa, Katie and I – and we all work on the same ward together. We got dressed up in my little room in the nurses' home and waltzed down the road arm-in-arm, giggling. There's something about working so hard together and dealing with the difficult things we do on a daily basis, that makes us really close.

It's hard to understand what it feels like to be a doctor or a nurse unless you've been one. It is a staggeringly tough job. Watching my colleagues, and myself, scrape a living and creep further into debt, after three or four years at university and spending our days and nights caring for people, really angers me. And always makes me shout 'Oh sod it, let's party, I'll put it on my credit card!' after a couple of drinks.

I'd read about the Sanderson Hotel and it was a stone's throw from the hospital (no cab to pay for – perfect!). I thought it was so beautiful inside. Much more aesthetically pleasing than the Dog and Duck, that's for sure. The cheapest bottle of wine was £25 – ridiculous, but I didn't care. We clubbed together to pay for one bottle and made it last all night.

We wouldn't let people buy us drinks though – that was the girls' rule. Firstly that meant the bloke in question hanging around you all flipping night, and secondly I wasn't going to be the kind of girl who used men to buy them drinks. I love to banter but I can buy my own thanks.

10th April 1999

Went to a bar called The Fine Line in Fulham with my friend Anthea. We'd graduated a few months ago and she's just got a job as a nurse in the Chelsea and Westminster Hospital. A tall guy kept looking at me across the bar and smiling. I recognised him from TV but couldn't put my finger on what it was he did.

He was very handsome though and didn't try to hide the fact he had his eye on me. He came over and introduced himself as John. 'That's it!' Anthea whispered afterwards. 'He's John Leslie, the guy who used to host *Blue Peter* and does *Wheel of Fortune* or something.' She reckons his last girlfriend was Catherine Zeta Jones. Blimey boyo. John asked if we wanted to come to a club called Crazy Larry's. We said we might, then followed approximately 7.6 minutes later (acting cool, obviously!).

In the club he kept telling me he wanted to take me out for lunch. He was acting pretty suave and confident, so naturally I pretended I wasn't the slightest bit interested. He was clearly used to getting the girls, so I wasn't going to give him my number just like that. He did sound nice though, and I don't think I'd been asked to lunch before. It sounded quite grown-up

I looked at him and said, 'Alright, I'll say it to you once and if you remember it then I'll come out with you.' He seemed to like that. Then I walked away, all full of myself. And full of 'house white'.

13th May 1999

I've worked as a staff nurse on Bentham Ward – Acute Admissions Unit – at University College Hospital for seven months now. On a good day this averages fourteen hours straight. I'm in charge of twenty-three beds and from the minute I get on to the ward I think of nothing except patients. And as rewarding as it is to know you've helped save lives, it's incredibly hard work, terribly underpaid and I have never felt like I fitted in. I fell into nursing because I was interested in becoming a doctor, but didn't have the right A-levels for medical school. My ten GCSEs got me straight into university for a nursing diploma, and I thought that if I liked it I could progress to medicine. Although I wasn't really sure what I wanted, to be honest.

Deep down my heart lies in neither of these professions. Acting – that's what I really want to do. I'd been in loads of plays at school, and I'd even been talent-spotted to act at other schools (ahh, *The Land Of Green Ginger* at Carre's Boys' Grammar. I was the only girl – it was brilliant!).

At university I had the chance to do some drama again. I joined the drama club and we staged a production of Monty Python's *Life Of Brian*. We played to packed audiences each night and I LOVED it. I remember us standing onstage on the last night, in the final scene, me as 'Mr Cheeky' in a stripy dressing gown, all of us on balsa-wood crucifixes, singing 'Always look on the bright side of life' and thinking, 'This is what I want to do!' Fame and money didn't even occur to me. I just wanted to act. And to learn.

By some strange quirk of fate, my nurses' flat is right next door to the Royal Academy Of Dramatic Art (RADA) on Gower Street.

The concrete wall that originally separated my block and the famous drama school was knocked down a few years ago, leaving their class-room windows exposed. I often sit and stare out of the window, craning for a glimpse into this other world, where young men and women can be whoever they want to be and seem to have so much ahead of them. But tonight was when it hit me. It's like I had a light-bulb moment. All these young faces were dancing around behind the glass. I think they were pretending to be trees. I know it sounds daft but as I watched their expressive, expectant features all lit up, it suddenly didn't feel like such an alien concept that I could be one of them.

Not that I have any burning desire to be a tree.

20th May 1999

Today was an exceptionally busy day on the ward, but I managed to snatch this little conversation with an elderly, hard of hearing patient. It was so sweet and funny, I scribbled it down on a napkin, for posterity.

It went like this,

'Hello, my name's Abi and—'
　　'AMY?'
　　'No, Abi.'
　　'ANNIE?'
　　'No, ABI.'
　　'ABBA?'
　　'ABI. Like Abbey National.'
　　'Oh! You're from the Abbey National!'
　　'NO. I'M A NURSE.'

Pause.

'RIGHT. WELL WHAT'S YOUR NAME?'

It made me think again about giving up nursing but despite that, tonight was the night I made the phone call to both my parents and told them the 'wonderful' news that I had changed my mind about going to medical school and instead, I wanted to act. They never quite know what I'm going to do next, and so they took it surprisingly well.

Now the decision's made it feels astonishingly liberating. It is also quite terrifying. What if I'm no good at it? I looked out of my window at the twinkling lights of London, full of possibility, and twirled around my little room.

I am free!

'No one can make you feel inferior without your consent.'
Eleanor Roosevelt, 1937

19th September 1999

John took me to *An Audience with Tom Jones* at the London Studios. It was being filmed for ITV. You couldn't move for celebrities. What a night! After the show we stood at the bar and there were hordes of girls trying to get John's attention. I leant across the bar trying to catch the barman's eye – 'white wine please' – it took me about a minute to realise I was standing beside the Australian comedian and TV presenter Clive James. He looked at me with a twinkle in his eye.

CJ: 'So, you're going out with him then?' [Motions towards John]
Me: 'Yes.'
CJ: 'Hmmm. Can't be easy. And what do you do?'
Me: 'I'm a nurse. But I want to act and maybe write. I'll have to change my name though!'
CJ: 'Why, what's your name?'
Me: 'Abi Titmuss [we both laughed]. Arggh! Any advice?'
CJ: 'Abi Titmuss. I'll remember that. Don't change your name. And write a novel – you can put anything in a novel.'

21st September 2000

Now it feels like my life can truly begin. Have enrolled on the Acting Foundation course at the Kensington and Chelsea College. I've done my year and a half as a full-time nurse but I now thank God I was able to go part-time for this. Three days a week for one year – and I'm going to love it.

16th March 2002

Have been doing a part-time course at the Central School of Drama (bit of a gap since Kensington and Chelsea but life with John just took over – you know what it's like when you're all loved-up). But am back on track. And tonight proved it.

One of my drama tutors, Mike Miller, took me aside and said I'm good enough to go to RADA! This is like a dream come true. Am thrilled. Picked up a prospectus on the way home, planning to pore over it in bed tonight.

July 2002

The course at Central was great, although I struggled to make every class due to having to work night shifts. Still, I got a certificate at the end. Now I've got an acting place at Westminster college – am so excited. I hope John will be.

November 2002

My life feels a bit out of control. Three years into our relationship, I feel like I am sliding further and further away from myself. I seem to spend all my time looking after John.

For the last three months the papers have been having a field day with him. There have been endless headlines, kiss-and-tell stories and vicious rumours. Overnight, he seems to be losing everything.

5th December 2002

The TV was on in the ward. Suddenly I heard John's name and froze. They were saying he'd been arrested over 'rape and sex allegations'. I knew the rumours, I knew what they were all saying – but it's not true. He shouldn't be arrested. I was shaking. It was the most terrifying feeling. But I couldn't let any of the patients see me. People started coming up to me in the corridor – 'Have you seen the news?' I couldn't breathe.

I called John to see what was happening and we arranged he would be outside to pick me up in the next few minutes. I was going out of my mind. It was all such a blur. His car pulled up outside the hospital. My mind was buzzing – how could he have kept this from me? What an appalling burden for him to have been carrying round. I felt so paranoid, were people watching?

We were silent on the way to his house. I looked at his face – he looked battered. Absolutely exhausted. Just as we were nearing his road, John pulled over and looked at me sternly – 'There're going to be a lot of people outside, Abi. This isn't going to be nice.' I looked down at myself, and as bad as it sounds, my first thought was, 'I'm in my nurses' uniform and I look like shit.' I had zilch make-up on, I'd been on the ward for eight hours, my hair was a mess . . . I felt so self-conscious. Instinctively I reached for the lipgloss in my pocket and put it on. Stupid mistake.

'What do you think you're doing?' John asked incredulously. 'Why are you putting on make-up?'

I immediately apologised.

We drew up at his house. Flashbulbs were going off everywhere. Reporters were running over at us – shouting John's name, asking him to tell them how he felt. He grabbed my hand and we walked indoors as fast as we could, locking the door behind us.

I felt so sorry for him. When we got inside he handed me the folders that the police had given him – full of statements from girls accusing him of things. All the information was there. They were thick with paper. I thought, 'If I'm going to stand by this man I need to know everything.' And I sat down in the sitting room and read them right through the night into the early hours. John sat numbly in front of the TV watching the news reporting his downfall.

I finished the last page and I felt relief. It's rubbish. I know it's not true. But I realised that this was serious now, that there could be no half measures. I had to stand by him. Despite our ups and downs, I know in my heart that John isn't a bad or violent man.

We can get through this. Together.

6th December 2002

Our picture is in the *Mirror*. It's in all of the papers in fact. The headline: 'I am no rapist – what Leslie told police yesterday.'

And then there's me. It is such a weird feeling seeing yourself on the front of a national newspaper – thousands of strangers seeing you, the anonymity that we all take for granted, gone with the publication of one headline. I started analysing the picture – I looked at myself hiding behind him in my nurses' uniform. I really hope I'm not going to get into trouble? You're not meant to wear your uniform off the ward, let alone in a national newspaper. I'm a mess. Don't know why I bothered with the lip-gloss – you can't see I'm wearing anything. I look about twelve. I wish I hadn't worn the long uniform, it swamps me. And why didn't I put on the belt? It would at least give me some sort of shape. It seems really funny that John's holding my hand too – makes me realise how rarely he does it. I stood in the kitchen staring at the page. And then, aside from everything going on with John, it suddenly dawned on me –

it's going to be really hard for me to be an actress now. I was in the middle of my drama course and it really felt like I was getting somewhere. But now this? Tears immediately started to come because I felt so selfish that I was thinking about myself when John was going through so much. It sounds awful, but it did flash through my mind for a second just how powerful this headline was: I was John Leslie's girlfriend, the nurse. Not the actress. Then reality kicked in and I decided John had to come first from now on.

31st July 2003

I don't know what to wear. It's absolutely boiling outside. All I care about is looking smart for John. I don't want to let him down.

I remember seeing a picture in the paper recently of a celeb going to court – who was it again? Victoria Beckham? She was wearing a white shirt and I thought, 'Gosh, I wish I could look like that.' If only I could be smart like her.

The only handbag I have is a really cheap grey thing from Oasis. It's definitely seen better days. This past year has been absolute hell; my appearance has been the last thing on my mind. We've been staying in the house, I haven't read fashion magazines for ages, I haven't been shopping – everything's been focused on John.

It sounds far-fetched but it's absolutely true. I haven't done anything normal for months as there have been paparazzi camped outside John's house, day and night. And they follow us EVERY-WHERE. Blocking our car at traffic lights so they can get a shot, following us into shops and supermarkets . . . It just makes you so paranoid.

Shit. How am I meant to look? All I have is a black dress that I've had for years. I don't want to show any cleavage. That should work – it goes up to my boobs and I can wear the black jacket I bought for my job interview as a nurse to cover my shoulders. Maybe a necklace to brighten it up a bit. I've got a cheap thing with a cross on, that'll do. Quite sensible. Wonder if I can just sneak in the side door and it won't matter? It won't matter anyway – this is John's day, not mine. Everyone around us is worried about what's going to happen today in court, concerning the indecent assault charges, but that's not what I'm thinking about. It's what's going to happen to John afterwards that is worrying me. The man has almost been destroyed.

The case was thrown out. All the charges were dropped.

The judge said he could leave the court 'without a stain on his character'.

I have never seen so many cameras. When we emerged from the courtroom it was like John was the President of the United States or something – there were scores of microphones lined up in front of us. My legs were shaking. We were all so upset. It wasn't even a happy time of relief. I was fighting back the tears, it was so overwhelming. John was in absolute bits. He'd been up all night because he wanted to watch everything on the TV – the build up to the verdict was running 24/7 on *Sky News*. He hadn't had any sleep at all.

With all the cameras on him, John said that he wouldn't have got through his ordeal if it hadn't been for me, his mum and his dad. I really appreciated him saying that.

After John spoke to the press we all went to the Electric Brasserie on Portobello Road to 'celebrate' – if you can call it that. We had a few bottles of champagne pretty much straight away, then the reality that it was over started to sink in and as result we got even more merry. When we got the car home there were press everywhere, swarming like bees outside John's house. I'd taken my jacket off by this time because it was so sweltering outside. As we pulled up outside the house I went to put it back on again. It didn't seem appropriate not to wear it somehow. John could see that I was unsure, but told me to leave it off if I wanted and not to worry. It was boiling hot after all!

The press went mental. And oddly they seemed more intent on getting my picture than John's. I think he noticed that too. He looked at me and laughed, 'You are allowed to smile, you know. We're alright now.' I climbed out of the car as flashbulb after flashbulb went off in my face.

1st August 2003

I opened the paper thinking it would be all about John. Instead in the *Sun* the headline is: 'Abby Ever After' beside a large, rather odd picture of me – climbing out of the taxi. I had mixed feelings. It's exciting, yet I feel guilty that the press is all about me and not John. It's not quite right, but I can't help being flattered. John's mates have been laughing about it all day. I guess it is quite funny in a way. He's just finished a massive court case and they're using a shot of me stepping out of a car!

It was a funny picture to use. I was leaning forward, about to stand up. But at that angle you could see my legs, I was bending towards the camera so it was clear I had a chest, and my shoulders were visible.

Basically, you could see flesh . . .

'I always say keep a diary – and someday it will keep you.'
Mae West

1st September 2003

I am trying to pick up the pieces of my life now. I have hardly any savings and I've neglected my friends too. It's time to try and move forward. Somehow.

12th September 2003

John Noel, John's agent, rang. He's been ringing loads over the last few weeks. Why is there such interest in me all of a sudden? People working in the media keep calling, wanting to know more about me. But why? Feel bad for John, but can't pretend not to be a bit excited. Especially today – 'The producer of *Richard and Judy* wants you to come in for a presenting screen test.'

What?

It hadn't even crossed my mind when we were filming John's Sky One documentary. Admittedly one of the producers had made a few comments about me being 'good on camera' but I was so busy focusing on John I didn't register. Now it's got back to Richard and Judy!

Considering the year I've had, just the word 'screen test' is exciting. Keep saying the word to myself. I don't understand the world of TV. I've never really taken much interest in John's career – unless you count him taking me to see *Wheel of Fortune* being filmed a couple of times (which was thrilling...). It's acting that really excites me – being able to morph into someone else altogether, taking the stage and making people believe and care about the character you've created.

Felt a bit odd telling John the news. He's the presenter, not me. He was really generous though, and said it will be a brilliant opportunity. That just served to make me feel even guiltier.

I asked him what they will make me do and he said that they probably just want to watch me on camera to see what I look like. He reckons I'll just have to say a few words – nothing to worry about.

13th September 2003

Been practising in front of the mirror but haven't got a clue what I'm meant to say. Started speaking into a hairbrush and realised I looked like I was about eight. Also realised I need a new hairbrush.

14th September 2003

Screen test tomorrow. Am so nervous as I have no idea what to expect.

15th September 2003

Really nervous. Stupidly left it till about thirty minutes before I had to leave to even think about what to put on. What do you wear for TV? Are there rules? Chose a brown V-neck top, dark jeans and some boots. John said I looked good – had to take his word for it.

A silver Mercedes drew up outside John's house. Felt very strange and a bit embarrassed. Am so used to watching flash cars arrive to take John to work, not me. Looked back at him waving me off at the door and it felt completely weird.

Amanda Ross – the executive producer – took me to the dressing room when I arrived. It had my name on the door! So bloody scary but so exciting at the same time.

'We're really pleased to have you here,' she said. 'We're going to give you a go in front of the camera shortly to see what you're like.' I took in my surroundings. Here I was in this plush dressing room with food, drink, flowers . . . everything laid on for me.

What was I doing here?

I suddenly got an overwhelming sense of regret. I broke down and sobbed. I had no business being here. This was John's territory, not mine. He's not working, what right did I have to be somewhere like this?

Amanda was understandably shocked. She must've thought, 'Who is this fruit cake?' but she didn't show it. She gave me a hug. 'What on earth is the matter?' she asked warmly.

I looked at my tear-stained face in the mirror and had a moment of clarity. 'What am I doing now? I'm going to fuck this up as well.'

Amanda was lovely and sat beside me until I got it together. My mascara must've been round my ankles by this point so she took me to the make-up room. There I was told that they'd got someone in for me to interview – as a bit of a test – and I was handed a brief. My 'guest' was a costume historian and his specialist subject was sixteenth-century clothing. I had half an hour to prepare my questions, and then I'd be interviewing him on camera.

How can half an hour suddenly seem like two minutes? We walked up a corridor and Amanda guided me through the back of the studio. It was all dark so I couldn't really see where I was going – 'Mind the wires' she laughed as I nearly went arse over Titmuss. Turned a corner and suddenly I'm standing on *Richard and Judy*'s set with about a zillion people swarming around.

Gulp.

Huge TV cameras, crew with head-sets, clipboards, important wires coming out of their persons . . . Then someone came over to put a microphone on me. Shit. This was seriously scary.

Someone else gave me an earpiece.

'The director will be talking to you from the gallery.'

I looked straight up to the ceiling expecting to see someone looking down at me. The earpiece provider laughed. 'It's not like *Romeo and Juliet*! A gallery's just a room where the director controls all the cameras.'

Someone took me over to the sofa. 'You'll be sitting here.' All I could think was, 'I'm in Richard's seat!' In came my costume historian, the camera pointed at me, a red light went on and . . . the nerves hit. The earpiece was bloody confusing – there were people talking in my head, how was I meant to concentrate? During the interview I was told I had to wind up to go into a break, had to look into an autocue, read the words and the music would start.

Somehow I did it.

In fact, I absolutely nailed it. I asked the guy about corsets and even managed to throw in a joke about Ann Summers, which raised a laugh. Then I went to the break – and didn't stumble on any words.

Afterwards, I felt like a superstar. The crew tried to hide their astonishment. The director even said, 'Are you sure you haven't done anything like this before?'

Amanda walked over. 'You were really, really good. Exceeded all our expectations in fact. We'll be in touch.' I was buzzing. Still am. John seemed genuinely taken aback at what I'd been asked to do.

He reckons they might have me in mind for something big . . .

16th September 2003

I took another shift at the hospital today. It felt good, but it was hard. I don't feel like I belong on the ward anymore. My mind wasn't on the job, and that's not right. But it's all I have at the moment.

19th September 2003

I'm just starting to process the enormity of what the screen test could mean for me. Was I really any good? What did they think of me? It's like waiting for my exam results.

20th September 2003

Had a huge row with John. Don't know how much more I can take. However, when it's good between us, it's incredible. He wouldn't admit it but I think he's jealous about the *Richard and Judy* thing too. And I can't blame him. Doesn't make his disposition any more tolerable though. I love him, and we've been through so much ... but I feel like this is impossible.

He drove me back to the nurses' flat. Need some space.

21st September 2003

The *Sunday Mirror* has written about our row. Someone must have spotted John driving me home yesterday. It says I 'threw' a suitcase at him. I didn't throw a bag at him! I chucked it into the back of his car – I'd used it to put some of my stuff in. How the hell do they find out these things?

23rd September 2003

John's tetchy again today. We're not normal anymore. Nothing is.

24th September 2003

Oh. My. God.

Got the call. They want me as a roving reporter.

I should be jumping for joy. But with everything that's happening with John, it's hard not to feel a bit guilty.

'What's a roving reporter?' I asked John Noel when he told me the news. 'Does that mean I'll be standing out in the rain? It sounds like I'm going to be covering a football match or something.'

After the screen test they'd made me feel I was the best thing since sliced bread. And now they're going to stick me outside in a rain mac.

John Noel laughed. 'What are you talking about? It's bloody great! This is a way in for you – it's a brilliant opportunity. You should definitely do it.'

26th September 2003

Ironically, John was a guest on *Richard and Judy* today. I sat at his house glued to the telly. This was his first big interview since the court case and I could see how incredibly nervous he was. My first thought was, 'Oh God, you look so old since you were last on TV. You've aged.'

I felt so sorry for him. Having to watch him being grilled like that was intensely upsetting. He kept doing this thing with his hand that he only ever does when he's feeling uncomfortable. Had a tremendous sense of sorrow. Why did he have to go through that? Despite the fact that they were Richard and Judy, old colleagues of his, and they were being nice to him – I felt so infuriated. What the fuck is going on? What the hell has happened to his life? Why? Hours ago he was sitting in this house as my boyfriend John, now I saw him through the eyes of a viewer. And it was awful.

I sat there thinking, 'You're not going to work again.'

Of course, I didn't repeat that thought when he arrived home. He opened the front door, I hugged him and told him how well he'd done.

But when he was out of earshot I spoke to one of his friends on the telephone.

'He looked terrible didn't he?'

'Yes' he said, sadly.

27th September 2003

The papers are running reports about John's interview on *Richard and Judy* as confirmation we've split up. He never said that! They'd simply asked whether we'd be friends and he'd answered 'Remain friends? I didn't know we weren't friends. We will be friends for life.'

Why does anyone care so much about our fucking relationship?

28th September 2003

John's documentary, *My Year of Hell*, went out on Sky One tonight. Our friends came over to watch. As soon as it finished, one of his mates looked at me.

'Well that was a good show about Abi wasn't it?'

Everyone laughed awkwardly.

He was right. I was all over it. When I wasn't in vision, they'd still used my voice. It was embarrassing.

Couldn't look John in the eye.

4th October 2003

It's in the papers that I've landed the *Richard and Judy* gig and that my first appearance will be next Friday. There are quotes from Amanda Ross saying how good I was in the screen test! 'She was fantastic. None of the crews could believe it was her first time on TV, as she was so good, a natural.'

Had another blazing row with John. I just can't seem to do anything right.

Couldn't sleep.

5th October 2003

Bloody hell. The *Richard and Judy* show are sending me to New York! John Noel rang to tell me. I nearly dropped the phone in shock. I've never been to America before! When I told John I could see something alter in his face.

'Fucking hell,' he said. 'That is massive, Abi.'

Although he was saying it in a nice way, the atmosphere was suddenly a bit serious. He said that for any presenter a trip to New York would be a big deal. It's going to cost them a lot of money to send me out there. He reckons that means they trust me to deliver the goods.

I've got to interview the world's first 'sleep concierge' whatever the buggery that means. We're going for two or three days! Feel a bit weird about John though. I hope he's OK with it.

Clearly not, as we've just had a huge row. Perhaps I was over-excited – who know, but whatever the reason, it really kicked off.

6th October 2003

The ward was particularly hard work today. Sister said that people keep calling and asking about me – journalists. The staff are fed up with it – and I don't blame them.

7th October 2003

I'm on the plane to New York! Wooooo!

That was all I could write before I got distracted by wine and pretzels. As we prepared for take off, I felt the stress of the last few months lift and promised myself that, for the next couple of days, I was going to have fun.

Arrived at the hotel. My room is massive – I've got an executive suite! The director Gareth had to come to my room and literally pull me off the balcony, I couldn't stop looking at the view. All the skyscrapers and the lights, it's breathtaking . . . I just want to stay here forever.

We're situated on Lexington Avenue in New York, right next to Grand Central Station. The sleep concierge idea is genius. Rather than calling for a taxi or to ask for a restaurant recommendation, you call when you can't sleep! There's a pillow menu, cookies, hot chocolate and a white-noise machine to block out the sound of the traffic. You choose between sounds like birds tweeting, woodland noises and a flowing stream. Although that's more likely to make me need a wee than sleep.

One of the first bits of filming we did was me having to get out of a yellow taxi, shut the door and say, 'Well they say New York is the city that never sleeps . . . ' The driver thought he was going to be in some big budget movie. He was dead chuffed. If only he knew what had just happened to me and why I was here. And that this was *Richard and Judy*.

Had food with the crew and got an early night. No need to listen to the sound of woodland creatures tonight. Shattered.

8th October 2003

Phew, this filming lark is full-on. Left the hotel at 7am and didn't stop. Loving it though. Not only am I in New York for the first time ever. I'm being *paid* to be here.

The director, Gareth, wanted to film me in my bed as if I was tossing and turning – having a bad night's sleep. Felt like a real film star. Had a special light shining on me while the cameraman stood on a stepladder filming me 'in action'. When I looked at it back on the monitor I nearly welled up. A few days earlier I had been emptying bed pans on the ward. Now I was in an executive suite in Manhattan and had an entire camera crew on me!

But by far the best bit was filming in Times Square. I remember when I first came to London and saw Piccadilly Circus; I thought *that* was amazing. Times Square makes Piccadilly look like my nan's Christmas lights in comparison.

People kept stopping and whispering 'Who's she?' So surreal.

We finished at about 10pm and Gareth said, 'It's time to go to bed, I'm knackered.' The producer Paul announced that he was off to the Village to get a beer. 'We've only got one night here,' he said excitedly. 'I'm not wasting it.'

I thought, 'I'd better make a good impression,' and signalled to get in the cab with Gareth and go back to my hotel, but Paul knew I could be tempted.

'Come on, come for a drink if you want.'

Gareth was concerned. He reminded me that the next morning we were due to film me having had my 'sleep concierge treatment' – it was essential that I looked rested. I'd already chosen a pillow from the pillow menu, cookies had been ordered and everything was waiting in my room to give me a brilliant night's sleep. I assured Gareth I wouldn't be late. I'd just have one drink . . .

Went into Greenwich Village, and I don't know how we found it but we came across this amazing underground karaoke bar. Paul and me were the only white people in there. We ordered drinks. 'Are you going to get up and do "New York, New York"?' I teased Paul. Then the singing started. Our jaws dropped to the floor. Every one who got up to sing sounded like Whitney Houston or Snoop Dogg. It was incredible. I've never been anywhere like it in my life.

Cocktail after cocktail . . .

I don't even know what time we went to bed. Think it was around 5 in the morning . . . I was so pissed I'd fallen out of the cab. It was starting to get light. Shit, Gareth was waking me up in two hours. I vaguely remember eating the cookie when I got in, couldn't even see to switch on the noise machine. As my body hit the bed I missed the special pillow altogether.

9th October 2003

The plan was for Gareth to knock on the door, I'd get out of bed and open it, then go back to bed allowing the camera to come in and 'find me' fast asleep. That was the plan.

After what felt like no more than two minutes' sleep there was the knock on the door. It was Gareth and the crew. I hadn't even got undressed. Oh fuck. Realising I hadn't even slept on the pillow I frantically started prodding it to make it look like there'd been human contact.

'Just coming,' I shouted and ran to the bathroom in a desperate attempt to sort my face out. There was mascara running down my cheeks. I plastered concealer on, trying to make myself look like I'd had a good night's sleep. I looked like shit.

'What are you doing in there?'

'I just want to freshen up.'

'No, no! We need you looking natural,' panicked Gareth from the other side of the door.

Natural maybe. Not pissed.

The camera came into the room. Good job it wasn't smellovision because it must've reeked of booze. I had to sit up and talk about what a restful night I'd had. I'm sure Gareth raised an eyebrow.

Only Titters could go all the way to New York to get a good night's sleep and end up looking worse than I did at the start.

When Gareth said, 'How was the pillow? Did it help?' I looked back at the space my head had totally missed. 'Oh, it was great. It made such a difference,' I lied. 'And the milk and cookies really helped too.'

In reality I could have slept comfortably on a washing line, the state I was in.

Got back to John's flat at 7am to find him ready to greet me. He asked me how the trip was but I could see he didn't really want to know. Welcome home to the real world Abs.

11th October 2003

Back to dreary England and my nurse uniform. How can I be so happy one minute and feel so low the next? Finished my shift (which after the last week's excitement was really hard work and a big jolt back to reality). Then got back to my flat and curled up on my bed. I'd had a whole day of people recognising me and asking after me. Reporters are starting to come into the ward on a regular basis. Sister was understanding but I could tell she was getting miffed.

Got a call from a journalist at the *Mirror* who started asking questions about John. Somehow, they've heard about our rows. How? Could one of the neighbours have heard and said something? God, is nothing sacred? I didn't know what to say – have been so upset. Think they could tell I'd been crying but tried to keep my voice steady.

'We're fine.'

Sometimes in a long-term relationship, it's easy to become what you think your partner wants you to be. I feel like that's exactly what's happened to me – I don't know who I am anymore.

It sounds pathetic, but it's true. I love him deeply and the physical side of our relationship is something that really keeps us together. But I was only 23 when we met, I'm nearly 28 now and it isn't enough for me anymore. And things are getting worse, not better.

12th October 2003

The *Sunday Mirror* headline is: 'John dumps Abi'. They've got full details of our screaming match last Sunday night. How do they find out this stuff? Says when I spoke to the journalist yesterday I wept.

13th October 2003

John called. He really wants us to try and put the rowing behind us. I can't function with him and I can't bear life without him.

16th October 2003

My New York report aired on *Richard and Judy* today! It was so exciting! I had to sit on the sofa and chat to them before and after the clip (or VT as it's known apparently) was played out. They were really lovely to me and I felt surprisingly comfortable.

Got back to John's still buzzing from being on live TV. He didn't seem that enthusiastic though.

21st October 2003

Went with John to a charity bash at Ronnie Scott's jazz club. Could feel people's eyes boring into the back of my head all night. People would look at John and give him an awkward smile. He was really suffering. Someone paid £5,000 to sing with Roger Daltrey. Should've been a great show but I wasn't really in the mood to be there. Not enjoying anything much with John at the moment.

22nd October 2003

Back on the ward again. Twelve hour shift. Two patients died today.

10th November 2003

Went with John to the opening of *Jerry Springer: The Opera* at the Cambridge Theatre. There were going to be celebs there so I knew I had to dress up a bit. Bought a little dress from Karen Millen. John said there'd be some cameras outside but I wasn't expecting anything remotely like what happened.

The instant John and I stepped on to the red carpet the photographers went crazy. Flashbulbs were going off like mad. All I could hear was shouting. We stood there together as they took our photo, then I started to realise the shouting was for me. The words reverberating along the throng of paparazzi were 'Abi! Abi! Abi!'

Without even thinking I instinctively turned round and flashed a smile. Almost as suddenly I felt John tapping me on the arm to remind me he was there too. I'd completely forgotten myself.

But what an adrenaline rush.

It's the first time anyone's ever shouted my name like that. After all the shit that's been going on, it felt amazing. I checked myself, realising they were more interested in me than John, but he encouraged me to go for it, so without thinking, I pulled away from his arm and stood on the carpet alone. I wasn't hiding behind him any longer. And it felt nice. It's like I'm really part of it all, in a good way.

12th November 2003

There are pictures of me from last night in the papers. And I look good!

The *Sun* says: 'John Leslie and girlfriend Abi Titmuss show their relationship is black on track by stepping out for the second time in a week. The couple wore matching black outfits to attend Monday night's opening of *Jerry Springer: The Opera* . . . '

14th November 2003

I thought I'd be doing stuff for *Richard and Judy* all the time but it seems to have all gone quiet. Called John Noel and he said I shouldn't worry – they don't always need reports for things, it depends what's newsworthy and what topics they want to talk about. Maybe I need to think of something myself. Show them I have initiative.

16th November 2003

Life at the hospital is getting so tough. I keep getting paranoid when I see people I don't know enquiring at the nurses' station in case they're reporters. Then I start worrying that the rest of the staff are thinking the same and that I'm more of a hindrance than a help. So I bit the bullet and handed my notice in. I know it's the right thing to do – my heart just isn't in it anymore. I feel a mixture of sadness and relief. My life has changed so much and it is time to acknowledge that – it's just not fair on everyone else. I am keeping everything crossed for *Richard and Judy* – a fresh start is just what I need.

17th November 2003

John Noel spoke to *R&J*'s producer who assured him they're still really keen to do stuff with me and why don't I come and hang in the green room and watch the show on Friday for a catch up?

18th November 2003

Night shift on the ward. Spookiest thing happened. Must tell Richard and Judy – I reckon they'll love it!

21st November 2003

Sat in the green room watching the show and afterwards Richard and Judy both came into the room with the producers and we sat chatting. They were all so attentive – really made me feel like one of the team. I told Richard I'd had a weird encounter on the ward. As I relayed it, he sat transfixed.

The other nurse I was working with went on her break and I was sitting at a desk at the end of the corridor. There was an elderly lady in one of the rooms. She'd only come in for a routine operation on her leg, nothing too serious. But for some reason, I suddenly got this powerful urge that I *had* to go and check on her. I couldn't explain why. I left my seat and went to her door. As I opened it a shape jumped up and shot past me out of the room. It startled me so much that I screamed before quickly putting a hand up to my mouth to stop the noise – I didn't want to wake the other patients. It was like nothing I'd ever seen or felt before but I knew intuitively that it was a man. Definitely a male presence. Despite my muffling, my scream had been enough to wake the lady. I couldn't tell her what I'd seen because I didn't want to frighten her, but my heart was going crazy. I walked to her bed and said, 'Sorry to wake you up there.' But she'd been in such a deep sleep that although the noise had woken her she hadn't fully comprehended what it was.

I leant over to switch out her light. As I walked away she said, 'Oh, hang on nurse! I'm glad you came in. I don't know why but I'm in absolute agony, this terrible pain has started in my leg. It's been getting worse all night; I really need some painkillers.'

'Why didn't you ring for me before?' I asked her.

'I just didn't want to bother you, nurse,' she grimaced. Her face was white, it was clear she'd been in a lot of pain.

It was like something had sent me in to check on her. It sent shivers down my spine. I went out to get her some painkillers and just as I got to the door I caught sight of the stool at the bottom of her bed. 'It is funny you know, nurse,' she said quietly, 'I had just drifted off to sleep before you came in and I was just dreaming that my husband was sitting right there.'

I paused.

'He only died recently, and I still haven't quite got used to it.'

Her face looked so upset and I really had to fight the urge to let her know he was there. It must have been his ghost that shot past me. And that was the reason I'd come in to check on her.

'It was such a lovely dream,' she smiled. 'I was talking to him.'

As I left I said, 'I'm sorry to have disturbed that. I do think he's looking out for you.'

When I'd finished telling the story, Richard was in raptures. He loves all that kind of stuff – storms, ghosts, anything dramatic. 'Abi, this is great, we can turn this into an item on the show!' That's just what I was hoping he'd say. I'm going to ask round the other nurses I know and see if they've had any similar encounters. If you want something sorting Abs, sort it yourself.

Perfect.

25th November 2003

John was auctioneer at the CLLASP ball in Edinburgh last night. Really good thing for him to do, he needs something to help get his confidence back up. It was a nice for him to be working again. But it still has that tinge of brokenness about it somehow.

Fire alarm went off halfway through and we all had to stand outside in the freezing cold. Felt really self-conscious – people kept staring at me. John noticed that too.

6th December 2003

A reporter came on to the ward today. It seems to be happening more and more lately. It's a bit scary actually. He was asking where I was and pretending to be a patient. Then he got thrown out.

7th December 2003

On the ward today I tried to do some investigation about the ghost situation. Not very successfully. One of the nurses said she had seen one but she was so spooked out she wouldn't talk about it. Another was too worried about hospital confidentiality to go on air. I'll just have to tell one of the team at R&J and hope they can persuade someone to come on. I hope they still do the piece. I haven't been used as much as I thought I might be. I don't want them to get bored with me.

8th December 2003

Richard and Judy have written about my ghostly encounter in their column in the *Express*, appealing to other nurses to come forward.

9th December 2003

John and I had a massive row again last night. Can't even remember what it was about. So we've split up again. Can't live with him, can't live without him. It still hurts though . . .

10th December 2003

He called and we made up. So we're back together. Until the next time.

15th December 2003

We finally did the ghost piece on the show. Afterwards the producer said what a great item it was. Yay! And it was all down to me. Hopefully this is just the start.

16th December 2003

John's becoming very difficult and volatile towards me. Hardly surprising with what's gone on. He's had no work while I'm suddenly having my picture taken when I'm out. Yet I'm finding myself retreating into a shell. I can't cope. People are noticing me, reporters are hounding me. I don't know what to do or think about our relationship anymore. We've been on/off for so long – nothing's real. I know I want out, but I can't do anything about it. I feel so low. I'm not going to be some big TV star like I thought I was. I've got no money, debt from acting classes, and I've just quit my job, what the hell does the future hold?

18th December 2003

I was on the A&E ward today and the sister got really cross. One doctor had come in asking after me and she snapped.

'She isn't called Abi Titmuss when she's on my ward, she is staff nurse Titmuss.'

She was partly saying it for my sake as well – I'm finding it impossible to concentrate with all the stuff that's going on. I can't handle it.

I know I've made the right decision to go.

19th December 2003

Reporters have been phoning all day again. It's so embarrassing, and difficult. There's a long desk with people answering phones – taking calls from A&E – and one journalist rang at least five times in the space of an hour asking what time I was starting my shift.

These phones never stop, there are *real* emergencies, so for one person to be taking up the line for that space of time can be lethal. Wendy, one of the healthcare assistants, got angry. Afterwards she said to me, 'I hope you don't mind Abi, but I told him to fuck off and stop calling.'

I didn't mind at all.

21st December 2003

Today was my last day on Bentham ward.

I felt emotional as I left. So many feelings: pride for the work I had done, fear for the future now I was unemployed, and sadness to leave a wonderful team of hard-working people that I had so much respect for. Three years slog at university, five years in the hospital and now it was all over.

I looked at the reflection of myself in my uniform for the last time and decided all I wanted from life now was to be happy.

24th December 2003

Went home to Sleaford. Have been so looking forward to some normality. Went out with some of my mates. This is what we always do at Christmas, we go on a pub crawl. But tonight it was so odd. Strangers were coming up to me, knowing my name! My mates were looking at me so weirdly. One couple even came up to me and asked for my autograph. What the fuck? (It was fun though).

25th December 2003

Went to Mum's for the day – going to Dad's tomorrow, that's the drill. Had pheasant, the usual. Just me, Mum and Alan – the lodger. He's an old hippy, a qualified reflexologist and aromatherapist. Keeps himself to himself. Reads a lot. He's become a great friend of the family.

One of my oldest friends came round. Went for a walk in the woods, one of my favourite things to do, then some of the others came over too. We played Scrabble. Very rock and roll.

26th December 2003

Went to Dad's. Such a different affair from being at Mum's. There's never any bad food at Mum's, everything's organic and from the local farm shop. But at Dad's I can stuff myself with all sorts and not feel guilty. Good job I'm not there all the time – I'd be like Humpty Dumpty.

Alison, Dad's wife, did an amazing buffet as usual. Loads of people came over. Drank stupid amounts of wine. Dad always has the best wine. He's handled this past year so well: the difficult headlines and especially having the paparazzi camped outside his house for weeks on end. Spoke to John again today – I'm looking forward to seeing him and drawing a line under this horrendous year.

2004

'I was Snow White – but I drifted.'
Mae West

13th January 2004

I got an invite to Jermaine Pennant's twenty-first birthday party at Attica. Apparently he's a footballer. I'm really rubbish with sportsmen, I don't know any of them. Recently, I've had a few offers of parties to go to – they all come via Taylor Herring, John's PR company – but I haven't felt like it until now.

John's PR, a girl called Sam, said I should go with a mate. Sam has become a friend over the last few months and it's like she's looking after me too. While John Noel is the 'agent' filtering offers of work and guiding me as to what I should do next, as the PR Sam or her boss James Herring are the people who look out for how the public see you. And now she's doing the same for me as she did for John, because believe it or not, people want to interview me all of a sudden(!). Sam said I should let my hair down tonight, it might be fun.

However, I'd already arranged a girly get together that day and, having zero interest in footballers, I decided I wouldn't bother with the party.

My friends and I were going somewhere nice for lunch, for a treat to cheer me up, so I made a bit of an effort. I wanted to look like a 'lady who lunched' so I wore a knee-length Marks and Spencer grey wrap-dress with cute blue shoes and matching blue necklace and earrings that my mum had given me. The dress showed a bit of cleavage so I didn't feel too dowdy. That's one good thing about having boobs. Even if you're feeling fat or not-so-great, you can cover everything up except a good bit of cleavage and feel sexy again.

Within two hours of arriving at her lunch, this lady was completely legless. Lunch turned into the afternoon and afternoon to evening . . .

'Anyone know any good parties tonight?'

'Actually yeah,' I piped up.

I must've been drunk to go to a nightclub in a Marks and Spencer's jersey wrap-dress. The rest of the night is extremely hazy but I do have a patchy memory of being involved in something exceptionally, mind-bendingly stupid. Not to mention illegal . . .

Once we were in the club, a guy called Jayson came over to me. Through my vodka-goggles I recognised him as an acquaintance of Calum Best. They had both come to a party at John's house last year. It had been yet another very drunken affair and had turned into a bit of a crazy night, ending up with me kissing Jayson's girlfriend for fun. We'd seen him a few times since then.

I've always been curious about women and after quite a few drinks and a lot of egging-on I had found myself in similar situations with girls several times during my relationship with John.

My interest in that side of things had started when I was younger and I was in love with my boyfriend at the time, but utterly bored with our sex life. I remember thinking, 'If I marry him, is this IT forever? Is this as good as sex gets?' I thought there must be something wrong with me, I loved him after all. I didn't know what was missing, so I questioned whether I might be gay. I remember walking up and down Oxford Street that day and making myself look at women to see if I fancied them. It wasn't the same feeling as I had for men though, and I knew I didn't want a relationship with a woman, so I definitely wasn't gay. But I did still feel that something was missing from my sex-life. I wanted to explore. At first when I started 'exploring' things it was incredibly exciting and liberating. I knew there was more to sex, and I was right.

Anyway, back to the rapidly deteriorating evening at Attica. I was now staggering around (so much for poise) and had lost all my friends. Jayson at least looked vaguely familiar. I had never really liked Jayson – there was something about him that gave me the creeps, but I was too drunk to care. As I called

John and slurred that I was coming back to the house, Jayson took the phone out of my hand and told John he'd 'look after me'.

The next thing I know I'm being led outside and suddenly there was madness. Paparazzi were all over me, there were so many flashes going off I couldn't see to put one foot in front of the other. I was genuinely shocked. I fell into the first cab I saw and just as it was pulling away Jayson jumped in the other side.

The only thing that could possibly make this mad situation worse would be if drugs were involved. So naturally that's exactly what happened next.

I'm cringing as I write this.

I have tried cocaine many times over the last few years. Having been extremely anti-drugs for a very long time, I finally let curiosity get the better of me at a show-biz party one night. Cocaine was everywhere, as it is at most show-biz parties, and I had said no to it a thousand times before. This night I thought, 'Oh fuck it, I wonder what it's like?' and I snorted a line.

In five minutes I went from self-conscious, under-confident nurse to Marilyn Monroe and Eddie Izzard rolled into one (in my head, obviously). Suddenly I could talk to anyone, dance all night and drink enough to kill a small horse, all without keeling over. No wonder everyone liked it. What a brilliant invention! This powder is genius, I thought.

What no one tells you about cocaine is that the following day (if you're not still up, drinking and talking utter bollocks to someone you met in a bathroom who is now your best friend, even though you can't remember their name), you will feel SO bad that you want to pull out your brain, wash it in the sink, stamp on it for being so stupid, and put it back.

But, slumped in a grossly drunken stupor in the back of a cab, I was not averse to the suggestion of cocaine. I didn't care, I just wanted to get home. Jayson said he would get some and the next thing I know I'm handing him money and watching him jump out of the cab and get back in with the coke. As soon as we arrived at John's, I staggered upstairs and passed out.

I came to at about midday the next day to find that Jayson had stayed the night in one of the spare rooms. I went in to tidy up the room and noticed that the cheeky sod had been using the phone.

17th January 2004

My mum called. 'Have you seen the *Daily Mail*, dear? You're one of the main headlines!'

In fact I was in every single flipping paper.

The *Daily Mail* front page read: 'Dear John, now I'm the famous one.'

According to them it was my 'plan' to go to Attica to get noticed. What? What a load of tosh. And why on earth is anyone interested in me going to a nightclub? Mates (which bloody mates?) have said 'she's changed over the last few months' and that John was 'surprised by what Abi was wearing as she'd always been critical of people courting press in the past and now she was using oldest trick in the book – a little dress and a navel-skimming neckline.' Bloody hell. I was actually thinking the opposite, but in the photo they've used, my 'bit of cleavage' now makes me look like Lola Ferrari.

Ooh, get this. I'm 'taking it all very seriously . . . taking advice from Denise Van Outen, Lorraine Kelly and Anthea Turner . . . ' (oh yes, I call them up on a daily basis, especially as I've never met two of them) and ask them how I can grab the limelight from John – you know, sock it to him, just when he's getting over a trial.

Oh God – I hope this doesn't affect my job at *Richard and Judy*. I've been charming the socks off them all, what will they think seeing me and my cleavage, splashed all over the press, falling out of a nightclub, trolleyed at 3am?

I had Richard's mobile number, I thought I'd better call and explain. He was brilliant.

'Don't worry about it Abi!' he said cheerily, and not without a hint of amusement. 'You look great. No harm in a bit of press.'

Thank God.

'Don't want you thinking I'm some kind of drunken floozy!'

Ha, phew.

18th January 2004

Today's headline reads:
'ABI AND JOHN, 4 IN A BED ORGY' and it went on, 'He took snaps of Abi having lesbian sex . . . we joined in.'

It seems like that bastard Jayson has sold a story about John and me. And it didn't stop there. He had PICTURES too.

Fuck.

It's an account of that night sometime last year where I ended up kissing Jayson's date. As I remember it we were only snogging a bit, but the paper has described it as an 'orgy' with girls and guys.

Oh my God. It also says there are fifty-three 'sordid' photos! I haven't done anything 'sordid'; sex isn't 'sordid' for God's sake. Where? How? When? Shit, that night . . . We were set up.

Did he plan this?

The night at Attica when Jayson got in the cab with me and stayed at John's house, John's camera was out on the kitchen table – it looks like Jayson must have got up in the night and taken things. Photos . . . oh my God.

I think I might throw up.

John is understandably livid. He checked through all his camera stuff and confirmed that a memory card had gone. They weren't some kind of home-porn archive, they were just full of all our regular photos, like any normal couple – holiday pictures etc. But there were a few sexy shots in there too.

As it started to sink in I began to shake. It isn't just the pictures printed in A NATIONAL NEWSPAPER that are flooring me, it's the thought of all the other photos of me that are on that memory card and are now probably being pored over by every journalist in London. Things that were on it kept popping into my head . . . Oh God, when the two of us were on holiday in the Caribbean last year, didn't I do a little striptease for him? And what about all the other times John had captured us for fun? These are PRIVATE, personal, intimate things for my and John's eyes only. Now who's looking at them? At me. Naked, vulnerable and exposed. OhGodohGodohGodohGod. I started to cry uncontrollably.

John reckoned that given how quickly the photos have appeared in the tabloids, Jayson must have even called the newspapers and done a deal from the spare room that night too. That must be what he used the phone for. Good God. While we slept in the room next door. I can't take this in.

Am numb.

Why did John leave his stuff lying around? Why did we let that man into our house in the first place? I feel responsible. Why did we take photos and film each other? John loved all that stuff. And yes I went along with it – but we'd be drunk, and it was all in private for heaven's sake. God, I would never have done anything like that if I thought it would get out. It was just a bit of private fun.

It's in the *People* too. It says Jayson had been touting the pictures about, trying to get the most money he could. The paper reckons he asked for £100,000! Are we worth *that* much?

Oh Lord.

'There were pictures of Abi giving oral sex to men as Leslie films, performing a sex act on a woman while a man pleasures her. Romping with Jayson and a mystery blonde . . . '

What? That's not how I remember it. But to be honest there have been so many drunken, wild nights in the last few years. They're all a blur. Have they got pictures of my entire sexual history for Christ's sake? What consenting adults do in the privacy of their home should remain exactly that – private. I'm beginning to feel very angry.

Reading all the coverage, I can't help but feel that Jayson has gone into absolute fantasy-land with his story. He's really gone to town, saying that I had dressed up as a dominatrix and all sorts of hyperbolic, titillating nonsense that I know didn't happen. It made me sound like Miss Whiplash.

Mum rang.

'It's not how it sounds, Mum, honest. There was no "orgy".'

'Abi. Try not to get yourself into a panic. If we were in Roman times, no one would bat an eyelid darling.'

If there is a more perfect, non-judgemental way for one's mother to deal with a front-page story regarding her daughter and an orgy, then I would like to hear it. She is one incredible woman.

John's been on the phone to John Noel all day. They've contacted the police who think we have a case for theft. We have instructed lawyers too. They are going to cost thousands of pounds. Where on earth is that money going to come from? We'll just have to find it.

Bit late now though isn't it?

19th January 2004

Got a call from Amanda Ross, the producer of *Richard and Judy*. I knew this was coming. They can't use me on the show anymore.

She was trying to be really diplomatic about it. 'We just can't use you at the moment; I hope you understand, it just wouldn't seem appropriate. Richard and Judy are journalists and because the story is so high profile we couldn't have you on the sofa and simply not mention it.'

I didn't even really try to explain to her. It wouldn't have made any difference. It doesn't matter if it's not true. The damage has been done. It's there. People won't forget it. I know only too well that in TV Land it's the headlines that do the damage. Am devastated.

John is beside himself. What else can possibly go wrong for him? Now I'm right down there with him and we just keep rowing. I have been nationally humiliated.

Cried and cried for what seemed like hours.

20th January 2004

The *Sun* is saying my job on *Richard and Judy* is 'threatened'. Got that right. Feel a bit confused. It seems to me I was booked for being sensational and now they've *dropped* me for being sensational.

It's not like Channel 4 only shows documentaries about nuns, is it? Looked at the TV guide and they're advertising a show called *A Girl's Guide to Sex*. And now they won't use me because I had sex. But I guess the damage was done.

Spoke to John Noel. He was extremely supportive.

'You're fucked.'

'Thanks.'

'You're in the same position as John now. You'll never work again. My advice to you is to go to America and travel for about six months. Leave the country.'

But my agent wasn't being an arsehole, he was just being his usual blunt self and telling me like it is. There are no frills on John Noel, but there is a warm heart under the gruff, Northern exterior and I have a lot of time for him. I had become close to him over the last year and I trusted pretty much anything he said, so this came as quite a blow.

'I can't leave!'

I put the phone down and wept. It's like my whole world is collapsing around my ears. I've left my job as a nurse, I've abandoned acting classes. I've focused all my last year on John, my boyfriend. I've got nothing. No future. But I am not going to let this man and one ridiculous story ruin my life. So I've had sex! BIG frigging DEAL.

'Fucked?' Fuck this.

I called John Noel back.

'No, this is not going to happen.'

'What do you think you're going to do about it?'

'I have absolutely no idea, but there is no way you're going to tell me I'm fucked because of one person who's sold a story on me. I haven't killed anyone. I've been through too much to let this ruin everything, it's crazy. There must be something I can do to redress the balance.'

He thought for a minute. 'All you could do is to tell your side of the story. You'd have to really be honest though.'

I was silent.

'OK, I'll do it. I have to do something.'

And he knew I was serious. We discussed it and he went ahead and called our PR – Sam's boss, James Herring – and told him to sort an interview. A few minutes later, James called me.

'Great, brilliant. Fantastic – you can do your side of the story, say it's all complete fabrication, the man's a fantasist, there's not a grain of truth in it and we can kill this beast once and for all.'

Oh dear.

'Yeah . . . about that, James . . . '

'Yes?'

'Well, there are elements of truth to it . . . '

'Right . . . '

But as I spoke to James I knew it was going to be a case of sink or swim. I have to try and salvage myself. I am not going to let that story, that piece, be the last thing that's ever written about Abi Titmuss.

James said he'll secure an interview. What's more it'll pay a substantial sum. He's talking in the £50,000 mark which seems like an inconceivable amount. At least it will pay the lawyers' bills.

21st January 2004

Haven't got out of bed all day. Am at Mum's and she's been devouring the papers in spite of herself. She said there's a nice account from someone I went to school with. She tried to cheer me up by reading out quotes.

'I can't believe it's the same person because I don't recognise the Abi I knew. She was a normal, fun-loving classmate. She was very popular at school and never had a bad word to say about anyone.'

There was another one too. A girl called Rachel says, 'Abi had a naughty streak . . . she was very good at imitating teachers and invented various methods of getting us out of lessons. The best was in French when I'd pretend to have a nosebleed and Abi would tell the teacher she needed to take me out and look after me.'

What the hell does that have to do with anything?

At least they were trying to be nice, I suppose. Wonder how much they got paid for saying those things . . .

22nd January 2004

Went back to John's. He's concentrating all his energies on getting these pictures back. Says the police are investigating. It's as if he thinks that once we've got them, everything will return to normal.

Normal?

There's a story in the *Daily Express* about me aged sixteen! There's a photo that was taken on my last day at school in 1992 – the report says I'm displaying my 'infamous cleavage'. Where did they get that from?

Some girl (whom I apparently went to school with) says she wrote to me recently and said I had friends back home and was proud I'd become a nurse as that's what I always wanted to do. But I never wrote back . . . I never got any such letter!

It goes on to say that I was 'pretty at school but nothing special . . . ' and then this girl added, 'when I saw her in Sleaford at Christmas she was a different woman. She is a celebrity here and all the men were flocking round her.'

What is happening here?

After another row, I left John's to go back to the flat. I know I've got to sort my life out, but with so much going on, it's hard to get focused. They have been great at letting me stay on as long as I pay the rent.

There were photographers swarming outside, so I tried to hide under a hat and just ran. Reporters were shouting questions but I said nothing. Don't think they got my picture.

23rd January 2004

There's a picture in the *Sun* of me leaving John's. Great.

Did my interview with *News of the World* today. I was so bloody frightened. Sam came with me. She briefed me beforehand – told me not to say too much, just to answer the questions as carefully as possible. That they'd try and trick me into saying certain things and that I should think about everything before I spoke. Oh God, I'm notorious among my mates for *not* doing that.

The journalist was called Polly Graham. She seemed really nice. I relaxed and we started having a bit of a jokey chat. Not so horrific after all. 'Didn't Jerry Hall once say "A woman needs to be a cook in the kitchen and a whore in the bedroom?"' she asked.

I couldn't remember. Probably.

'Do you think you're a bit like that?'

I joked 'I guess so, it's a bit like me saying I'm an angel in the courtroom and a whore in the bedroom.'

She laughed. See, I can be funny at times. Neil Wallis the editor came in to meet me during the interview. He told me he'd come especially because he thinks I'm great.

By the end of the interview though I felt utterly drained. And cheap. Polly asked me so many intimate questions about sex and my private life, it was horrible. But of course she did, that's what the story was about wasn't it? And I answered most of them. Doing this awful, humiliating interview was the only way I thought I had to grasp some semblance of control over what was happening to my life.

All the time she was looking at me I was wondering what stolen pictures she'd seen of me. Then, as if she knew what I was thinking, she looked at me and appeared to smile as she told me that she'd seen lots of them. Of me. And so had Neil and all the other men in the office.

I felt violated. No amount of money can ever take that away.

One of the tabloids has spoken to someone from the Royal College of Nursing. They're not going to strike me off the Nursing Register.

'Although it is not ideal to have your private life splashed across the newspapers, I can't see how it would affect her ability to do the job, should she wish to return to full-time nursing.' Well at least that's something.

24th January 2004

Neil Wallis from the *News of the World* phoned.

'We've got the drugs thing.'

'What are you talking about?'

'We've got a story about you ordering drugs. It's come from the taxi driver. It's in your best interests to talk about it now and we can add it on to the interview.'

I couldn't believe what was happening. Does this mean they knew all about it when they spoke to me yesterday? Have they deliberately left it until the eleventh hour to get me in a corner?

'I need to speak to my agent.'

'Fine. I'll call you back in fifteen minutes'

I rang John Noel. No answer. Frantically tried James Herring. He's not there either.

My phone rings.

'It's Neil from the *News of the World.*'

I sobbed and sobbed. 'Please don't do this to me . . . Please.'

'You've got to speak to us, Abi.'

'What have you got?' I cried.

'You were in the back of a cab with someone called Jayson and you stopped to buy some gear. You paid for it. You bought the drugs.'

Oh my Christ. It's neverending. What next?

'So what do you want me to do?' I asked desperately.

'We need to add this into your interview. We've already written your answers.'

'What do you mean?'

'We've written your words.'

'What? But I have not said anything to you about that . . . You've made up my answer, as if I have talked to you?'

'Yes. So I'm going to read it to you and you can say yes if you think it sounds reasonable.'

Oh my fucking God.

He read it down the line to me ' . . . I had money on me . . . I bought drugs.'

The crying was getting uncontrollable. I felt like I couldn't breathe.

'Please don't put that, don't do that to me.'

I didn't know what to do. In the end I didn't have any choice.

25th January 2004

The *News of the World* came out today. I couldn't face going to the shops. I knew it was going to be horrible. I called James Herring.

'You won't want to see it,' he said.

Go on . . .

'The headline is "Abi: I confess" and inside, "I'm an angel in the courtroom and a whore in the bedroom."'

Why did I say that? I was joking! It must look horrific in print. Like I'm some dirty slapper. Why did Sam let me say that . . . ? She must have known what they'd do with it. Still, it came out of *my* mouth . . .

James continued.

'Abi Titmuss has sensationally admitted buying cocaine and snorting lines of the class-A drug in lesbian sex romps to satisfy lover John Leslie . . . The blonde now faces police prosecution – which could lead to up to seven years in jail – following her astonishing confession.'

Seven years?

In jail?

I want to kill myself.

It's horrendous.

Mum called, she'd just bought the paper. She began reading it down the phone. I pleaded with her not to. I can't have her knowing about the drugs. That's the worst, worst thing.

But she said she wants to know everything about her daughter. No surprises. She's being so good about this, but I know she's shocked and hurt. Scared too about what I'm getting myself into.

Dad phoned. He didn't read it. He's good like that. He says he doesn't want to know. But the embarrassment for them . . . They're my parents.

It's done now. I did what I could. All I can do is sit back and see what, if anything, happens. Will I be vilified, or will anyone anywhere at least give me some tiny modicum of respect for trying to stand up for myself, and being ridiculously honest? Or do I deserve all this for being drunk and allowing myself to get into a dangerous situation?

Oh God. Seven years?

26th January 2004

John Noel rang.

'You've got two job offers.'

Is this really happening in the same week?

'What? You're kidding.'

'Yep, Playboy TV and Television X.'

I burst into tears.

'It's one day's work, just a few links to camera. Easy money.' He was trying to make it sound like it was a normal presenting job.

'John, it's porn.'

I was at breaking point. Didn't think I could take any more. Is this what it's come down to? I have nothing: nowhere permanent to live, no job, no self-respect, nothing. This is what I've become – a porn star.

That's it then. That's how people see me. In two years I've gone from being a nurse on a ward to being offered a job on a porn channel.

John quickly backed down. 'Don't worry, forget about it. We're not going to touch it with a barge pole.'

I hung up the phone and slumped to the kitchen floor. Numb.

An hour later the phone rang. John Noel again.

'Right, I've changed my mind.'

'What do you mean?'

'They're offering a lot of money, Abi. This is going to be your last paycheque. It will get you out of that nurses' home, pay all your lawyers' bills and give you a deposit on your house. It's that much.'

I was hesitant. My head was all over the place. My personal boundaries had become so blurred by now that I felt as if I was losing sight of reality. John Noel was like a lighthouse in a storm to me. He was the person I really trusted and looked to for guidance. If he said do something, I should.

There was a long silence.

'What do I have to do?'

'It's a day's filming and a day's press. You have to do pieces to camera. It might be porn Abi, but it's *a lot* of money.'

Somehow, he started talking me round.

'Abi; it is what it is. All you have to do is say "Tune in and call this number." That's it.'

Maybe I have to go with what he says. He knows what he's talking about. He advised me to go with the Television X – Fantasy Channel. They were going to pay me a Six. Figure. Sum. I've never dreamt of that kind of money.

Playboy TV had offered me even more, he said, but the owner of Television X is Richard Desmond who owns *OK*, the *Express* and the *Daily Star*. If I went with them, it would mean coverage in the media. I needed to be smart.

I'm starting to learn. And it's not over. I won't let it be. Something good has to come out of this nightmare. I can buy my own place. A positive from a negative. I hope.

27th January 2004

'Miss Titmuss?'

It was the police.

'We need you to come down to the station. We're going to arrest you.'

'Oh God, no'

'Don't worry; we're not going to just turn up at your door with handcuffs. If you come down to the station we can do this quietly.'

Oh well, that's fine then. I couldn't even speak. My mouth had gone so dry. I was terrified.

By some bizarre coincidence it was the same policeman who had helped us with the investigation of the stolen memory card. I wanted the ground to open and swallow me up. He sighed, 'We shouldn't tell you this Miss Titmuss, but if you ever do any interviews never mention drugs as we have no choice but to proceed with it and investigate. The police cannot be seen to be ignoring an issue like that.'

I started to explain that I hadn't said anything to the paper, that they had written 'my words', but what was the point? It was true that I had paid for drugs, wasn't it? I felt so ashamed, and very frightened. I could have sworn he felt sorry for me.

'We can't even just caution you and let you go. Because you technically bought drugs for someone else we're going to potentially have to charge you with supply of a class-A drug. It's serious.'

My heart was pounding. I couldn't take this in.

'You need to get yourself a lawyer. We're not going to rush round and arrest you, it will happen in the next month or so and I will arrange for you to come in.'

I called the lawyers. It's going to cost thousands. And they said that the fact that I am looking at 'supply' is 'very worrying'.

'What's the worst that could happen?'

'"Supply"' is a wide area. It's definitely a jail term. You can get anything up to a life sentence.'

I have made the decision tonight that the only way I can deal with this is to put it out of my mind until the police call again. There is absolutely nothing I can do at the moment. Otherwise I'm going to lose my mind. All this for a couple of grams of stupid, disgusting cocaine. I can't look at myself.

Don't panic Abs. This is going to be OK. It has to be.

How have I got here?

Everyone hates me, and I'm going to go to prison. Can life get any better?

28th January 2004

'Hi Abi! Everything okay?' It was Sam from Taylor Herring.

'Oooh yeah, yeah, great.'

'Good. I've got some exciting news, are you ready?'

'Yep . . . ' Christ, now what?

'*FHM* want to shoot you! It's the biggest-selling magazine in the country, did you know that?'

'Nope.'

'You won't get paid, it's basically an honour that they're doing it and you'll get great publicity from it. It'll just be one shot, one page somewhere in the mag but it'll be really fun for you and something to keep forever you know? It's amazing. That interview you gave to the News of the Screws has really caused a stir.'

Yeah, you're not kidding.

'You don't sound very excited, you should be happy about this!' She was right.

'I've just got stuff on my mind, that's all.'

It started to sink in. Hang on, this is great – me, a model? In the top-selling magazine in Britain? Are they sure? Have they SEEN me?

'Oh by the way, you know it will be in lingerie, yes?'

HOLY CRAP.

29th January 2004

Stood in front of the mirror this morning in my bra and pants. They have definitely seen better days. So has my body. I bear absolutely no resemblance to any of the gorgeous models in those magazines. Have *FHM* gone mad?

I looked down at my wobbly belly and held my stomach in. Hmmm, that's slightly better. I can't exactly hold my breath for a seven-hour photo shoot though, can I?

OK, question: do you want to do this? Take your clothes off for a glossy, glamorous, once-in-a-lifetime sexy shoot, that is also potentially a fantastic opportunity to start to turn your life around?

Answer: Absofuckinglutely.

FHM want to do it in three weeks.

Right, we need drastic action.

30th January 2004

Had a consultation with a personal trainer who works with John Noel and lots of his celeb clients today. They weighed me, which was awful, and I am nine and a half stone. At five foot six that's not exactly obese but I am, well, jiggly, and I certainly have *no* business taking my clothes off for a magazine in this state.

It's going to cost at least a grand and a half for an intensive program but I can use some money from the interview. No half measures now. I've got to go all out for this. I start tomorrow.

Got the train home to Dad's tonight, for his birthday dinner. It was so good to have a hug from my dad. We didn't talk about the *News of the World* and I was glad about that. I don't think he wants to think about it and I don't blame him. He just wants to know that I'm all right, that's all he cares about.

I hope he's not ashamed of me. He said he wasn't.

31st January 2004

The *Sun*:

'Abi is getting £150,000 to launch the spring schedule for Television X Fantasy Channel next month. A spokesperson says "She will be our public face ... doing interviews and posing for photos. At this stage there are no plans for her to appear on the channel itself, although the offer is open.'"

No going back now. It's out there.

My new trainer, Matt came for my first, unbelievably hard session today. He had a slightly terrified demeanour when I said I had three weeks till the shoot, which I tried to ignore. He doesn't know how hard I'm going to work. I'll show him. I'm going to work my arse off. Plus I've read the Atkins Diet book from cover to cover and I've started it today.

I'm already having visions of myself in a Rocky-style montage, running up and down steps in a ripped T-shirt soaked with sweat, doing press-ups on one finger, boxing for hours and drinking raw egg, stomach like a xylophone . . . Oh yes.

1st February 2004

Can barely move. Every muscle hurts. Hate Matt. Hate my body. I must be mad thinking I can do this. Give me a cake.

The headline in the *News of the World* is 'Cocaine Cop Quiz For Abi,' followed by

'Disgraced Abi Titmuss has been quizzed by police after the *News of the World* exposé of her secret cocaine-fuelled sex sessions. A police source said that she was likely to escape prosecution but the incident will remain on her file. This may affect Abi's likely £150,000 new job as a presenter on the TV porn Fantasy Channel.'

Don't think about it. Just don't think about it.

2nd February 2004

In preparation for the photo shoot I did something I've wanted to do for years today: went to a private dentist and had my teeth whitened. Fantastic. Has given me a real lift and a bit of confidence back.

3rd February 2004

Trained again today. I'd better get used to this.

4th February 2004

More training. Talked about diet and nutrition. I'm on a strict plan so no booze . . . Argh! The Atkins Diet sucks; I'm having a piece of ham and an egg for breakfast every day. Yuck. I'm sticking to it though. Got to be done, I want results, and fast.

5th February 2004

Trained and had massage. Needed it, body is in shock.

6th February 2004

Am seeing more of my trainer Matt than my friends. I now love him though, despite the fact he makes me work so hard. He's brilliant. Time to see the girls tonight though; it's been so long since I went out and enjoyed myself. It's my birthday on Sunday – going to be twenty-eight – so we're having a night out tonight. Meeting Katie and Zoe (nurses) and Miranda at the Sanderson at eight and going from there.

Better be a bit more prepared for paps tonight I guess.

8th February 2004

Today is my twenty-eighth birthday.

I cannot believe what has happened. John is furious. He's thrown me out of the house. Literally chucked my bags out on to the street. All thanks to the *Sunday Mirror*:

'Slapper about town Abi Titmuss kissed and canoodled with a yummy male model in the storeroom of a London nightspot.'

What?

I had a brilliant night with the girls on Friday and we'd ended up in a nightclub called Pangaea. We had a drink and a dance and I came home. All fine.

A guy called Zac works there; I've seen him quite a few times before and we always say hello and have a quick chat, as we did on Friday. That was it.

How, after everything we've been through and what he knows about the press, can John throw me out because of one salacious story? I only said hello to this Zac guy. After all the things I've had to read about him . . . I'm reaching the end of my tether.

Can't stop crying, how can he believe them?

Happy birthday to me.

10th February 2004

Had to attend the launch of the Fantasy Channel today.

I didn't want to go. They sent a hairdresser and make-up artist round to my little room in the nurses' home and I was given a long, black designer evening dress to wear.

The irony that I was looking classy for a porn channel was not lost on me. Classy was the last thing I felt when I arrived and suddenly realised how incredibly exposed and raw I was. I'd been expecting a few people, a little smattering of curious press attention. But it was nothing compared to the reality.

It was crazy. Have never seen so many cameras. There were reporters swarming around me, cameras flashing, people shouting my name – I was shaking so much. What's more, I had to stand up and do a speech. And somehow justify the fact that I've agreed to be the face of a porn channel. Possibly the worst thing I've ever had to do.

I kept telling myself, 'Think of the money and what John Noel said, I'm getting paid by these people, I'm here to promote the channel. It's only sex, there's nothing wrong with that.'

Looking around at the sea of cameras and notepads there's no doubt as to why they hired me.

It was a huge press call – I had to stand and pose amongst a herd of scantily clad girls pulling sex faces around me. It was so cringingly awful and tacky. But I'm learning. Every day I'm getting a tiny bit wiser about the media. You have to give them what they want.

I was to give a little spiel about how great it was to be here and how excited I was about joining the channel, then there would be a small promo on the screen behind. I waffled something about the fact that we all like sex and it's nothing to be ashamed of but all I really wanted to shout was 'I don't want to be here!' Then I sat down in the front row to watch the presentation.

Of course they'd failed to mention what was going to be on it.

It was a montage of hardcore porn. I don't know what I was expecting, but, I guess rather naively, it wasn't this. There was an audible gasp from the row behind me. Fuck fuck fuck. There were reporters all round me. No one was watching the film, everyone was watching me. I could feel them all craning for a reaction, their eyes boring into the back of my head. I wanted to die, but I had to keep smiling, maintain the appearance of cool. If this wasn't so real it would almost be hilarious. Afterwards a swarm of microphones filled the space around me, TV cameras thrust in my face.

First up was some guy from BBC News

'Do you think this . . . porn . . . is all right?'

Quickly I replied, 'Well there's nothing wrong with it, they're consenting adults.'

There, I managed to come back with something.

Another reporter asked me why I was doing the job.

'Compared to what I used to earn in a year as a nurse, this deal is worth a hell of a lot of money. A year ago I would not have thought I'd be here but I'm working for the best. I don't see anything wrong with a girl whose life has been turned upside down trying to make a living. I watch adult films. There is nothing wrong with having sex.'

Job done.

Now, more tea, Vicar?

My picture is all over the papers. Every single one. How has this – how have I – turned into such a big deal?

Trained again with Matt at 10am. I'm only a week into it but I've lost 5lb already and my tummy is flatter! Hurrah! Just as well, because the car came to pick me up for a photo shoot at midday.

My first-ever photo shoot on my own. Sam had arranged it. Apparently the papers and magazines are now clamouring for pictures of me. Sexy pictures of course. And, OK, I can go with that, at least things seem to be looking up and also I'm starting to see that I can make some money for the future here. Could my 'I'm not fucked' vow to John Noel somehow be starting to come good?

They took a few nice shots of me in a dress, one in hot-pants and a vest and one in vintage-style underwear (not skimpy, phew).

It was quite hard work, I didn't like my hair and make-up and I didn't think I looked very pretty. I didn't know how to stand or pose at all, but by the end of the afternoon I had found out for myself by listening to the photographer and checking all the shots myself to see how I could improve, and which poses worked with my body shape.

It was over in five hours and I was glad. I'd found the whole thing tiring and it hadn't done much for my confidence. I wish I'd gelled with the photographer more and also spoken up about being unhappy with my hair etc.

I gave a quick interview to the *Daily Star* at the end, as they were going to buy some of the pics. I'd spoken to Sam a while ago about whether to mention that I had studied drama and wanted to be an actress and we had agreed that it would sound ridiculous to bring it up at the moment. No one would take me seriously, or worse – I could be criticised for it. After all, I was known as a nurse. So I decided to keep it inside me.

Well, for at least half an hour anyway. As I was leaving the reporter started talking to me 'off the record' and I blurted out that acting was my real passion. Am sure she won't write anything about it though. Or Sam will be cross.

12th February 2004

I am marking today in my diary as a 'day to remember'.

The most incredible thing happened today.

Sam called. She'd just been on the phone to *FHM*. Apparently their readers have been voting to add me to the list of their '100 Sexiest Women in the World' poll! I'm not in their list of choices for people to vote for but guys have been sending in my name. Unbelievable. I had no idea I had been noticed so much in the papers. Clearly I had. And I hadn't even had the glamour shoot published yet, this was just from pictures of me with my clothes ON.

Hmmmm, and the orgy story plus my revealing interview probably have a lot to do with it too. What a twist of fate that some good should come of all that. It is literally the best of times and the worst of times.

This is undeniably exciting. I am a sex symbol with *FHM* readers! Am so chuffed. But it's so surreal. That means someone actually likes me.

Then I went to the bank. Lloyds Bank on Oxford Street. The exact same place I have been in many times over the last few years, all through the hardship of university days and then more hardship as a nurse. I remember crying in here once and begging the account manager to increase my overdraft limit as I could not even withdraw ten pounds to go and get some food, and I was too ashamed to ask my parents for more money. It was a truly humiliating experience.

Today, they treated me with kid gloves and asked me if I would like to join their premier account, for high earners. I was also offered a credit card with a ludicrous limit. Why is it when you need money, no one wants to lend you any and when you've got plenty suddenly it's available?

13th February 2004

The shoot I did on Wednesday was on the front cover of the *Daily Star*! Ha, check me out! Madness. Interesting which picture they chose for the front. Not the one I would have picked. Hmmm . . . I'm learning. Also, no sign of the shots I did with clothes on. Pored over the article for any snide comments but it was all nice. Oh, and she did mention my acting though, but just a sentence at the end. No harm done. Trained and had sports massage today. I'm starting to love it, and so is my body.

I spoke to a financial adviser too. The next big thing I need to do is finally get out of the nurses' home. When the money comes in from Television X I can start thinking about buying a house! I've lived in this little room for a long time now. Just think, my own front door for the first time. And no more communal showers and people nicking food from my fridge. Or having to walk six floors down to do my washing in the basement. Wow, that is such a thrilling thought.

Just as I was feeling happy and excited, the whole police thing came screaming back into my head. Bang.

Couldn't sleep tonight.

14th February 2004

Couldn't sleep again tonight, the police are bound to call any day now. Am so freaked out. It would be typical if it happened just as things are looking up for me. What if everything is blown to pieces again? What if I am charged for God's sake? Calm down, calm down. Breathe.

16th February 2004

Ran around Russell Square a million times with Matt this morning. He said to channel all my frustration and fears into exercise. Plenty to go on there then.

Had a lunch meeting at Claridges with James, my new financial adviser. Did I really just write that? A 'lunch meeting' you say? At 'Claridges'? With your 'financial adviser'? I'm going to wake up soon.

After that I met a property agent woman that John Noel recommended, who's going to help me find a house. For a fee of course. But I need the help, I don't have a clue about buying property.

17th February 2004

Amazing news today! I've been asked to do AN AUDITION FOR A PLAY! Astonishingly, someone did notice the single sentence about acting at the end of the *Daily Star* piece on Saturday. A theatre producer called Marc Sinden, and he has sent a script to John Noel for me to look at.

I raced over to John's office and stood hopping up and down as I waited impatiently while he printed it out. When he finally handed it to me I stared at it and welled up. John looked at me like I was a bit mad.

'Bloody hell. You really want to do this acting nonsense, don't you?'

I nodded.

19th February 2004

It's the *FHM* shoot tomorrow. Have trained for two hours solid every day this week and stuck to the diet like a military regimen. Have not starved myself, in fact have eaten the equivalent of a herd of cattle, but inconceivably have lost a stone! I am under eight and a half stone, my lightest ever. Oh, praise be to God and all His angels in heaven.

Matt can't believe how quickly my shape has changed; we are

both very pleased with ourselves. He's really impressed with how much work I've put in, and it's not going to stop here. I am in love with my new body. And teeth. And possibly Matt, ahem.

For the *pièce de résistance* of my makeover, I had my hair high-lighted and long, blonde hair extensions added today. Took six hours but who cares – I feel like Rapunzel.

Then I had a set of pristine French-manicure-style, white-tipped acrylic nails glued on. I always had to keep my nails short while I was a nurse, so with talons to be proud of for the first time in my life, I felt preposterously glamorous and chic, almost Parisian.

That's until I dropped a coin when I was paying for a coffee and could *not* pick it up off the floor, for about five minutes, in front of a queue of people. I was like a baby vulture trying to grasp a postage stamp.

For the finishing touch, I went for a spray tan. I'd always fake-tanned myself at home but I figured that this warranted a professional job. I couldn't exactly see Pamela Anderson turning up at an *FHM* shoot saying, 'Would you Adam-and-Eve it boys, I couldn't reach my back? Can you just shoot me from the front?'

Total cost of makeover, not including a grand and a half for personal training, came to around £1,150. Not counting the fifty pence I left on the floor of the coffee shop.

Hope it's all worth it.

20th February 2004

FHM shoot today! I was picked up at 9am, nervous but excited. In the car I imagined what it might be like. As I was going to be wearing 'lingerie and swimwear', I assumed probably some kind of dignified, 'closed set' like on a film, with just myself, the photographer and some quiet words of encouragement and direction. And it's only one picture anyway.

I arrived.

It was like Sainsbury's on a Saturday.

I couldn't believe it. Hair, make-up, styling, set design, set-design assistant, lighting, artistic director, photographer's assistant, publicist, deputy tea-lady's assistant's cousin's uncle Jim . . . It went on and on. I counted twelve people. Surely I haven't got to get undressed in front of all of them?

I kept waiting for some of them to leave but no one did.

Okaaaay.

A scary woman came up to me,

'I'm the artistic director. I've seen your hair in the papers and it's not good enough so we'll be putting extensions in.' She waved at someone, 'Hair, we need hair!'

Nice. I'm below-par already. Except I'd thought of that, hadn't I? I flicked my head round to reveal my long, golden locks.

'Oh! When did—'

'I had it done myself.'

'Good.' She marched off.

Someone else appeared.

'And this is what you'll be wearing.'

Oh. Holy. Jesus.

The stylist was motioning towards a clothes rail full of what can best be described as, very expensive, glitzy, beautifully made, designer . . . pieces of string.

I thought I was reasonably racy as far as lingerie was concerned but I had never in my life seen underwear and swimsuits as small as this. The bikini tops were like two peanut shells on a hair and the bottoms looked like they would barely contain Barbie's labia, let alone mine.

And talking of hair, I'd done my bikini-line, but for a *normal* bikini, not for these Dairylea-size triangles! My own knickers suddenly felt like a World War Two parachute. And I'd been feeling confident about my body, but Jesus. I suddenly felt very naïve and out of place.

I started to panic. Then Sam arrived, thank God! I grabbed her and had a quiet word. She was great, calmed me down and said not to worry, that there were lots of 'outfits' to chose from, and something would work.

Before I could worry any more, I was whisked into hair and make-up. Now this was fun. They were much more professional and friendly than on the other shoot. As well as enjoying it, I saw this as an opportunity to learn how to do it better myself and asked for lots of tips, which I got.

Next I had to face 'the rack'. I was feeling a hell of a lot better with my hair and make-up all done, and I started trying things on. I'd never seen G-strings on a hanger before, which made me laugh, but not the stylist, who was taking it all very seriously.

Sam was right, I found some gorgeous things that did fit my bits, just, and I began to relax a bit. You're here now so enjoy it you idiot, I told myself. Bloody go for it. I slipped into some killer heels and strode into the studio in my absurdly tiny pants, like Elle McPherson's shorter, chubbier cousin.

The photographer was the coolest guy I'd ever seen, a caricature of what you would imagine a top photographer to look like. 'Flown in' from New York, Chinese, with trendy black specs and known only as 'Man' (are surnames out now?), luckily he seemed to like me straight away.

With slightly shaky legs, I took my stance on a big black box, under various enormous lights and facing the huge dark room full of people. Standing up there practically naked, I felt a surprisingly heady mix of vulnerability and power. I had a second to store this moment in my memory bank, then some music started up from somewhere and we were off.

I had no idea what was expected of me but I just started posing and as the camera clicked and Man called out encouragement I really began to enjoy it. A wind machine whirred into action and was directed on to me. Woo-hoo! I'd always secretly wanted to try this! Who do I think I am, J-Lo?

In the middle of the studio was an enormous Perspex screen with a water pipe connected to the top, pumping a cascade of water down the front of the screen.

'Stand behind it Abi and I'm going to shoot you through the running water.'

Cool. I was really getting into it now.

A few pictures later the female artistic director asked how I would feel about taking my top off. I thought for a minute and replied that I didn't mind posing so I appeared bra-less as long as my nipples were always covered. There was no way I wanted to show my nipples. I was dead sure about that.

'We won't show any nipple, we don't do "topless",' she assured me, 'it will be shot through the water and we'll Photoshop steam on to it to hide your nipples.'

Admittedly, on reflection, this does sound vaguely funny. Steam and water to 'hide' my nipples? But this was the biggest-selling glossy magazine in Britain, not the *Sunday Sport*. So I trusted them. And this was another woman reassuring me, after all. Also I had every intention of pushing the boat out on this shoot and making an impact. I looked at Sam.

'You don't have to do anything you're not comfortable with,' she said.

'I don't mind appearing to be topless in the picture, as long as—'

'Darling, we can cover your nipples in Photoshop. No problem,' said Man.

I might never do anything like this again, I thought, so I went for it. The whole thing felt very professional, and very sexy.

I was surprised that the shoot seemed to be more than just the one shot I was expecting, but they explained that they would just pick the best one. Fine with me, I'm loving this! And can't help thinking I might not be doing a bad job. I've totally clicked with the photographer and we seem to have real chemistry. I can feel it.

Next I picked a vampy black bra, knickers and suspender set and did some shots lying on a huge glass box thing that was lit from inside. Man was up on a stepladder shooting down on to me. He told me to look into the lens as if it were his eyes, which isn't as easy as it sounds actually. But I concentrated and totally focused on him and the dark, open lens and I believed what I was doing. Like acting really.

Because I switched into it so much, writhing around, with Man saying things like 'Oh yeah, now wet your lips. Yeah!' I was genuinely feeling sexy, and getting pretty turned on, if I'm honest.

Another shot was to be me sitting on a Perspex chair, leaning forward. I said quietly to Man that I was worried this wouldn't be a flattering position, imagining my belly all squished up and on display. He laughed and told me not to worry, I looked great and he would position me so everything was covered.

The team seemed to really like this shot. I was topless but had my arms covering my breasts, and was wearing silk knickers that tied with ribbons at the sides. I glanced down at them and had a thought. I was sitting side-on to the camera. If the ribbons on one side were undone and tucked in, my modesty would be intact but it would appear as if I were naked in the shot.

Am I really going to do this? Of course I am! It's only a bit of ribbon, and I'm practically naked anyway. Just go for it. So I did. They loved it.

Finally we were finished. I received a round of applause from the team. I was tired and my back ached from arching it and holding poses, but I was sorry it was over.

As I teetered out of the studio in my heels and underwear, with a silk robe slung over me to protect my modesty (bit late now, and anyway I was so relaxed after five hours in front of everyone that I felt like a life model in an art class), Man asked me out for a drink. What a cliché! I declined but I was a bit shocked; after all he is regularly in the company of proper models who are really beautiful, unlike me. It was flattering though.

Arrived home, still with fabulous hair and make-up and full of adrenaline from the shoot.

I called Miranda. 'Fancy a drink, buns?' (my girlfriends and I all call each other 'buns', short for bunny).

'Why not, Mrs Top-Model. I'll come round to yours and get ready. You can tell me all about your big day.'

Miranda's been one of my closest friends for years and I love her. She's one of those gorgeous, dead slim, shiny-long-haired girls who could wear a plastic bag and make it look like Dior.

She can (and does) throw on some boots from a second-hand shop, mixed with bangles from India and a dress from Topshop and look like Kate Moss. When I try to do that I look like a homeless person.

22nd February 2004

It was John's birthday tonight. I hadn't seen him since my birthday but he had called and asked me to come over as he was having drinks at the house. After everything he's been through I have to make allowances for the fact that he's not himself. I also felt guilty that I had just done an exciting photo shoot when he was at home doing nothing. Against all my better judgement I went to his party, laden with presents to cheer him up.

It was a terrible mistake, on my part.

We had a horrible row in front of everyone. But for the first time in five years, something finally just clicked in my head. It was so definite and absolute that it was almost tangible. As if the invisible rubber band that had kept me attached and always pulled me back to him, had suddenly been severed. Just like that.

It was over.

As I left in a taxi I was unable to get the words out to speak to the driver, tears pouring down my face. We pulled away and I turned and looked out of the rear window at the house that held so many good and awful memories. We had been through so much together. I wished I could have been a better girlfriend and helped him more in this last dreadful year. Had I done enough? I felt so guilty for not having been stronger, for drinking too much, for going crazy at times . . . it went on and on. I felt responsible for the entire relationship. If only I'd been smarter, prettier, thinner, a better person . . .

I had not an ounce of strength left in me. My forehead rested on the car window, tears streaming and nose running but I hardly noticed. The driver silently passed me a big handful of tissues. We locked eyes in his mirror for a moment and he just nodded at me. I appreciated his stillness.

I would not be making this journey again.

23rd February 2004

Very low today. The initial sense of relief you experience when you finally break free from a difficult, passionate, destructive long-term relationship is overwhelming, but that is soon replaced with gut-wrenching loss. A relationship like that is like a drug. Time and again it spins your head around and gives you an incredible high and then pulls the rug from under your feet and you come crashing to the ground. But you become addicted to the cycle and as the lows get lower and your self-esteem plummets, you desperately cling on, hoping for the high that will fix you both again. It's as if you were addicted to the person.

I was twenty-three when we met, I'm twenty-eight now and I've realised I don't know who I am. It's time to pick myself up and start finding out.

24th February 2004

Trained with Matt. I had no energy and it was boxing today. I put the gloves on and Matt told me to try imagining the pads he was holding were the faces of anyone who'd ever been horrible about me. Now that helped! I started with every journalist who'd written disgusting things about me and John . . .

'Whoah! Bloody hell!' exclaimed Matt. 'Got some pent up frustration there I see.'

At 3.30pm I had an interview with Dom, from *FHM*, to go with my picture. It was at Soho House, a super-cool and fiercely private members-only club. I'd always wanted to have a look in there, which was a bonus.

The interview was a lot of fun and, after a couple of glasses of champagne, I was rather trigger-happy with my tongue and Dom was blushing. My sex life was already so out there after the *News of the World* pieces that I felt pretty comfortable giving Dom what I knew their readers wanted. This was a job after all, and I saw it as exactly that. You don't talk to a lads' mag about your passion for embroidery, after you've just posed naked for them do you?

So I played the 'naughty nurse' role that everyone wanted. Not that this was entirely disingenuous of me, on the contrary, there was truth in it. However, I still know that this won't last forever and I am keeping my acting dream close to my heart.

25th February 2004

Today I had my audition for Marc Sinden. I had learned a long monologue he had chosen from the script. I'd dug out all my books and notes from drama classes and gone through the piece, breaking it down into units and objectives. Matt had even helped me by testing me on my lines.

Marc was absolutely lovely and put me at ease. I was nervous but I loved doing the piece. Marc directed me and got me to do it a couple of times. He told me at the end that he hadn't known what to expect from me but that I had really surprised him. He wanted to recall me for a second audition.

I skipped straight round to see John Noel to tell him. He was pleased for me, and a little surprised, but I think he's wondering where I'm going with 'this acting nonsense' as he puts it. He's not really an acting agent, but he's supporting me nonetheless.

Anyway it's OK, *I* believe I can do it.

26th February 2004

Came down from the high I was on after the audition today. Spoke to Sam about some nasty piece a female journalist has written about me. Back to reality then.

Trained, which helped, and picked up some scripts for a demo CD I'm going to do to try and get some voiceover work.

Went for a spray tan to perk myself up.

27th February 2004

Now the pressure's off and the *FHM* shoot is over, I'm going to come off the Atkins diet gradually. I can't bear it any longer and I'm sure it can't be good for me.

Feeling a bit anxious today. I've got the recall for Marc Sinden next week but that's about it. My thoughts turned to my old colleagues on the ward, slogging their guts out. I don't feel worth-while anymore now I'm no longer working as a nurse. In fact I feel quite the opposite today.

28th February 2004

Trained with Matt this morning and I'm going out with Aisha, my good friend from the acting course at Kensington and Chelsea College. I haven't seen her, or had a drink for weeks. I can't wait to catch up and let my hair down. Well, I say 'my' hair ...

I'm having a blow-dry at 2pm. I know now that I will probably get papped so I need to make the effort, especially with these flip-ping hair extensions. When I dry them myself they look like a small child has been playing with them. If I'm going to get any other work then looking good in the papers will help.

1st March 2004

Oh, in the name of arse. Looking nice in the papers = good. Looking pie-eyed in the papers and as if I'm snogging my friend = not so good.

I'm all over the tabloids again. Which is oddly exciting and sickening in equal measure. This is because there's a picture of me whispering in Aisha's ear as she turned her head and they've made it look like we were kissing. They've gone crazy for it. So basically I look like a tart. Oh God, am I turning into a tabloid tart?

Sam said, 'Don't worry, it's just upping you in the sexy stakes.'

OK then. I was sorry for Aisha though. She didn't ask for this.

2nd March 2004

Well, one good thing that came out of the Saturday night debacle was that I met a man! A hot Italian man, called Joe. Get this (now this is the way to do it, boys) he sent the *sommelier*, not just the barman, over to Aisha and I, at the bar at the Sanderson, who handed us the champagne menu and said, 'The gentleman over there would like you to choose a bottle of anything you like, with his compliments.'

Classy.

The smartest thing that Joe did was that he didn't even come over to us. At all. He just smiled at me and then ignored me. Which had me absolutely gagging to meet him. Finally, as he was leaving he casually walked past, introduced himself, asked me for dinner, took my number and left in a trail of exquisite aftershave. I wasn't quite sure what had happened.

Joe called me today and we arranged dinner for tomorrow night. I'm so excited! I haven't dated for five years!

And I've certainly never been out with a handsome, rich, well-dressed Italian before. God, what shall I wear? I'll ask Miranda. She's style-bunny.

3rd March 2004

John and I released a statement through Taylor Herring that we had split and the *Sun* have run a story on it today. It never ceases to amaze me that anyone would be interested.

I don't feel good today.

I've cancelled the dinner with The Italian. The timing just doesn't feel right, my mind is on what was in the papers. Maybe I'm not ready to date yet after all.

5th March 2004

I had the recall audition for Marc Sinden today. I put my heart and soul into it. When I'd finished he sat me down, looked me in the eye and said,

'Before I say anything else I first want to say this and I want you to listen. I can see how important this is to you and how unsure of yourself you are. I want you to know that you don't need to feel that way because, in my opinion, Abi, you can do it. You can act. You have got that special something. I think you need someone to tell you that don't you?'

I was embarrassed to find I was crying. I knew he was going to say I hadn't got the part but it wasn't just that. It was the sound of someone validating my shaky belief in my ability. Telling me that I was worth something.

I didn't get the job, and he was right, I am far too raw to be put straight into a professional theatre job right now. But I did walk out of there with my head held just a little bit higher. Marc's kind words had encouraged me to follow my dream, that it was the right path.

He said to come back to him one day when things had calmed down a bit, that he would remember me. I wonder if he will?

6th March 2004

Have rearranged my date with Joe for 8.30pm tonight. He's asked me to meet him at the Blue Bar of the Berkeley Hotel, in Knightsbridge. Nice choice. It's a beautiful, swanky cocktail bar that I have seen in magazines but never been to. Have been nervous all day.

Will I recognise him? I only met him for a moment.

I wonder if he knows anything about me from the papers?

Oh my God, what if he recognised me and only asked me out because he thinks I'm up for a frigging orgy? What if he thinks I want sex because of the way I came across in my raunchy interviews?

At least he's Italian so maybe he doesn't read the papers.

Oh, stop worrying and just go, Abi. It's only dinner. There's absolutely no way I'm going to be sleeping with him.

7th March 2004

Oops.

Did the walk of shame in last night's outfit this morning. Joe was charmimg, I was tiddly, his apartment was nearer . . .

It was a lovely evening. We drank fabulous cocktails, had a delicious dinner, went to a cool little club. It was so much fun. His Italian accent makes everything sound better. He could probably say 'let's go to Stringfellows and wash glasses,' and make it sound sexy.

Anyway, I don't care.

I am modern woman and I am single and liberated!

Oh crap, I left my bra there.

8th March 2004

Had a lovely day with my old friend Katie today. We worked together as nurses on Bentham Ward and became really close. She supported me throughout my turbulent relationship with John and even more so in these last two years. I'm very lucky to have her.

She's met a man now and moved out of town, so I got the train to see her. She can't believe all the fuss in the papers,

'What are they so interested in you for? Sex symbol? I might ring up and tell them that this is the girl who took Weetabix in her suitcase to Lanzarote!'

9th March 2004

On the catching-up (and reasons-to-go-out-drinking-as-am-not-working) theme, I had dinner with Zoe, another nurse friend from the ward. We went to the Slug and Lettuce, no swanky cocktail bar tonight, although I didn't let her pay for anything. Christ, she was still a nurse and I had just earned thousands. I knew exactly how much she had to live on and how difficult it was. I was in the same boat six months ago. It was the least I could do.

All I wanted to hear about was life on the ward, how was it? How is she getting on without me? (I mentored her a bit when she first qualified.) What patients did she have today? Did Mr So-and-so die in the end? I wanted to feel part of it again and I think I wanted to feel missed, that the hospital could barely function without my Florence Nightingale-esque benevolence.

Actually the doctors were more likely to miss me because there was no one to sneak them paracetamol and anti-sickness pills for their hangovers.

As Zoe talked about her day I listened, thinking how much respect

I had for her and all of them on the ward, doing such a wonderful and difficult job. My day job seemed pointless in comparison.

17th March 2004

Another night out tonight. I keep getting invited to parties, it's unbelievable. At least I'm catching up with the girls! Tonight was the opening of some fabulous new bar/restaurant called Taman Gang and I was on the VIP list.

Miranda came round to get ready as usual. Before she arrived I had been practising a pose in the mirror. I'm fed up with looking like someone's drunk auntie at a wedding in pap shots. I once read Liz Hurley say, 'To take a good picture I don't just stand there, I have my pose.' I scoffed at that at the time but now I can see what she means. So I need to have my pose.

I tried a few. Ha! this is hilarious, I feel ridiculous. OK, feet together . . . no, I look like I'm guarding the Crown Jewels . . . How do I look side-on? Christ, my tits look like a shelf. Hmmmm.

The *FHM* photographer had told me to create a shape with my body, because it makes a more interesting picture. So, hand on waist, hip tilted, leg out, stomach in. OK!

I look slightly like I'm doing 'I'm a little teapot' but it will do. I must remember how I did that. Especially after I've had a few.

'Wow you look hot!'

'Cheers, bun!'

Miranda liked my outfit, so did I. I actually felt good about my body for the first time in years. I took a last look in the mirror.

The training had really paid off, I was my slimmest ever, plus I had nice hair (another blow-dry today), nails, a tan and I'd learnt how to do my make-up a bit better. I was never exactly a dog's dinner on a Friday night, but now I had really made the best of myself.

It was a brilliant feeling to actually like my reflection. It was unfamiliar.

Joe, The Italian, called before we went out. He wants to see me again. I really like him but I'm not ready to jump back into a relationship again. I'm too busy partying! After a miserable couple of years, I want to have some fun!

I do want to see him though. He's lovely.

18th March 2004

Well, what a night.

The paps didn't recognise me at first, with my new look, and I was almost up the red carpet when they realised it was me. They went bananas.

Shouting at me that I looked great. For the first time ever, I enjoyed the paparazzi. I admit it. I'd worked so hard on myself and I had a bit of my body-confidence back. It's a powerful feeling to feel comfortable in your skin. It doesn't tend to happen often, or last long for me. I even remembered my teapot pose! Just.

I had a great night and surprise, surprise, got completely mullered. I met a posh polo player (PPP) – he was really cute and absolutely lovely. Met loads of people actually and danced all night, really let our hair down.

By the end, after I'd put Miranda in a cab home, there was a big group of us and we went back to someone's hotel room to carry on partying. Someone even tried to give me a gram of coke (for free? What was all that about? Is this what happens in the showbiz world?)

I finally went home at around 5am. PPP said he'd like to see me again.

Keep reading about my big transformation from frump to glamour puss. Makes me laugh. People are basing their view on one unflattering shot of me in my nurse's uniform. But they forget that photo was taken just after I'd finished a nine-hour shift, had no make-up on and had just discovered my then-boyfriend had been arrested. What's wrong with wanting to go out looking nice? Is that such a problem?

19th March 2004

There are pictures of me outside Taman Gang absolutely every-where. The *Star* said 'fellas couldn't keep their hands off Abi as she partied at a swish London bash.' The *Daily Record* says 'Abi cadabera ... she's finally shed her angelic image.' There's a full-length shot in the *Daily Mail*, the *Sun* has called me 'Abi Fitmuss,' and it's all over the *Mirror* too. Good Lord. Sam rang.

'Abi. Do you understand how hard it is to get this kind of coverage? You make my job look easy!'

Joe rang today and came over all strong and very Italian. I loved it. He is insisting on seeing me tomorrow. He said, 'Eef you have plans tomorrow, you cancel them. I amma peeking you up atta eelevenn a.m. We are going forr deener. You breeng your passaport and an eevening dress.'

Whaaat? He wouldn't tell me anything else. Oh my God, how exciting! I'm so going.

Where am I going?

22nd March 2004

I have just spent two nights in Milan.

Ha!

Joe took me to MILAN for dinner.

HA HA!

It was like a dream. He treated me like an absolute princess, but not in a flash or show-off sort of way. It's as if he's been sent from somewhere to make me feel lovable.

We stayed in one of the most expensive and beautiful hotels in the city (the one the Queen stays in, don't you know). Joe ordered champagne and olives up to the room before we went for dinner. I'd never seen olives like these! They were as big as golf balls and an exquisite soft green colour. You had to eat them like a squirrel eats a nut. I showed myself up and had too many, naturally.

He took me for dinner, then to a cool bar, then dancing. I remember one of the clubs had dancers hanging from the ceiling on long, coloured sheets and doing acrobatics. We drank champagne all night. I felt like Cinderella.

Naturally, by midnight Cinders was steaming.

Joe didn't seem to mind, he looked after me. Such a gent. The next day he took me for a walk around Milan. The architecture is so beautiful. Then we test drove a Ferrari, as you do. I want one now! Then he took me to meet one of his handsome friends. Are they all like this over here?

Joe had intended on coming home on Sunday but we were having such a nice time that we stayed another night.

I floated home this afternoon on a pink fluffy cloud . . . to a story in the *People* about me, Miranda and Posh Polo Player, from the night at Taman Gang. Says I was dancing with PPP, then flashed my boobs at Miranda in back of cab (I would never do that!) The journalist adds that the party continued at the hotel but what follows is a load of utter fiction: I 'seduced' PPP after dragging him into the hotel bathroom . . . then we both emerged from the hotel the following lunchtime full of smiles. If only.

I feel so angry, more for Miranda than me – she didn't even come to the hotel! It's Mothers' Day for heavens sake. What's her poor mum going to think?

I spoke to Sam, who calmed me down and also had some good news. *FHM* have been in touch to say they're really pleased with the shots. So pleased in fact that they're now going to give me two pages. It was only meant to be a quarter of a page!

I was really pleased but still a bit upset by the story yesterday.

So I did the only thing I knew that would make me feel better – I went out.

Went for food with one of the bunnies then popped into Chinawhite. As we were walking down the stairs we saw Eddie Irvine walking towards us on his way out. Eddie and I simultaneously did a double-take as we passed each other and he smiled warmly at me. 'All right?'

'Hello,' I smiled back. We paused for a second and then both just carried on. The girls were behind me and I wanted to get to the bar. He had a nice smile though.

Stayed for one drink, then left. It was rubbish.

23rd March 2004

I do not believe this. There's the most horrible piece in the *Mirror* today. It's on the '3am' pages. Says that days after 'canoodling' with PPP, I was shamelessly chasing Eddie Irvine around Chinawhite.

'She was begging to be introduced but he wanted to be left alone – and at one point got pals to stand round his table so she couldn't get near . . . she followed him to bar and in end he left early.'

Sam's really angry and she's fallen out with the 3am girl Jessica Callan – they're meant to be really close. She says it's the only time she's ever rowed with her in the many years they've been mates.

'Jessica hadn't even bothered to check the story,' fumed Sam.

It's sweet that she's so livid on my behalf, but I think she feels protective. She knows it's not true. I've just got the feeling she also knows the tide is turning very much against me. Am starting to realise I have no control over what people say or think.

Besides, if I was reading that story about someone else – I'd believe it. And I'd probably hate them. I feel so disliked.

Joe wanted to see me tonight but I've said no. My head's in a spin and I keep crying. Not a good look. Besides, he's almost too perfect, it's too much. I can't understand why he likes me.

24th March 2004

FHM don't dislike me though.

Sam called me. 'Guess what?'

'*FHM* have seen the papers and are now dropping me altogether?'

'No, they're going to make it three pages – maybe even four! They want to use more shots. They love them so much Abi! This is amazing. You've done really, really well and should be proud of yourself. It paid off, darling.'

I couldn't believe it. I've done this. I prepared, I trained my arse off and it worked. Just one picture would have been achievement enough.

25th March 2004

Sam again. 'Are you sitting down?'

Never in a million years did I expect her to say what she said next.

'They're going to put you on the cover.'

Oh.

My.

God.

'Abi – do you know who was the last person they had on the cover?'

'Who?'

'Halle Berry.'

Wow.

'You have done it, lady. Try and forget about all the shit you've been through. This is one thing you can feel proud of.'

And I know deep down that it's all because the shoot was good – it's nothing to do with the fact that I'm any more famous now than I was then. It's down to my pictures. I've earned it.

I had a meeting this afternoon with some TV producers from ITV about a new show called *Hell's Kitchen*. They seemed really nice and they want me to be in the show. It sounds a bit mad though – two teams of celebrities working as proper chefs in a kitchen run by Gordon Ramsay. I've no idea why they want me in there, I'm not a celebrity.

Am I?

After that I had another meeting, with a man called Darryn Lyons. He runs a picture agency and told me that I am insane not to be capitalising more on my current fame. He said he could make me thousands from sales of photographs to papers and magazines.

'Just give them what they want,' he said in his Aussie twang. 'It's simple.'

He talked about shots of me on a beach holiday – taken as if they were paparazzi snaps, but that I actually had complete control over (meaning I looked good in them too). He said that if I worked with him I would pocket the money from the sale, rather than some greasy pap who's been trailing me, trying to catch me when my top falls down.

'Why hasn't anyone done this before?' I asked.

Darryn fell about laughing, 'Jesus facking Christ giddy-up girl!' he shouted. 'We've been doing it for years!' and he stood back to reveal a big whiteboard on the wall.

It was covered with the names of about fifty celebrities from massive A-list Hollywood stars to C-list British ones, with locations that they were going to be at on a given date and time this week.

It was staggering. I ran my eye across the names, wow . . . So she does it? And him? And her?

Darryn was a bit full-on but I liked that about him. More than that, I liked the idea of taking control of my own image very much indeed.

26th March 2004

Viewed some houses today and came up with a shortlist. I really can't believe that I am going to be able to buy one of them.

27th March 2004

Did a trial set-up shoot with Darryn. I went into the expensive, sexy lingerie shop Agent Provocateur and shopped while he took a few quick shots through the window. It was fun and easy. It did feel a bit cheesy, pretending not to know he was there, but then I thought of some of the names on that board and didn't feel so weird.

29th March 2004

Had a talk with John Noel about finding another agent to represent me. John Leslie was his first-ever client, he's been with him for fifteen years and it just doesn't feel right that he's looking after me too. Besides, John Noel had always told me – 'What I can do is help you make as much money as you can in six months, but that's it. I'm not really an actors' agent.'

Besides that, I'd got too close to him in the last year. I needed a new start and he said he would help me find someone to look after me.

He called Taylor Herring and James Herring set up a meeting with an agency called Money Management. They were great, really encouraging about the acting but also realistic about what I need to do to get there. They have lots of plans – not least of which include paying for my own photo shoots so I get a cut of the profit when they're used. It means I get control of my image. They told me to think of myself like a company – 'Abi Limited' – that way I'm always in charge of my choices, and my career. They really seem to know what they're talking about. What's more, James trusts them – and that's good enough for me.

30th March 2004

The top boys at *FHM* took Sam and me for a fab lunch today in a cool restaurant called Hakkasan. They wanted to congratulate me on making the cover (which still hadn't sunk in). I could get used to all these lovely lunches and dinners. It's like I'm finally experiencing the side of London that I've always read about in magazines. I still feel like it could all end tomorrow though, so I'm appreciating all of it.

1st April 2004

There's a story in the *Sun* – saying that I'm 'desperate to land a part in Channel 4's *No Angels*' and that apparently approaches have been made. First I've heard of it, but at least it tells people that I do want to act, so maybe something will come of it.

2nd April 2004

Flew to Dublin today with ten girls for Katie's hen weekend. She doesn't know it but I've booked a stretch limousine to pick us up and take us out on the town tomorrow night. Tacky? Pah. It's a hen weekend!

4th April 2004

Wow. The *News of the World* is sensational today. According to them David Beckham's been having a secret affair with his personal assistant in Madrid. Blimey.

Katie absolutely loved the limo last night. We did have a laugh. However to my horror she insisted that we all wear pink bunny ears and pom-pom tails all day today, as her hen 'theme'. She is rabbit-mad. We almost fell out. I did NOT want to wear them! They were ridiculous! All the other hen parties in Dublin were staggering around in matching cowboy hats and Supergirl outfits. At least they were vaguely sexy. What if I got papped?

I was soon put in my place by the others. 'Get over yourself, Titmuss,' was the general consensus. 'You're one of us, not some superstar celebrity. As if you're going to be papped.'

I don't know all of the girls here so they must think I'm a right silly cow.

I smiled, put on the giant pink rabbit ears, stepped out of the hotel and immediately got papped.

6th April 2004

I'm in the *Sun* and the *Star*. The shot in the *Star* is much bigger. I'm getting on to a bus in Dublin, with a massive hangover, straggly hair, droopy rabbit ears, a pom-pom tail and a bow tie. To top it off there was no one else in the picture so it looked like I was just strolling around like that on my own. Hilariously it reads: 'blokes were ogling her like there was no tomorrow.'

7th April 2004

Sam set up a meeting with Darryn Lyons from the Big Pictures agency to discuss doing a formal deal. He's certainly a character that's for sure.

Darryn explained the premise. He'll take me away on a few 'holidays' – the Caribbean, St Tropez, Majorca – all flown on his private jet and I'd stay in first class hotels. Naturally I was blown away by the prospect. 'All expenses,' he said, 'will come out of the costs made from the sale of the pictures.' So nothing was needed up front. He also assured me that the costs incurred would be peanuts in comparison to the money we'd make from the sale of the images. As a parting shot, Darryn showed me some of the 'set ups' he's done in the past. Was nothing actually for real in the celebrity world?

8th April 2004

Took my nurse friend Zoe to a *Loaded* magazine party last night. We got ready together and had a drink to calm our nerves. She was so excited, it was lovely. She couldn't believe it was a free bar when we got there and squealed in my ear every time she spotted someone famous.

After a few drinks I completely forgot that anyone knew who I was and it turned into a nurses' knees-up as usual. We got so well-oiled that we could barely walk out of the place.

And it was only Wednesday. This celebrity lifestyle has non-stop parties if you want them.

12th April 2004

Having just about recovered from the *Loaded* party, I had a call today from CID. I have to go into the station tomorrow with my lawyer.

This is it.

13th April 2004

Well, now there's one thing I can tick off my list of 'things to do before you're thirty' – get arrested.

It was terrifying.

The officer was very nice, and I could tell he didn't really want to be doing it, but he was serious. It was just like you see on TV and films, a little interview room with a table and a tape recorder and my lawyer beside me. I felt like I was in *The Bill* or something. Actually, I felt like I was in John's shoes.

As the questioning started I tried to answer as best I could but it was very hard to remember details of that night back in January with Jayson as I had been so drunk. As the icing on the cake – it turned out that the cab-driver that night was a frigging retired policeman who had gone to both the papers and the police. Astonishing.

I just wanted it to end, I wanted to plead with the officer to let it go, that I would never touch drugs again. But of course I didn't.

Eventually he said I would have to wait to hear if I was going to be prosecuted. He couldn't say how likely he thought that was. This is certainly punishment for having ever taken drugs but surely I don't deserve to go to prison for what happened that night?

Now I just have to wait.

Again.

14th April 2004

Trying desperately to put yesterday out of my mind. It's hard. I feel sick every time I think of it. What's even worse is that I can't tell anyone.

I had asked the policeman if he thought the *News of the World* knew that by printing that 'confession' the police would take action against me.

He said yes.

15th April 2004

I need to stop thinking about the police and what could happen. It's going to send me insane.

Been invited to yet another party tonight at a club called Embassy. It's like suddenly I'm on every guest list in town. This one's a fashion party for a designer called 'Wheels and Dollbaby'. They sent me some clothes to wear. Was thrilled. Sam said it's because they know I'll get papped and that way they get free advertising. Free ads for them, free clothes to me. And at least I can forget my worries for a few hours.

Jordan was there, so was Myleene Klass. As if the papers are going to use my picture over theirs.

16th April 2004

Shots of us arriving at the party are in the *Star*. I've got half a page, while Jordan and Myleene's pictures are minuscule. Not bad, Titters.

17th April 2004

Story in the *Mirror* again from the Embassy night. Apparently I told a reporter, 'These are my fuck-me pumps. I hope I get lucky tonight.'

I would never say that – every girl knows it's fuck-me heels! Actually, I was joking with my friend. As if I'd say that to a journalist. Does that mean people are listening to everything I say?

19th April 2004

I'm off to Barbados with Darryn Lyons to do some pictures tomorrow. He doesn't waste much time. After the stress of last week I am so glad to be getting away. Am so excited!

20th April 2004

On the one hand this whole trip seems insanely odd but on the other it's just a brilliant piece of business. Darryn flew club-class and I was economy. Bit miffed about that at first, and he could clearly tell by my face, because when we got to the lounge he casually mentioned that whatever I did would come out of my budget. That soon shut me up. I haven't got that kind of money, and I'm certainly not paying a fortune for a seat.

21st April 2004

Darryn's got an amazing villa out here, it's idyllic. As soon as we arrived on the island he introduced me to the paps who work for him overseas. They're based here all the time because there's a constant stream of celeb holiday-makers. Darryn laughed, 'If you don't want to have your picture taken, don't go to Barbados.'

One of the photographers was quite cute. Things are looking up. Quite nervous when we went to do the first 'shoot'. I've never done this kind of thing before. But after a few minutes I soon loosened up. Then there was no stopping us. They had me sitting by the pool, sipping cocktails, coming out of the sea with wet T-shirt clinging to my body, the lot. All very cheesy but Darryn said the key was to be 'doing' something or to have an 'accessory' – that way the picture was easier to sell. 'It needs to tell a story so there's something to write about.'

22nd April 2004

We're doing loads of set ups. And anything goes, it seems. I had the idea of riding a horse along the beach, so Darryn arranged it.

Unfortunately the horse decided it didn't want to walk after all. So I ended up sitting there like a twat.

23rd April 2004

'We're going to St Lucia today,' announced Darryn. Wow, this was the life.

Jet-ski time. We looked back at the pictures afterwards and some of them looked really cool. There was one of me wearing a cowboy hat and the lighting was beautiful. God, I never need look like a munter again! Genius.

Am learning so much about the whole business. Knowledge is power and all that. Darryn explained that if some pictures are out on the news wires straight away that means other paps can't sell theirs. So, he advised, 'If you ever go on holiday, do some set ups at the start, then you can relax for the rest of the time.' To be honest, I don't even care how much they would sell for. It's quite simply about being in charge.

27th April 2004

Flew home. Back to reality and a reality TV show. The meeting I had with the producers a while ago went so well that they've made a firm offer for me to be in *Hell's Kitchen*. Blimey.

I can't cook to save my life, I burn water, but I'm going to have proper training from Gordon Ramsay. So I'll earn some money *and* come out a Cordon-Bleu chef!

They want to film me 'cooking at home' on Friday. This could all go horribly wrong . . .

28th April 2004

Walked into Sam's office and there it was. My *FHM* cover. I was tingling with excitement. I couldn't wait to see it.

She handed me the issue and there I was, near-naked on the cover.

'Oh,' I said. It didn't look like me. My face looked weird.

'Everyone's critical of how they look, Abi. You look really pretty.' Sam smiled.

I didn't think I looked pretty at all. I looked odd.

Opened the magazine and – oh no, oh no, oh no. After everything they'd said about not showing nipples in that shot, there I was. Completely, full-frontally, nipple-glaringly TOPLESS. I was standing behind a Perspex, transparent screen and you could see everything.

I burst into tears. Sam looked at me like I was completely off my rocker.

'What the . . . ? I thought you were going to love it . . . ?' But I was devastated. It was such a shock. I'd gone further than most people, but you have to have some boundaries! Otherwise I might as well have opened my legs and let them take a picture of my fanny.

Feel so stupid. But what could I do now? Also, this was *FHM* and being such a focal part of it was a huge deal. They'd see it as them having done me a favour. Nevertheless, Sam made a call.

'They've said they're sorry, there must have been some miscommunication back in the office.'

Bloody hell, I hope they don't think I'm being difficult. I loved doing the shoot – and the rest of the pictures are stunning, I must admit. But something tells me it might be my last . . .

The *Sun* has run one of the set-up shots we did in Barbados. Kerching! It sold for loads! Thousands! Their columnist Jane Moore has written a sarcastic piece about it. Of course she knows it's a set up but who cares. 'Alone in Barbados . . . unaware the photographer was there . . . . The fact that her head was thrown back in porn-style ecstasy while a see-through top resembling a wet tissue clung to her breast implants was entirely by chance.'

But who's the winner, her or me? She's the one writing about me.

29th April 2004

A huge package arrived at the flat with my name on. It was from *FHM*. They'd sent it to say sorry. It was a massive maroon leather case. Looks so bloody expensive. When I opened it it was filled to the brim with all sorts of amazing stuff: champagne, perfume, Calvin Klein goodies.

Despite all that, what affected me most was the address label. It arrived in a soft green bag. On the outside was a sticker bearing *FHM*'s logo. And it simply said: 'ABI'.

I couldn't stop looking at it. What a moment.

It's like I'm part of the *FHM* team.

My wet T-shirt picture's in the *Sport* and the *Sun* have used the one of me on a jet-ski. Darryn knew they'd go mad for that one. The *Sun* has run theirs with the headline 'I want to bed Britney.'

Hilarious. When we knew they wanted the picture I agreed to do a small chat to go with it. The journalist asked, 'If you had to choose four or five people to have a celebrity orgy with who would it be?'

For a laugh I'd said 'Britney Spears, the lead singer from the Red Hot Chilli Peppers and Jenna Jameson. And Robbie Williams. I didn't actually say 'I want to bed Britney!'

The *Star* has got some of the *FHM* pictures. There are quotes from my interview about kissing girls. Can't even remember me saying that, must have been all the champagne! But if that's what they want . . .

The headline is: 'It's lovely – you don't get stubble rash for a start.'

They've also run the results of *Loaded* magazine's 'Sexiest' list 2004. Get this: the world's sexiest women – Angelina Jolie is 60, Jordan is 1, Paris number 2 and I'm number 3!

1st May 2004

Sue called, laughing.

'Stephen, eh? I didn't know you were into teenagers!'

So much for me liking the *Star*. Turns out there's a ridiculous story about me dating some nineteen-year-old called Stephen Johnson. I'm twenty-eight, for God's sake. I want sex, yes. But not that badly! Called Sam. Stephen is Charlotte Church's ex apparently.

Sue brought the paper round. Stephen finds me an 'inspiration' and 'texts all the time'. Oh and we've been out on a few dates too. How lovely.

2nd May 2004

The *People* has somehow got wind of the fact that I'm not happy about the pictures in *FHM*. Well, I say 'got wind' – I'm pretty sure Sam planted the story to generate publicity:

'A close pal of John Leslie's ex said: "She was assured fake steam would be put on the pictures so they didn't look too saucy." Seems odd that Abi – who became a soft-porn TV hostess after losing her job on *Richard and Judy* over revelations about her sex life – is now so shy.'

Too right I am. Women are going to hate me when they read this. I would despise me.

4th May 2004

My friend Marisa was home from Australia today. Hurrah! We were really close for a few years, after working on the ward together and living in the same nurses' home. We even moved rooms so we could be right next door to each other. She left to work in Australia a year ago and I've missed her hugely.

It was so good to see her. I sat her down and watched her jaw drop as I filled her in on what's been happening to me.

She could not believe it. I was still a nurse on the ward this time last year when she left.

5th May 2004

Had dinner in Gordon Ramsay's restaurant in Claridges tonight with all the other celebs that are going on *Hell's Kitchen*. We had a private alcove with a big round table. The restaurant is so beautiful, all art-deco with gorgeous pictures, huge chandeliers, white flowers on the tables and the most flattering, atmospheric lighting I have ever seen. It took my breath away, It's like stepping into an old movie.

I sat next to Matt Goss. Ha! I couldn't help being a bit excited to meet him; I used to love Bros and there is definitely something a bit weird about having dinner with someone whose face you used to kiss goodnight on a poster every night (which, incidentally, I told him and he loved!).

ITV filmed the dinner, which felt strange. I kept looking down to check I hadn't spilt anything on my dress. I felt very out of place and nervous at first but I think some of them could sense that and everyone was so nice to me – especially Al Murray, James Dreyfus (who is hilarious), Matt, Jennifer Ellison and Belinda Carlisle.

James and I ended up getting the most squiffy I think, but I don't care. Haven't laughed so much in months.

6th May 2004

The *Sun* ran a story today saying '£500,000 Abi lives in bedsit for nurses.' You nasty, nasty bastards. Now everyone's going to think I've left some poor nurses out on the street, hungry and homeless because I've got the room that they could have. Half this building is empty! The manager has told me time and time again that he wants me to stay as long as possible until I can find a place to buy.

Called him to see if he really does want me out. He told me not to be so ridiculous.

God, even I'm beginning to believe all this shit. Besides which, I'm trying to find a flat to buy as quick as I can. I've got some more viewings today.

8th May 2004

Thank the Lord for Richard and Judy. They have a column in the *Express*. They stuck up for me.

'One of our former colleagues' – ah, they see me as one of them! – 'is rarely off the front pages since we parted company. I refer of course to Abi Titmuss, John Leslie's ex. I don't think I've ever seen a transformation like it. When she worked on our programme as a roving reporter, Abi was demure, ever-so-slightly boring and always fully dressed.' Ever-so-slightly boring? I cracked jokes! . . . actually, they have a point . . . 'Overnight, since those three- and four-in-a-bed revelations, Abi has become a no-holds-barred lads' mag babe. At first I felt extremely sorry for her parents and even for Abi. But now it's becoming obvious she relishes her new public identity, not to mention earnings of around half a million.' Er – half a million? Who's got that then?

' . . . So I think it's time everyone stopped judging her – she's doing what she wants, she's not breaking any laws and, since her split with John, she's in control of her own life. What's wrong with that?'

Thank you. Thank you. At least someone likes me. Am so grateful to them for everything they've done. They've only ever had nice words to say about me, and they could so easily have turned their back on me.

We're starting work on getting my own set of photos done straight away – my agents, Money, said I need to get a load of shots in the bank to be sold to the papers whenever they write anything about me when I'm on *Hell's Kitchen*.

10th May 2004

The shoot is going to cost thousands of pounds and I'll be paying for it out of my own pocket. Christ. My management assured me I'll get that back with two or three shots and then after that I'll be the one laughing all the way to the bank. I hope they're right. What if no one wants to buy a picture of me?

12th May 2004

Day of my first 'Abi Ltd' shoot. The photographer was great. It was a woman which helped, and made me feel so much more comfortable. We did loads of set ups all based around a kitchen so the papers could link them to the new TV series.

Know I'm never going to be a top model, but I have to make this work. I need to be real and make people want to see pictures of me. I asked the photographer what makes a good shot. She confirmed what the *FHM* snapper had told me: it's all in the eyes. Sounds crazy when you're standing there nearly naked, but what makes a really successful picture is what's going on up there. She said, 'If you're really feeling it and getting into it, the reader can tell.'

Focus. It was like acting, I just knew instinctively what to do.

Licking ice lollies, doing the cooking in a pair of leopard-print pants, kneeling with pink frilly knickers on a worktop, licking a spoon, washing up with long black gloves on . . . At one point I was crouching in front of an open fridge, in a see-through nightie, holding a bunch of grapes to my lips thinking, 'This is ridiculous. What in the name of arse am I doing here?' But you know what, I think they're going to work.

13th May 2004

Yay! Found a lovely flat on Islington Green. Soooo excited.

14th May 2004

Sam called.

'Are you sitting down?'

'What now?'

'*FHM* have called with their sales.'

'Shit. It bombed didn't it?'

'When they make a magazine, they estimate how many copies it will sell that month –'

'Yes, yes, OK . . .'

'– If it sells 5,000 over the estimate that is classed as very good. Ten thousand over is brilliant, and the absolute best possible result would be up to 50,000 over.'

'Wow. Have I sold 5,000 over? That would be amazing.'

'Abi, they sold 100,000 more copies than they'd estimated!'

She was nearly screaming into the earpiece. I'd never heard her so excited.

'Ten times over their expectations! That's power, young lady!'

Power.

I have power.

I know my worth.

I'm worth something.

Mum came down to London today from the village, with her best friend Val. To celebrate my news I took them for a posh lunch at Hush, which they loved. I'm starting to know where the top restaurants are now, and feel even more comfortable when I'm in them. It's a wonderful feeling to be able to spoil your mum. Especially the mum who once, when I had nothing, offered to sell her house to pay for me to go to drama school.

Neither of us can believe what is happening to me. After so much pain and stress in the last year it is so nice to be able to enjoy a positive moment. I want to be a better daughter.

15th May 2004

Nurse Katie got married today! Marisa and I went together. The three of us used to be inseparable. It was a beautiful day. I had gone to Katie's wedding-dress fittings with her so I knew what she would look like but I still burst into tears when she walked in.

Wonder if I will ever get married? Carole Malone once wrote about me in the *Mirror*, 'No one would ever want her as their wife, mother or daughter.' She had never even met me. Still, it doesn't do wonders for your self-esteem. It's hard enough to find a bloke, even without comments like that.

21st May 2004

Hell's Kitchen starts in two days. Am so excited. Over the last week we've been doing hygiene and food preparation classes (yawn) and some cooking classes at a catering college. As a test, Gordon got us all to make an omelette. Pretty much everyone's was crap. Gordon had a field day. He's quite scary. Oh dear, maybe this isn't going to be a walk in the park. We're all being put in a shared house. I hope no one judges me. At least this gives me a chance to show people I have a personality, I'm not one-dimensional. I am human.

The survey on the flat's come back. Not good. Been advised to pull out. Shit. Haven't got anywhere to live. Have told the nurses' home I am moving within the next month now. How can I do that when I'm cooking all day?

23rd May 2004

Arrived at *Hell's Kitchen*. Very nervous.

There are so many nice people here. Amanda Barrie – she was so beautiful in *Carry on Cleo* – seems really friendly. Really want to learn from her, she's a great actress.

Matt Goss had been living in LA before the show which meant he obviously didn't know who I was before we met at Claridges, and with the cameras on us then we hadn't really had a chance to chat normally. It also meant that the inevitable question had to be asked: 'What do you do?'

I didn't know where to look or what to say. Felt so embarrassed. This was a guy who used to be in one of the most famous boy bands in the UK – what was I meant to say to him? 'Oh, my boyfriend was in a scandal and I stood by him. Oh, and then some guy sold some photos of me and him in a foursome.' I was mortified. I knew it was a privilege to be asked to appear on a show like *Hell's Kitchen*, but no one in their right mind wants to get famous by being dragged through the tabloids.

I felt really self-conscious. Why am I even here? No one's going to care about me.

Part of me wants to curl up and hide. The other part wants to show people that I'm not just some sleazy wannabe.

Jennifer Ellison from *Brookside* is really sweet and giggly. Really pretty too. Belinda Carlisle – another icon! She's nothing like I imagined – really dry and witty. And such a filthy laugh. She called my name and I nearly fainted.

Love James Dreyfus, he's so naturally funny. Al Murray is brilliant, makes me laugh all the time and he's a real family man. He told me all about his wife and kids. Not seen his stand-up act but he's got such a jolly aura about him. Out of everyone, he's been the nicest to me.

As for Gordon, I thought he'd be really scary but he was OK. Powerful yes, and quite sexy in a way. If you look past the lines on his face that is. He's like one of those wrinkly pug dogs up close. But he doesn't give a shit, and he's so passionate about what he does.

And swears a lot.

We had a 'blind taste' test. As soon as I had the blindfold on I knew Gordon was going to make some sexual comment.

'You must be used to these,' he laughed. 'Do you swallow, Abi?'

Everyone giggled.

I felt sick, and thought, 'Why did you have to say that in front of all these people?' But I didn't show I was upset. It would only give him more power over me. Couldn't let him see I was vulnerable.

Instead I had a comeback – 'Do we get handcuffs as well?'

Afterwards Al came over to me sympathetically. 'You must get that all the time . . . '. Think I've got an ally here.

Some of the food we tasted was disgusting . . . calves brains nearly made me throw up.

The rest of the day was fun though. My tarte tartin got top marks! Nice to have a different kind of tart associated with my name for once.

24th May 2004

We had to kill a live lobster! I was so nervous. I couldn't stop looking at it, like it was a person with feelings. It was horrible. Had no choice in the end. The look on Gordon's face told me if I didn't kill it, he'd do away with me instead.

By the end of the day we were rolling pasta for Gordon's trademark dish – ravioli stuffed with the lobsters we had murdered. I still felt bad but they tasted delicious! Sorry, lobsters. Feel absolutely knackered, but so proud of myself. I'm learning to cook!

We've got a practice run tomorrow. Have to produce six starters, six main courses and six puddings.

25th May 2004

For the next fortnight we're all living together under one roof. Not that there's going to be much time for enjoying ourselves. Am fast realising there's a good reason it's called *Hell's Kitchen*.

There's a girls' section and a boys' area in the house. Mind you, if we wanted to make them into one big room I'd just have to stick my chest through one of the walls – they're so thin. Me, Belinda and Jen are together while Amanda and Edwina Curry are in a separate bit. Outside there's a garden area with deckchairs – it's up on the first floor, but we've got astro-turf and decking. Decided to toast our last evening of freedom (and unburnt, unsliced fingers!) with some vino.

26th May 2004

Woke up this morning and the horror of what we were facing washed over me. Over the next fifteen days, we've got to prove ourselves in a specially built restaurant, Hell's Kitchen, in East London, serving Michelin-quality food to celebs, food critics and members of the public. And just to add to the pressure, TV viewers will be watching us live every step and cock-up of the way on ITV! Angus Deayton's hosting it and getting viewers to vote for which of us deserves the chop first.

As soon as I entered the kitchen it was like all that training had gone in one ear and out the other. There were seventy-five people in the restaurant and they were all hungry. And by the end of the night, quite a few left in the same state. Gordon refused to let anything be served unless it was perfect. And hardly anything was.

Fuck me this is hard.

Jen is so sussed and confident. I'm older than her but I feel so much younger. You can tell she's done the whole showbiz stage-school thing – she knows intuitively how to hold herself. Some of the bunnies came into the restaurant tonight – it was so difficult seeing them and not being able to speak to them. Of course, that didn't stop me trying to get their attention.

Why do I never learn? I made joke hand-signals to them through the glass from the kitchen, suggesting Ramsay was all talk and no action.

But he spotted me.

'Why don't you just pull your knickers down and stick your butt against the glass?'

Had to bite my tongue to stop the tears. I know I shouldn't have done it. But that was below the belt. It's just perpetuating the opinion everyone already has of me.

Thank God for Al Murray. I don't feel judged by him at all.

His wife came in and ran up to the kitchen. The security guard tried to stop her and Al was shouting 'That's my bloody wife!' He had tears in his eyes. It's harder than you think being in a TV show like this, with no contact allowed from your family and under immense pressure.

They had a kiss across the hot plate. Bless them.

Caught a glimpse of myself in the glass this evening. I look dreadful. Jen looks so pretty in her chef's hat. People are going to see me and say 'Ah-hah, so that's what you really look like! Dumpy and plain.'

I feel like Amanda Barrie's being odd with me and it's making me really uncomfortable. Hope I'm imagining it.

The producers rewarded us all tonight (for actually having fed the diners!) with takeaway pizzas and wine back at the house.

We made Matt play 'When Will I be Famous' on his guitar which was hilarious. Feel a bit star-struck by him actually.

Not that he was awake for long of course – the women had much more staying power than the men. In the early hours, we took our microphones off and started telling stories. Belinda started talking about when she was in the Go Go's. I didn't realise how much of a rock star she was. I thought she just sang about circles in the sand. She told us that they were voted number two in a chart of 'the most debauched rock videos of all time.' Motley Crue were number one.

Belinda and I eventually bowed out at 3.30am and Jen followed a bit later. Amanda outlasted everyone. Good girl.

27th May 2004

Our celebrations were short-lived. When he saw the state of us today, Gordon ripped into us for having a late night.

By the time we reported for duty at 9am, he was ready to tear strips off us.

'This is only going to get harder. You all need your sleep and not late nights, wine and fags.'

Things just went from bad to worse after that. I feel like Gordon has got it in for me. He was so intimidating. At one point he pressed his face pressed inches from mine. His reasoning? He caught me giggling on two separate occasions.

'Every time I look around you're fucking giggling. This is fucking serious. We're so fucking close to getting it spot on and you think this is a fucking joke.'

I was so shocked. Couldn't even speak at first. I was laughing more out of nervousness than anything. Then I broke down in tears.

Couldn't sleep tonight. Shouldn't be here. Everything's getting too much, feel really unhappy. Terrified because have to do the meat section tomorrow. Haven't got a clue what to do or how long things should be cooked – and daren't ask Gordon because he'll shout again. Want to run away.

Got back to the house and sat in my room with my head in my hands. Suddenly there was a rustling noise coming from the other side of the door. I lifted my head and looked over. Someone was pushing a piece of paper towards me. It was a letter.

I picked it up and slowly flattened the creases. It was two pages of beautifully written script. And it was from Al.

He told me a funny story about something that Matt had done that day and laughed about the way some of the others were behaving. It was as if he needed to let off some steam too and it was lovely.

And of course, it made me cry. At the point where I'm feeling my most vulnerable, this means so much. I turned the page to see he'd written out instructions of how to cook all the meat, the names, correct timings – everything. Do this, don't do this, don't panic. He's even worked out how I can get away with bringing this piece of paper in with me! 'You can hide it behind the salt . . . '

He's done all this to help me.

29th May 2004

Amanda and I haven't spoken to each other properly for two days. And the silence between us must be all the more difficult for everyone else because we're both in the same team.

Amanda tried to slap Gordon during a row yesterday, but he grabbed her wrist. He called security who rocked up and prised them apart.

The producers have called a psychiatrist in to see her. Wish they'd come and see me too.

30th May 2004

Amanda walked tonight.

Am so relieved, I can't tell you. The tense atmosphere has lifted – no one's said as much, but you can tell they feel it. It's Jen's birthday too.

James Dreyfus is genius. The pressure was really on but he just seems to thrive on it and it makes him act the clown even more. I was on desserts, really panicking, and he waltzed over, smashed an egg all over the counter and walked off. It was so funny. Even Gordon raised a smile.

And James keeps doing impressions of us all. I was desperate for him to do one of me. And he did:

'Hi I'm Abi and I speak reallyquicklyandIneverfinishmysentences . . . '

Everyone was in stitches. He's so right! Matt and Al are always telling me: 'Be calm . . . don't talk so fast . . . finish your sentence . . . breathe.'

Had a few drinks for Jen after work. Well, actually we all got completely pissed and ended up dancing around and singing. How funny to have your birthday on telly.

31st May 2004

Although we're living in a restricted house, friends and family are allowed to email us at certain times. The emails are vetted by producers so they can't tell us anything about what's going on in the outside world. Which to me is a good thing.

Earlier this evening, Edwina came over and said her husband had a message for me because he could see I was so down.

She read, 'You're looking great, keep going.' It was incredibly sweet, yes. But I felt a bit odd. Edwina seemed uncomfortable. So did I.

What can I do? No wonder people think that way about me if people's husbands are emailing me.

1st June 2004

I was standing in the line-up of cameras, live on ITV, with Angus Deayton clutching the card with someone's name on and praying it wouldn't be me out first. I would feel like everyone in Britain hated me if I was. Then again, why would anyone vote for me?

It was Belinda. Each of us had to develop a 'signature dish' to serve. Mine was venison and celeriac mash with chocolate sauce. It sounds horrendous but when I said I wanted to use venison, Gordon secretly suggested that I make a dark chocolate sauce as that's what he does in Claridges.

Suddenly it's really starting to feel like a competition.

2nd June 2004

Competition it certainly was. And Titters is no longer in it.

Gutted. Even before the votes came in, I knew it was going to be me. Suddenly felt overwhelmingly sad. The team were fantastic. Don't want to leave but I can't deny it was getting difficult.

Gordon seemed horrified that I'd lost out to Edwina. Never realised he thought so highly of me. He was strutting about, calling it 'a fucking disgrace'. Still, I'm the second person to get the boot.

When I agreed to take part in the show I had two hopes:

1. That at least a handful of people would say 'You know what? She's all right.'
2. That I wouldn't be the first one voted out.

At least I've achieved them. I think. I still haven't been myself though, and there hasn't been one minute when I haven't felt out of place.

What's more, my nails are ruined, I'm covered in burns, my feet are in bits from standing from 8am till 1am every day and I've got one finger practically hanging off where I'd slashed it with a fish knife.

My evictee interview with Angus Deayton was conducted with me complete with sweaty kitchenwear. All I kept thinking was 'I'm sitting here, on telly and I look like shit.' I wanted to crawl under one of the tables and hide.

'It's been really hard work, hasn't it?' he said.

'Yes, it has actually, we've been getting no sleep, finishing really late, getting up really early in the morning.'

'Yes,' he smiled ' . . . let's have a look at that, shall we?'

Cut straight to a shot of me, pissed as a fart on Jen's birthday, dancing round the lounge like I didn't have a care in the world. The time at the bottom of the screen read: 3.30am.

The cameras are always watching.

After the show I was driven to a suite at the Great Eastern Hotel – all the contestants are to stay here when they get voted out. A bit of luxury as I get used to reality again.

Spoke to Sam. I was desperate to know how I'd been received.

'It's all been really positive – there's been loads of interest, you've been all over the papers with your kitchen shots, magazines are keen and GMTV are thinking of you for a job as a presenter.'

I'm elated.

Nevertheless, still can't shake the nagging disappointment that I didn't have the confidence to shine as much as I could. Feel like I was just chopping spring onions and crying the whole time.

3rd June 2004

Had to get up at 5am to go to GMTV. Had the funniest sensation on the way there – felt really disorientated. I know it sounds silly but I've been holed up for almost two weeks with no contact with the outside world and it seemed so bizarre to be in a car and see places whooshing past me – the traffic, the radio playing, the people – it was all oddly unsettling. Unless I just needed some more sleep.

I was nervous. When I arrived, Eamonn Holmes showed me a scrapbook that he'd been making – full of pictures of me – they'd obviously made it as a joke but it was nice all the same. He was immediately welcoming and did everything he could to make me feel comfortable.

Fiona Phillips didn't.

Eamonn patted the sofa and joked, 'Do you fancy a job on here? . . . Go on Fiona – let Abi sit down.'

She had no choice but to get up and let me take her place for a few minutes. And she absolutely hated it. I could see it in her face. I hadn't forgotten what she'd written about me before *Hell's Kitchen* started, either:

'Hell's bells! Abi Titmuss, right, has got herself a job on ITV1's new primetime reality show *Hell's Kitchen*. So the former nurse, best known for her three-in-a-bed romps, has literally shagged her way to the top. Pardon the unladylike language but what sort of message does that send out to Britain's work-shy, fame-obsessed young-sters?'

Not that there was anything I could do about it. I was out of my comfort zone. Fiona was the one in the position of power; it was her place I was sitting in. Felt a bit of a wimp that I couldn't have it out with her, but I know it's not in my interest. It would only make things worse and people hate me more. Eamonn did most of the talking anyway.

'It strikes me that there are two yous. There is Abi Muss and there is Abi Tit.'

'There are lots of sides to me. There's the side that went to university, there's the nurse, the side that goes out with my friends . . . I'm still a twenty-eight-year-old single girl having fun.'

Am sure Fiona Phillips raised an eyebrow at that one. Eamonn also asked me why I wanted to go on Gordon's show in the first place.

I said, 'There is the caricature of me that has been painted and there is the real me. Hopefully it might mean people change their perceptions of me. I just wanted to come out and have people say "She's not bad really."'

Naturally I was asked about John.

God, I wish the whole thing would just go away. I know it's the reason I'm doing all this, but feel like I have to keep defending myself, as if I've used him and that all through our relationship I'd been secretly plotting my 'I want to be famous' master plan.

There were questions about Amanda Barrie too. Tried to be as diplomatic as possible. Said we got on well and that she was funny but that it was an odd environment to be in – lack of sleep etc. What I really wanted to say was that she wasn't very nice to me and it had really upset me.

'Why did you want to go into sexy modelling?'

I answered as honestly as I could: 'At that point in my life things had gone awry. I wasn't sure what else to do . . . but it's given me a deposit for my first flat. Look at how many other actresses do it. I don't think there's anything wrong with a girl being sexy and attractive . . . I think it's great and I enjoyed it.'

That seems to be the problem though.

That I enjoyed it.

All I've ever done is stand by my boyfriend and had a story sold on me. Then, because I was asked to do some photo shoots and I agreed – I'm now some kind of tart. What if I said, 'Oh I hated every second of it . . . I felt used and violated' – would women like me more?

I bet if no one had known anything about my background and suddenly I sprang up on page three of the *Sun* they wouldn't give a shit.

Spent some time later with Sam looking at cuttings of articles that appeared when I was on *Hell's Kitchen*. The set of pictures we took before I went in have worked a treat. They've been used all over.

And that means money for me!

The leopard-print pants, marigolds and soapy sink shot made front page of the *Star* – with the headline 'Abi: how I got Roger Cook up again.' Touché.

Next day there was another shot in the *Star*, and this time the words were: 'Saucy Hell's Kitchen babe Abi Titmuss got her hands on a mighty chopper last night. And the plucky star put it to good use, beating a rival celeb to carve up a pigeon in expert style on the reality telly show.'

The pics I took with Darryn in Barbados are still selling too. The *Sport* has one alongside the header: 'Abi topless and touching herself.'

Nice.

And guess what? *FHM* want to sign me up as their columnist for a year! It's big bucks. All I have to do is some saucy shots and answer readers' sex questions. This is more like it.

The only problem is that I feel like I'm moving further and further away from what I really want to do – acting. I am becoming, what? A celebrity chef? A glamour model? A sex columnist? What am I?

I don't think I have any choice but to keep going, all these things are a massive step forward compared to where I was a few months ago and I do appreciate that. I will never lose sight of my dream though. Never.

Did a phone interview with the S*tar* (they've bought another one of my shots they want to print!)– am getting used to what they want from me now. Sam told me to give them just enough tittle to make a good headline and they'd be back for more. In a funny way it's a bit like acting in itself – I could be in a *Carry On* film the amount of innuendos I'm coming out with. The 'Abi Titmuss' they want to write about is a character from a saucy seaside postcard.

And so be it.

Got back to my room at 10.30am and slept till 3.30pm. Was absolutely shattered from the entire experience of the last two weeks.

My management sprang on me the news that I'd got a gig as a guest presenter on Virgin Radio. Love the idea of being a DJ. Well, until I recorded something at lunchtime and I was absolutely rubbish.

It goes out tomorrow. Thank God it wasn't live. Sounded like Alan Partridge. All I had to do was sit there and record links but I was awful. The producer was nice enough but didn't give me an ounce of guidance – merely kept saying 'Yes, just do that once more . . . do that again.'

Lord knows what it's going to sound like. Am not going to tell anyone I know.

Also did my first big interview with the *Sun* this morning – it's harmless stuff. Naturally the questions were all about sex, not cooking. Talked about not having had a boyfriend for ages and, yes, of course that meant I was sexually frustrated. Told them I thought Matt Goss was gorgeous but added that I wouldn't consider anything as he has a girlfriend (they'll probably leave that bit out). Somehow the journalist managed to get me to admit that I'd love to have had a massage from him – can't even remember how we got on to it – something about the long days and being tired and achy. Waffled about how sweaty it was in the kitchen. They seemed to like that bit.

Predictably it wasn't long before we moved on to the subject of Mr Ramsay. I admitted my relationship with him was tough at first and that it seemed like he was picking on me at times. Then the journo kept pushing me on the possibility of sexual tension, which bored me a bit, but I didn't show it.

Such a busy day.

The afternoon was spent doing an interview with the *News of the World*. The journalist was called Sharon Marshall. I'm being paid for it but for the first time ever this was a really nice chat. It was funny, girlie and warm – sex wasn't mentioned at all. My manager had arranged for copy approval so I was safe in the knowledge that even if I said something I regretted it could be taken out afterwards.

Came away feeling like I'd really achieved something. At last I was going to appear in the paper in a manner that my parents could be proud of. We did a photo shoot to go alongside the interview – it was a tiny bit sexy but not tasteless.

Just had to move from the suite in the Great Eastern Hotel. I've gone back to my old nurses' pad. At least the paps can't hide outside my window quite so easily now though – the tree was chopped down weeks ago. Ha ha.

Listened to myself on Virgin Radio. It was so cringy. I was speaking ten to the dozen. Could hardly understand a word I was saying.

5th June 2004

The *Sun* interview has come out and guess what the headline is?

Abi: 'I fancy Gordon and Matt.'

Smack-bang wallop next to a picture of me in my bra and pants. I guess I asked for it really. I've just gone to all this trouble chopping vegetables, spending fourteen-hour days in a rotten kitchen and now I've blown it. Stupid cow. What are Gordon and Matt going to think when they see it?

I never actually said 'I fancy Gordon'. I just said that he was attractive and powerful. I was being light-hearted! But of course that doesn't come across in print.

Had a whine to Sam about it but she soon put me straight – if I want to carry on getting paid for interviews, then that's what I need to be prepared for.

'It's simply the way it is.'

And let's face it, no one's going to want to read an article with me spouting off about how much I enjoyed making tarte tartin.

There's a piece in the *Daily Star* which is a bit better. It splashed on what a bright future I've got ahead of me. And if I get as many job offers as they're suggesting I've had already, I'll be a very happy lady. They've run quotes from me about the fact that I've been doing drama classes over the last few years which is good. They've also said I've just been recalled for a top West End show! Hollywood beckons eh?

The *Mirror* is saying I've been offered a show on Virgin Radio after being a guest presenter. Must be a PR spin from them. Can't believe I'd be given a show after that performance!

Got the copy over from the *News of the World* interview to read and approve. Really chuffed with it. It's precisely as I hoped it would be and a complete step away from the usual titillating business. For the first time I can hold my head up high and be pleased of something that's in print. Phoned both Mum and Dad to instruct them to read it tomorrow.

'Make sure you go out and buy the *News of the World*. I've done a story and you'll like it. Promise!'

At last, something they can be proud of. They've long stopped looking at the papers for obvious reasons. This time they'll be so happy.

Mum, Val and my friend Cheryl from my home village, Ruskington, are coming down tonight to have a meal in the Hell's Kitchen restaurant – we're planning on meeting up for lunch tomorrow. I'm feeling really happy for the first time in ages. My hard work is paying off and there seems to be light at the end of the tunnel. The future is starting to look a bit brighter at last.

Tomorrow evening it's the live final and all the contestants are on the show. I can't wait! I've got a new dress and it'll be good to see everyone again. Have a hairdresser and make-up artist coming over to the flat especially. Very exciting.

6th June 2004

News of the World came out today. Am ruined.

I don't know where to start. Feel numb. Am still not really all there. Wish I wasn't here at all. I have never felt so low in my life.

I had woken up at about 10am, blissfully ignorant. Mum phoned. She sounded a bit strange.

'Are you OK?' I asked.

'Yes.'

She didn't sound very convincing but I didn't think anything of it. 'Have you seen the paper?' she asked hesitantly.

'No, not yet,' I replied breezily.

'Oh, OK,' she mumbled.

'What is it?' I was a bit annoyed because she'd called me earlier than she said she would and she wasn't making much sense.

'Have you spoken to Sam yet today?' she asked.

'No, of course not, it's Sunday morning.' I was still half asleep and clueless. 'Why would I?'

'Nothing, nothing. Don't worry about it, see you later.'

'See you later.'

Weird.

Then Sam rang me.

'Are you sitting down?'

This was becoming a bit of a theme. I wasn't. 'Why?'

'I think you should sit down.'

'What is it?'

'You're on the front page of the *News of the World* – the headline is: "Abi's New Sex Video Shame".'

My legs literally just gave way underneath me. I fell to the floor. I couldn't believe it. I was in shock. I denied it at first. I didn't even remember. I didn't want to remember.

Then she went on to tell me that there were screen grabs of me and a black girl. I was racking my brains, what the hell was she talking about? Then I went cold. Memories were creeping in. Over the five years I was seeing John, he had had quite a few wild parties and the flipping video camera came out a few times too. It was only for fun, there's nothing wrong with that, but I hadn't done anything like that for ages and how *on earth* has it ended up in the hands of a national newspaper?

'The pair are then seen writhing on a bed exploring one another's bodies. As Leslie fights to control the camera Abi performs oral sex on him . . .'

It was everywhere. I felt so utterly violated. And I'd actually told my mum and dad to go out and buy the paper. So many feelings hit me at once that I physically couldn't move. They kept coming like huge, sickening shockwaves through my body as it sank in and another thought hit me, then another, then another . . . My dad seeing me like that, my mum, their humiliation in front of the newsagent, everyone in the village, at their workplace. Oh God, my poor dad. He is a teacher at a posh public school. For boys.

It got worse . . . What if people I've worked with have seen it – everyone on *Hell's Kitchen* and ITV, doctors and nurses on my old ward, the male receptionist downstairs who gives me my post. Has he seen me having sex now? And men on the street, in bars, in the supermarket . . . It went on and on.

Then I felt a jolt in the stomach. It wasn't even just John and I. I was in a threesome with a girl. Lesbian sex. None of my girlfriends even knew I'd done this, let alone my parents. Now it was national, front-page news and fully illustrated in glorious technicolour for every delighted reader.

The feelings of utter humiliation were profound and debilitating. I felt as if I'd been molested by every man on the street.

I couldn't move. At first I just lay on the floor for several hours sobbing and shaking, repeating the word 'no' over and over again.

Sam kept calling. I was too embarrassed to answer my phone and talk to anyone but eventually I did. I felt light-headed now and as if this wasn't really happening and I would wake up at some point.

'Abi, you need to get yourself together and start getting ready.' Oh FUCK. It's the live final of *Hell's Kitchen* on ITV1 tonight and I'm expected to be there, alongside Gordon and the other celebs. After all my hard work on the show I'd been looking forward to it so much. A few hours ago I'd been so happy and excited. I looked over at my wardrobe and grimaced at the sight of my new dress hanging there expectantly. Fuck, the hairdresser and the make-up artist would be turning up soon.

I felt sick. 'There's no way I can go,' I said quietly to Sam, 'I can't face everyone.' I couldn't speak without filling up with tears. Sam was adamant I should go. 'Are you going to let whoever did this win? Why should you let them stop you? You have absolutely nothing to be ashamed of. If you don't go it will be even worse. This is your show, you earned your right to be there, and it's your night.'

'But how can I possibly face people?'

Sam wasn't giving in. She battled on and reasoned with me until I saw no other choice. 'What are you going to do if you don't go? Hold your head up, Abi.'

'OK, OK, you're right. What else can I do? If I sit here on my own for much longer it feels like this room is going to cave in on my head. But I don't think I'll ever stop crying.' I felt trapped. I couldn't think straight, my head was spinning. But I knew I had to face it head-on, like everything else I'd been through.

But it was so, so hard. It was one of the most difficult things I've ever had to do. To go outside and face people like Al, Matt and Gordon?

Mum came round. I couldn't speak to her. She was downstairs. She kept pressing the intercom, asking me to see her just for a second. There was no way I could face her. I begged her to go home. The guilt I felt knowing how much pain she was in because of me was heart-breaking.

The first time I opened my door it was to the hairdresser. I could barely look her in the eye. I just sat there numbly; I don't think I even spoke. She could've shaved all my hair off and I wouldn't have noticed. Or cared.

When my car arrived I was shaking. I didn't want to look the driver in the eye. It was like the whole world had seen me having sex. All the people I'd been on the show with thought I was a sweet nurse, an ordinary girl – were they all going to think I'd deceived them now? I was convinced they'd think I wasn't really who I said I was.

I got to the restaurant and tried to put a brave face on it. When people asked me how I was I replied, 'I've had better days.' Followed immediately by the sick realisation that it was the exact phrase John used during his court case. He used to say that to everyone. And now I'm in his position.

My friend Al Murray was fantastic. I knew he would be. He didn't even need to say anything and he made me feel calm. I was next to Belinda Carlisle at the table – nervously waiting for Angus to have a dig. But Sam had assured me he wouldn't say anything awful.

I just didn't know who'd seen it and who hadn't. But I knew they all knew. I hadn't eaten all day. I couldn't. I ended up getting completely pissed.

Then it's a bit of a blur. I have a vague recollection of dragging a few of the crew with me to the Great Eastern Hotel at 4am where we demanded a room. This resulted in me and one of the guys from *Hell's Kitchen* sat in an empty bathtub, fully dressed, drinking and talking rubbish till about eight in the morning.

Then I somehow got home.

7th June 2004

I felt sick from the instant I opened my eyes this morning. It was that gut-wrenching moment you experience when something terrible has happened and your brain has blissfully forgotten it while you were asleep. Like waking up the first morning after your boyfriend has left you, or you've lost your job. Today is a million million times worse.

I have no job, no future that I can see and absolutely no shred of dignity or privacy left.

I stood and looked at myself in the mirror and wondered how on earth all this had happened to me. Two years ago I was a part-time nurse happily, and doggedly, pursuing my dream of being an actress. I wanted to start a degree in drama and spent three years doing acting classes and supporting myself with night-shifts at the hospital. Now look at me. I've got nothing.

I hate myself. I feel dirty and guilty. Who's going to want to have anything to do with me now? How can I possibly ever continue with my acting or any job in television or theatre, or any job at all for that matter? Will there always be one person who has seen it? And I can't imagine any man wanting to introduce me to his mother now. I can't even face my own.

I haven't left my building today. All I can see are the grey walls of my flat as I lie on the futon. I don't have the energy to get out of bed. I've just been curled up in a ball blankly facing the wall. I can't eat or drink. I don't even have the TV on. And I can stay like that for hours.

8th June 2004

The police want to see me again about the drugs charge. I feel like I've been on a terrifying rollercoaster that I can't get off, for six months now. Every day and every time the phone rings I don't know what to expect. Up, down, up, down. Am exhausted.

My lawyer picked me up this evening and took me to a police station out in west London, where no one would notice me.

After grilling me again they told me that the Crown Prosecution Service (or 'Criminal Protection Service' as they jokily call it) had still not decided what to do with me and I would have to wait again.

No one knows what to say to me or how to help. I can't speak to anyone anyway, I'm too humiliated. This is the lowest place I've ever been in my life. Ever. I don't even want to go across the corridor to the bathroom.

9th June 2004

I can't speak to anyone. I just want to shut myself away forever. I don't know how to cope.

Sam's the only person I answered the phone to. All the job

opportunities have disappeared. I could tell Sam didn't want to tell me – but I asked. She tried to break it to me gently by saying 'The offers have gone away for now.'

But I've been through it once before. Might as well get used to it. Going through the thing with John, then getting sacked from *Richard and Judy* – and now to have it happen again. Publicly shamed, nationally humiliated. Can it get any worse?

10th June 2004

Have hardly eaten and had no food at all at home so had to force myself to go to Tesco. I went in the early hours of the morning so that no one would see me, my cap pulled down over my eyes.

I'm terrified of being recognised on my own now and I feel intensely vulnerable. What if a man that has seen the film of me having sex thinks that I am somehow 'up for it' and that he can approach me?

My heart raced all the way there and back and I also constantly looked over my shoulder and into cars for paparazzi.

It's always worse at night when it's dark and you're not expecting the flashes, it really shakes you up. Kept my head down and sped past the spot where a group of them (all men) had jumped out on me one night. I'd thought I was about to be attacked and screamed out loud – I was so shocked. I remember I started crying but they just took pictures of that.

How can I be so paranoid, jumpy, vulnerable and stressed on a simple walk to the supermarket? This has got to stop. I'm starting to feel very angry.

By the evening I was thoroughly sick of the four walls of my room. I was supposed to be taking Miranda and Sue out tonight to the opening of *Tonight's The Night*, the Rod Stewart musical. There was no way I wanted to go but my bunnies came round and sorted me out.

'You need to get dressed and get out of this frigging room. It's ridiculous, hiding away. Come on, out!'

Good old, straight-talking Sue.

As soon as the curtain went up I was glad I went. At one point I looked at Miranda and Sue, singing along in their seats, so happy and 'normal' and such good friends to me, and I started crying. A big part of me wanted to be like them again.

There had been one pap outside when we'd come in and I hadn't minded that. I'd smiled for a nice picture. But when we left there must've been fifty. They surged around me, flashing away and shouting my name. I didn't know what to do, I kept smiling but it was very intimidating. Sue got scared and ran ahead to try and find us a taxi. Miranda was trying to hold on to me so I could see where I was going but we got separated.

I was shouting at them to keep calling out so I knew where they were. Then a photographer shouted 'Abi, you've dropped your keys!'

'Oh no! Where?' I turned around and bent down to try and spot them. As soon as I did a blast of flashes went off and all the men started laughing.

I hadn't dropped any keys.

Finally Miranda and I made it into a cab, after the pack followed me all the way up the street. Sue had jumped in another one; I hoped she was OK. My friends hate all this attention. Miranda glanced at me, she looked scared. We shook our heads. 'Fucking hell, Abs, that wasn't funny.'

I'm going to try and sleep now. I honestly don't want to wake up in the morning

Deeply unhappy. I wish that someone would help me or tell me what to do. I'm frightened and I feel very alone.

11th June 2004

Woke up this morning and realised that I may be depressed but I am still breathing and have therefore survived the worst week of my life. Also, the rollercoaster is now click-clacking it's way up, as I'm on the front cover of *Nuts* again. They've used the pic of me licking a lolly suggestively from my shoot – without the cowboy hat this time. That picture is proving to be a bit of a winner. The fact that my two friends are saying 'hello boys' might have something to do with it. Not only that but there's a whole five-page feature about me entitled 'is there a more perfect woman in England?' and they've bought nearly all the shots I did to go inside – licking the spoon, the leopard pants, apron and oven shot, saucy fridge shot . . . And deep down I know it was sparked by the *News of the World*'s 'exposé'.

Last night's pictures are in the paper too. Seems Victoria Newton from the *Sun* has an important question: 'What's the point in Abi Titmuss?'

What have I ever done to her?

'We all know she has big boobs but we've seen them already. And let's face it, they aren't real. And what is she wearing? It's not a case of Da Ya Think I'm Sexy? More like, Da Ya Think I Got Dressed In The Dark?

Going on *Hell's Kitchen* was Abi's latest attempt to be taken seriously as a telly presenter. But all it did was confirm she has zero personality . . . So please, Abi, disappear.'

OK then – stop writing about me, otherwise I won't disappear, will I? 'What's the point of Abi Titmuss?' Then they go and print a big picture of me.

12th June 2004

Off to Majorca today. Darryn Lyons has been hassling me to do another lot of set ups since I left the show.

'The papers are gagging for you – we need to give them what they want!'

I'm taking my friend, Cheryl, as a treat. We've been friends since I was sixteen and she's been ill recently.

A couple of friends of mine have a friend who knows someone who has a yacht, so while we were out there they said I could get some pictures done on the boat as it would look a bit glam for the papers.

At least that was the plan. But while I was out there on the boat someone else gazumped the pap I was with. Darryn was fuming. Says this other guy must've done the shots from the shore with a long lens because he sent the pictures back straight away before we had a chance to deliver ours.

Very strange dichotomy. Part of me feels arrogant to have been setting up shots of myself in the first place.

I've got to get my head round the fact that someone is probably going to take my picture, so I need to get there first. On this occasion I got the timings wrong, that's all.

14th June 2004

Darryn rang, still fuming. The other pap's shot is in the *Daily Record*, among others. Headline is 'Abi Titmuss cools off from the heat of *Hell's Kitchen* with a cruise off Majorca', something about me taking a dip just like my 'popularity' did after the release of my 'porn videos'.

15th June 2004

It's ten days since the *News of the World* story ran. I wonder if someone else will be going through their own hell today courtesy of the tabloids. Makes me feel strange; I am now old news. The rest of the world has moved on and I'm left battered and exposed.

Had a stilted phone conversation with Mum today. It was awful.

My parents have both been unswervingly supportive, loving and dignified through all of my troubles but I can tell Mum is very confused by the fact that there was another girl with me in the video. Even the idea of making a 'home movie' is so alien to both my parents – it probably seems a bit perverse.

There was a genuinely worried air of 'what on earth is going on down there in London that we don't know about?' in Mum's voice. Can you blame her?

I attempted to explain that I was just curious about women and experimenting with John and lots of people make 'home movies' and . . .

Oh fucking hell, stop, stop, stop.

It was toe-curling.

'Actually, Mum,' I said gently, 'do you know what? I don't think any adult should have to explain to their parents exactly what they have done in the bedroom. It isn't right or normal for us to be having this conversation. All you need to know is that there's nothing for you to worry about, I haven't done anything wrong or abnormal. And I'm not gay.'

'Because if you were you know that would be absolutely fine and you could tell me?'

Mum, you're fantastic but this is so humiliating . . .

'I know, Mum, thanks.'

16th June 2004

We all went to Jewel for Jennifer Ellison's belated birthday celebrations. Was so good to see the guys from *Hell's Kitchen* again. Especially when we were all dressed in something other than smelly old kitchen whites.

We got absolutely wasted – seems to be the only sure-fire way to blank things out these days. The night was such a blur. Ended up going back to the Metropolitan Hotel with Jen and her boyfriend Tony, just sat talking nonsense and thinking we were all comedians for most of the night. At least it took my mind off things.

18th June 2004

The 3am Girls are saying that Jade Goody's ex Jeff Brazier 'couldn't keep his eyes off' me at Jen's. If I recall correctly, I was introduced to him and said, 'Hello, how are you' and that was that. Whoopee do.

It's getting mental just leaving the flat at the moment. There are paparazzi lurking everywhere. Am also reaching the point when I have to have a security guard with me to get me out of clubs.

Another night out tonight, this time at Pangaea. Sophie Anderton was there. I'd met her a couple of times before and always thought she was a bit 'off'. Her boyfriend Mark is nothing but lovely, such a friendly guy. He runs the place, and whenever I come in he always says hi, never in a flirty way either. But Sophie is awful. Tonight proved that.

When I walked in and spoke to Mark I could almost see the thunder cloud hovering above her head. Suddenly, she said 'Come here,' and dragged me to one of the booths in the back.

'What's the fucking story with John?'

She was referring to some newspaper story making out she'd been with him recently doing drugs.

'You tell me.'

I soon realised she was convinced the whole thing was a conspiracy between me and John! She accused me, John and John Noel of planting the story to bring her down.

'I was never even with him! What are you doing to me?' She was just ranting madly.

'Why are you shouting at me?' I cried. I didn't have a clue what she was talking about. I was shocked. People could see us . . . this was embarrassing.

Instinctively I switched into nurse mode – I knew I needed to calm her down so I could get away. But she wasn't listening to me, she didn't care.

I glanced behind me and noticed a woman standing there, obviously listening. Oh God, this is going to end up in the papers. I wasn't having it.

I turned. 'I'm going to leave now.' I almost expected her to hit me.

As I left I said to Mark, 'You need to sort your girlfriend out.'

He simply looked at me as if to say 'Not again, I've been here before.'

19th June 2004

Had an interview with Ben Todd from the *Sunday Mirror*.

'Why do you think men like you so much?'

'I guess because other models are so untouchable, and, well, maybe I'm normal. It's known, unfortunately, that I do like sex. I guess people think I'm genuinely sexy, rather than just pretending to be.'

20th June 2004

The *Sunday Mirror* interview is out.

'It's an extraordinary moment in an extraordinarily frank interview in which Britain's naughtiest nurse reveals all her sex secrets ... Abi says "I'm not like those glamour girls who say 'I'm really dirty, I'm really bad', then just pose around," says Abi Titmuss. "I really am dirty AND bad – I just love sex."'

I didn't mean it like that! I keep getting myself into this. It looks so sleazy when it's written down. I said it in jest, but I was a fool to think it wouldn't be paraphrased into tabloid talk.

The *People* have got the story on my row with Sophie Anderton:

'Party girls Abi Titmuss and Sophie Anderton lashed out at each other in an astonishing nightclub catfight. And, amazingly, the hand-bags-out tiff was sparked by a row over shamed TV star John Leslie. Clubbers couldn't believe their eyes when the glamour girls – dressed to the nines in skimpy dresses – went in for some no-holds-barred wrestling.'

Who do they think I am, Hulk Hogan?

21st June 2004

Had a series of shots for the *FHM* column done – all scantily clad because obviously if you need any help with your problems, you also need to see a picture of me in my knickers.

Each week I simply have to speak on the phone to a guy from *FHM* I've never met and answer problems like 'How do I have anal sex with my girlfriend?' and 'I've just been in the army for five months, how do I know it's going to last for longer than five minutes?' They told me I didn't even need to do anything – just putting my name to it was enough. But I want to get involved – prove I'm doing the work.

Went to see Al Murray's *Pub Landlord* show at the Cambridge Theatre tonight. It was the opening night and I went with Edwina, Matt, and James. He was brilliant – I'd never seen him at work, only in the kitchen. Didn't really realise what he did, or why he was famous. I thought, 'Look at him up there on that stage!' Felt so proud to call him my friend.

22nd June 2004

Thank God I didn't have to stay in this evening. Was invited to the premiere for *Around the World In Eighty Days*. I'm so glad I had the balls to go. Firstly because my friend Suzanne cheered me up brilliantly as always, and secondly I had no idea who I was about to meet . . .

It was the first premiere I'd ever been invited to as a celebrity in my own right, which felt weird but undeniably exciting. Instead of being the 'plus one' I had my own.

The girls 'drew straws' and Suzanne won. We decided that if I ever got invited to another one it would be someone else's turn to come with me and so on, although I thought this would probably be the first and last.

After I'd 'run the gauntlet' through the paps outside the Odeon in Leicester Square I met up with Suzanne in the lobby. Like most of my friends, she hates all the shouting and being photographed so we agreed that she would get out of the car first and nip ahead of me unnoticed up the red carpet. Quite frankly I'd have preferred her to have held my hand as I was nervous.

The flashbulbs went crazy. It was an amazing feeling. For a few minutes I forgot caring that the main reason they were all getting so excited was because of my notoriety. The more scandalous I'd become, the more they wanted my picture.

In the cinema we couldn't stop giggling and glancing around to see which celebs were there. There was a whole sea of them scattered around the huge auditorium but it was David Walliams and Nick Knowles who we noticed first. Hard not to – they were sitting in the row right in front of us.

Nick struck up a conversation straight away – he had a cheeky grin and seemed really nice. I was very surprised when he knew my name. I remember each seat had a free bag of Doritos and M&M's on it, which we all joked about being high-class premiere-snacks but then immediately troughed as soon as the lights went down.

The film starred Steve Coogan, but it wasn't very good so we were gagging for it to finish and get to the party. I wanted to drink, have a laugh and meet people.

I was a bit disappointed that the party was in the Hippodrome nightclub though. The last time I was there it was at a crappy '999 night' for the Emergency Services when I was a nurse. But I didn't recognise the place tonight; it was all dressed up to look like different countries of the world inside. I thought, 'You can make a silk purse out of a sow's nightspot.'

We stuffed our faces with food from 'around the world', gawped at fit male dancers twizzling around on long, colourful sheets hanging from the ceiling (wondering what possessed anyone to put them there in the first place, although it reminded me of being in Milan with The Italian. (I must call him) and had our champagne glasses constantly topped-up by geisha-waitresses.

Suzanne made me laugh all night as usual, something I hadn't done for ages, but we were constantly interrupted by circling journalists trying to talk to me. I smiled and just concentrated on trying to keep my mouth shut (not easy for Titmuss). They were persistent though. Sometimes they followed me to the loo or stood close to us to try and listen in on our conversation.

I'd noticed David Walliams again at the party. He kept looking at me from across the room so occasionally I'd return his gaze and hold it that little bit too long. It was exciting and made me feel nice, especially after feeling so low recently. Seems like someone still finds me attractive!

When Suzanne was in the loo he came over and introduced himself. I liked him instantly. He was nice and tall and I liked the way he was dressed. We spoke briefly and laughed about how long the film was. Then he asked how he could contact me. He did it in such a sexy way that I looked at him for a moment with narrowed eyes. 'Why? Would you like to try and seduce me?'

I was a bit cocky thanks to Messrs Moet and Chandon.

He laughed and then I clocked that quite a few journalists were watching us. I told him that I didn't want to give him my number in front of them. Whoever I dated next I was going to make damn sure it was in private.

He said that I shared my publicist with his friend Jimmy Carr so could he get hold of me that way? Perfect.

23rd June 2004

My head hurts. Drank so much last night. But when it's free booze it's hard not to. Keep thinking about David. He was surprisingly attractive. And very intriguing. Wonder if he'll try to get my number? Why didn't I just give it to him?

Sam rang and said that Jimmy Carr's been on the phone. Can David Walliams please have my phone number?

Bingo. I said I'd think about it! No harm in making him wait, it'll tell me if he's really interested. And besides, I bet girls usually rush to give him their number.

I really knew very little about him. I'd missed most of *Little Britain*, the first series that had just finished. I remember catching a 'Lou and Andy' sketch near the end of it though and thinking it was brilliant.

This might be too.

24th June 2004

The *Sun*'s Bizarre column has made out I was running around after David Walliams and got knocked back. The headline is:

'SAD ABI UP AGAINST A WALL-IAMS.

It seems even London's top swordsmen are going off Abi Titmuss. The sleazy ex of John Leslie tried desperately to chat up Romeo *Little Britain* star David Walliams, below right, at the premiere party for *Around the World in Eighty Days*. But even David, who dated Patsy Kensit, wasn't interested and Abi was alone when she left the bash at London's Cirque nightclub.'

Little do they know, eh? Half of me is furious at the fact that they just want me to look like some idiot who'll try her luck with anyone famous who comes her way. The other half is glad they don't know the truth. But David – PLEASE ring me now! So I don't look such a twat.

It's typical of journalists trying to put me down. When they see you talking to a guy at a party they know they can go one of two ways with the story – either saying you're getting it on or saying you're desperately trying to pull them. And they seem to prefer the latter with me at the moment.

There's also a bit in the *Star* about us both being at the same premiere. But they mention David and me separately. They say he's 'nursing his broken heart' because Lisa Snowdon's back with George Clooney. And according to the journalist who wrote the caption next to my photo – there's 'nothing green' about me 'apart from this cheeky top'. Whoever it was needs a long holiday.

Half an hour after Sam gave him my number, David called. He's completely charming. Made me chuckle a lot.

This could be an interesting one. Am not going to agree to a date just yet though. Need to be 100 per cent sure first.

Went to watch England play in the championships against Portugal with one of my mates. In a pub called The Mitre in Fulham. Got drunk.

There was a group of rugby players in there and a few came over and started trying to chat us up. One was six foot seven!

They invited us to carry on with them but my mate cried off and went home. My problem is I don't know when to stop. Went to a place called Sugar Hut, then back to one of their houses for more drinks. Had a real laugh. They were absolute gentlemen and we sat on their balcony under the stars, drinking champagne and talking about how one of them was going to propose to his girlfriend. I think the tall one was a bit miffed I'd turned him down, but hey. Then I fell into a taxi home.

25th June 2004

Did my first 'phoner' for *FHM*.

26th June 2004

David rang – we're going out tomorrow.

27th June 2004

First date with David. He picked me up in his vintage car, which was very romantic (although that's exactly what John did on our first date . . . Oh, forget that, this is different). We had a lovely dinner.

He's great company. He was a gentleman and just gave me a kiss on the cheek as he dropped me off. Not completely sure how much I fancy him either, so it's probably best to wait.

A strange man keeps sending me a lot of letters and hanging around the nurses' flat. He says he's a doctor at the hospital I used to work at but he's starting to worry me. He was outside again today. It's like he's following me. I really hope I'm imagining things.

28th June 2004

Texts from David. He's so sweet. He's invited me to dinner tomorrow.

Apparently my 'sex video' is top of the charts on Scotland's black market. According to the *Mirror* 'Crime barons are netting a fortune', and get this – it's even outselling pirate copies of *Shrek 2* and *Harry Potter*. They make it sound like I'm in *The Little Mermaid*.

29th June 2004

David came and met me and a few of my friends at the Blue Bar (funnily, where I'd had my first date with The Italian. Now I go there all the time; how things have changed).

The two of us had dinner then went back to his flat. I love talking to him, he's incredibly intelligent and I can actually have a decent conversation about all sorts of things. I feel I can learn from him, especially true when I talked about my wish to act, and I like that. There's also definitely a lot of chemistry now, a real spark. But more than that, I feel very safe with him. I can't explain it. I feel at home.

I didn't want to leave him tonight.

30th June 2004

Phone call out of the blue.

'Hi Abi, it's Sophie.'

Sophie Anderton. And she was speaking really bloody quickly, like she just wanted to get whatever she had to say out of the way, and go.

'I'm just ringing to say that I might not have been right when I spoke to you the other night. Mark asked me to call you and I suppose I should.'

Great apology.

Then I had another call, my lawyer. The police wanted to see me again. Oh Jesus. Once again, I got there, nerves in shreds, to be grilled and then told the CPS still hadn't made a decision. The officer said he had recommended to them that it be dropped but that they may have to proceed as it was so high profile.

I came out of the station to a message from David, wanting to see me. Oh God, if he knew where I'd just been he wouldn't want anything to do with me. I must be mad thinking I can get involved with him. I can't see him. This is all too much.

That doctor was outside again. I'm glad I live in a block with lots of other people around me, other nurses and doctors from the hospital, and not on my own. Might be harmless. Hope it is.

2nd July 2004

David's been texting. I want to see him but I can't. I don't want to drag him into my mess, it's not fair.

8th July 2004

Went to Matt Goss's gig at La Scala tonight. He was brilliant and it was so good to see him and catch up over a drink afterwards. During the show, I was up on the VIP balcony with some of the celebs from *Hell's Kitchen* and he pointed us out and smiled at me. I'd never have believed that would happen when I had his poster on my wall as a schoolgirl!

9th July 2004

Woke up with a hangover, again. Texting with David all day as usual. I can't see him.

13th July 2004

Today we shot my first calendar. Well, half of it anyway. The pictures we're doing are such a smart idea – my management suggested we just totally turn the media image of me on its head. So we're playing 'Madame Ironic'.

One of the shots is me with a suitcase full of X-rated tapes spilling out as a policeman tries to arrest me. Another one was taken in a confessional box in a church in Hackney. There's one of me lying naked on a bed surrounded by tabloids, and another of me filming myself.

It was such a long day, fourteen hours solid, but I was used to that as a nurse so it didn't phase me – I loved every second of it. Looked at the Polaroids when we were finished, they're so classily done, it just looks really clever. Also, my management says the pictures will be bought up as images to go with interviews I do. So it's win-win.

15th July 2004

Went to the premiere of a film called *King Arthur* this evening. Was knackered after the shoot but so buoyed up and excited, it didn't matter. Took Sue, as it was her turn. The minute I got out of the car and the flashbulbs started going, she just gave me a knowing grin.

'Off you go, Ari.'

The girls have recently coined a name for the 'showbiz' me.

Her name's 'Arabiatta'. They've been taking the piss out of how I act when I step on to the red carpet. Sue laughed, 'You're hilarious when you get in front of the photographers – flicky, flicky hair, tits out, big flashy smile – its like you're a real posing pro. You're not Abi, you're Arabiatta.'

And Arabiatta was out in full-force tonight.

It feels strange posing for photos and smiling when inside I know what's going on. Trouble is, I'm getting rather used to it all now. I cannot possibly imagine going back to obscurity. Let alone jail.

The after party was amazing, like a medieval banquet. All flaming torches, knights on horseback in suits of armour and princesses constantly refilling your goblet with wine. Made the most of the princesses, waltzed into the VIP area and straight into the three stars of the film – Clive Owen, Hugh Dancy and Ioan Gruffudd. They were all gorgeous, but on screen they had looked like huge, muscley knights and in the flesh they were about my size! A little disappointing but the funny side of it was not lost on us. Until Sue pointed out that means I'd look enormous in a movie. Oh God!

Probably no need to panic about that just yet, Abs. Hollywood isn't exactly knocking your door down.

18th July 2004

Came home today and the stalker was waiting for me again. I could see him in the entrance clutching a bunch of flowers. My heart was beating hard. I waited for him to turn his back so I could sneak in.

I ran upstairs. I was going out for dinner so I dashed across the hall into the shower. Then I heard a noise. The door had opened. It's a communal shower, I thought, 'Be calm, it's just one of the other nurses.' But I could hear heavy footsteps, and I could see his feet. I felt a chill. Then he began shouting my name.

I was terrified. I froze. Hoping he didn't know I was in there. It felt like I was in there for about ten days, but then I heard the steps subside. God knows how, but somehow I managed to escape and run into my room. I shut the door, then it came from nowhere – banging on my door. 'Abi, Abi, I just want to talk!'

I was screaming at him to go away. I grabbed the phone and my shaking hands dialled for the police.

I don't know how long it took; I was rooted to the spot, but the police came, and he was arrested. I called David; I needed someone to look after me and I wanted him.

He was like my knight in shining armour. He rushed over and picked me up. I felt so safe in his arms. He took me back to his and made me a mug of fresh mint tea. Would've preferred a whisky, but was in such distress, I didn't care.

23rd July 2004

Saw David again last night – I can't stop myself now, I like him too much. I told him about what was going on with the police and also exactly what had happened that night. I was prepared for him to not want to see me any more and made it clear I would understand if he didn't, but he took it incredibly well and was very supportive. First the stalker and now I have to tell him this. The poor guy's only known me a month.

Could it be that he actually really likes me?

Today I went to Bournemouth for a girls' mini-break with Sue. Hurrah! We go quite a lot in the summer. We giggled and ate sweets all the way there in her car. Love Sue.

24th July 2004

The sun was shining but I had a massive hangover. Sunbathed a bit and then headed home. Met David for dinner, looking a bit ropey. I think he thinks I party a bit too much. I think he would be right.

Oh, and the papers now know about me and David. The *Mirror* says we've 'Enjoyed discreet dinners and dates', but according to the *Express* I'm already two-timing him with another man:

'It looked like love at first sight for blonde TV presenter Abi Titmuss and *Lock, Stock and Two Smoking Barrels* gangster actor Nick Moran. The pair met at a party to mark the London premiere of movie blockbuster *King Arthur* on Thursday night and appeared to be inseparable.'

Can't even remember meeting him! Was he there too?

25th July 2004

Went to the Engineer for lunch with David. After about half an hour, the barman came out and announced that there were paps outside. First thing I thought of was to ring Darryn.

'I don't know what to do.'

Immediately Darryn started going mental and panicking.

'It's not one of mine, you mustn't let them get a picture!' He was really laying it on thick.

Told David, who got annoyed. He had a point, I mean we couldn't stay here forever.

Started to feel really uncomfortable. Darryn kept calling:

'You must stay there! Don't leave together whatever you do.' It feels like he's starting to get so controlling.

David was more than happy for them not to get a picture though, so we decided to leave through separate doors. Got the bar to call us two separate taxis – I went out of one door and he through the other. I jumped in a taxi, lay on the back seat and headed to his house.

Part of my panic today was because I'm frightened of the paps getting a bad picture of me – therefore giving the papers another reason to slag me off. At least by going through Darryn I can have some say in which shots they farm out. But what if another pap took a shot of David looking nice and me looking all ugly? I want the first picture people see of us together to be a good one. Otherwise people might think 'What's he doing with her?'

27th July 2004

Was an extra in Matt Goss's new video today. Thrilled that he asked me in the first place. The shot involved a whole crowd of us running down the street in Primrose Hill. Had a St Tropez spray tan done this morning because I was so worried about looking like a milk bottle. The beautician told me not to put my knickers back on for an hour so it wouldn't mark. I had a knee-length skirt on so thought, oh it'll be fine – I'll just put them on later then. But I completely forgot. So excited to see Matt that they probably would have dropped off anyway. Typical, scatty, Titters.

Sat down on the pavement, in-between takes. Next thing I knew there was a clicking noise and I peered across the road to see a reflection of light. On a lens. A camera lens.

A pap was lying on the floor under a car.

Fuck. Shit. Arggggh! Am mortified. Now everyone in his office will see my bits. What an idiot.

Sam checked it out afterwards. It was someone from the *Daily Sport*. Just have to hope no normal people read that dodgy rag.

28th July 2004

Flew to the real St Tropez on a private jet today. As one does. For crying out loud, this is the life! I'm going from the sublime to the ridiculous. I went with Darryn Lyons to do some more pics. Miranda got the long straw and came with me. We were sooo excited.

There is something inconceivably, outlandishly 'rock-star' about flying on a private jet. From arriving five minutes before departure, your driver dropping you off on the runway and lifting your bags from the boot straight on to the plane, to the six cream leather reclining seats and shag-pile carpet, the two handsome pilots and the champagne and canapés. It is pure luxury.

Once there we boarded Darryn's yacht and started 'work'.

While Miranda soaked up the sun, I frolicked around in a bikini and Darryn snapped away. I was jumping off the back of the boat into the turquoise water, hosing myself down, stretching, dipping my toe in the water and so on. All very cheesy but it sells. I knew what to do this time and I knew which shapes looked good on me now.

We are going out in St Tropez tonight.

29th July 2004

Never, I repeat, NEVER have a hangover on a boat.

Darryn has been putting pressure on me to give Big Pictures the first shots of me and David together. That first shot of us as a couple is going to be worth a lot of money. A lot. But David doesn't want to do it. I tried to explain that after all that's happened it's not just about the money for me, it's about the control.

I've got greasy paps following me every day taking pictures of my fanny and sticking their lens up my skirt . . . there's no way I want one of them to get all the money for our picture. They don't deserve it. Why should someone else profit from a picture of me? It's my image, I should own it. If I know someone I can do a deal with – it seems completely smart and sensible to me.

But it's all foreign to him.

All got a bit heated.

I want to throw myself overboard. And Darryn.

30th July 2004

Have decided it's not worth falling out over at all. Setting up photo opportunities might seem perfectly sensible in my world, but I can see it's not in his.

Told Darryn and he got really shirty.

31st July 2004

Came home yesterday and went straight to David's. We're getting on so well. As soon as he opens the door to his flat and smiles at me I feel warm and happy. It's like a sanctuary. We just stay in the house most of the time because all we want to do is see each other.

Feel very emotional at the moment – I have realised that as soon as I stop running around or drinking away my feelings, and am still for a minute, I can't contain my emotions. They are so bottled up, bubbling away under the surface.

1st August 2004

Did my first PA (personal appearance) this evening in a nightclub called Time in Northampton. Emma, my agent at Money, says there's a huge market for these – and it's easy cash.

'All you need to do is stand on stage for a few minutes answering questions and you'll get between £3,000 and £10,000 a pop.'

Blimey.

The money didn't make me feel any less nervous though. Hadn't a clue what to expect. I had a tour manager with me who's going to accompany me to all these gigs in future. He's like a security guard who knows what's expected of me and how to get me in and out as painlessly as possible. When I arrived I was whisked into a back room. The club manager introduced himself (seemed unnervingly excited to meet me) then I poked my head through the door to the main room, and recoiled in horror. There must've been about 3,000 people in there, mainly blokes, but girls too. And they were all so loud!

Petrified. What if I got bottles thrown at me? The girls wouldn't want me to be there, surely? The manager must've seen how scared I was because within minutes he appeared with a large vodka and gave it to me.

When I finally got on stage, my knees were knocking together. But there was a compère who introduced me and he pretty much held it together. And the crowd went berserk! They were all screaming my name and waving. It was crazy. Even the girls were smiling and shouting.

When I said that to the manager afterwards he nodded. 'Being famous creates a slight awe in people, Abi – even if girls don't like you, they wouldn't do anything nasty to you. They'll either want to be your friend or won't come near you.'

That's one of my biggest hang-ups about the 'career' I'm carving for myself. I know how most women view me, and it's certainly not in a nice way. They think I rate myself, that I somehow orchestrated John's downfall so I could hog the limelight myself, and that I'm about to steal their boyfriend. I wish they could see me as my friends do. I'm the first person to take the piss out of myself. I'm much more comfortable at one of my bunnies' flats, trying on their clothes, eating chocolate with a face pack on and complaining about my figure while they all laugh at my chubby bits, than I am standing in front of flashbulbs in full make-up.

2nd August 2004

I get the feeling that everyone on the outside thinks we're an unlikely couple, but to me, we're completely right for each other. I could chat to David for hours – I want to soak up everything he has to say. He fascinates me.

Really hot day so we went to the Lansdowne for lunch with a couple of his friends. Drank rosé and sat outside. Twenty minutes into the meal, Darryn called.

'Do you know you're being papped?' he asked accusingly.

'No, but thanks for letting me know.'

'Stay there because I'm sending one.'

That was his way of saying, 'This is my picture now. You won't get a cut of the money, because you didn't tip me off you were going out.'

I walked out of earshot and started pacing up and down. I didn't want David or his friends to hear, I certainly didn't want him to think I'd set something up behind his back. I felt intimidated and the thought that it might jeopardise my lovely relationship frightened me. I wanted to detach from Darryn now. We'd done some good pictures, had some good times and both made a lot of money but it was starting to interfere with my 'real' life.

'Darryn, you know what? This is my relationship; I'm not going to tell you every time I go out. I'm going back to the table now; I want to enjoy the rest of my afternoon with David. Do what you like. I'm not going to live every moment of my life as a picture opportunity.'

3rd August 2004

The *Sun*:

'Here are the first snaps of Abi Titmuss and David Walliams on a cosy date. One drinker said: "He had her in stitches and she gave him passionate kisses in return."'

It's in the *Mirror* too:

'Randy David Walliams is already introducing his new squeeze Abi Titmuss to his pals. We revealed last month the couple had enjoyed several dates together since meeting at a premiere in June. The Little Britainer and the ex-nurse turned TV star/DJ/calendar girl were taking it slowly. Until now.'

Glad it's finally done and dusted and the fact that both the *Sun* and the *Mirror* have done it means it might all calm down now. It's quite a sweet picture actually.

Had a meeting with my management to discuss the concept of a fitness video. Hilarious, but it's no joke. They're real money spinners apparently.

Told them that I didn't want it to be the same as every other celebrity keep-fit video. We came up with the idea of making it a bit saucy – teaching women how to do the striptease for their boyfriends while toning up at the same time. That way it plays to my market – blokes who read the red tops.

4th August 2004

Was booked as a guest on a TV sketch show called *Bo Selecta!* today. Hadn't given much thought to why they wanted me on there though. Maybe I should've done. Went into the studio and the cameras rolled. The host, 'Avid Merrion' was sitting there in his pants.

'Abi Tatmuss, I am loving your tats!'

I laughed and sat down. Then, a door opened and a black guy came in with a video camera. I froze.

Avid announced, 'And now we're going to watch your video!'

'What?'

I didn't know what was going on. There was a big TV screen behind us. I instantly shrieked, 'No you're not!'

I looked around the studio imploring one of the producers to help me, to stop this happening. But before I could do anything, the screen flickered and something started playing. Were they really going to show the video? The actual thing? I could hardly bear to watch.

Quickly realised they'd done a re-creation – Avid was wearing a blonde wig, plastic tits and a neck brace. It should have been hilarious – and everyone was laughing around me – but I was still in shock about what was going on.

Somehow managed to mask my horror on set, but as soon as I came out of the studio I burst into tears. Was so angry, ashamed and demeaned.

Why did I feel so upset? It was only a joke and I like Leigh Francis, the comedian. I'm sure he would be upset to know I was so sad. Luckily I had dinner with Al Murray tonight to cheer me up.

'What's up, Titters?'

Love Al. He knows that the real me struggles with all the sex video stuff. He always teases me that everything I say sounds like an innuendo. Ha, he's right.

7th August 2004

Went to Majorca with Sue. Booked it ages ago, before I met David. Pathetically, when it came to it this morning, actually didn't want to go. Don't want to be apart from him. Is that strange?

As soon as my feet hit the sand, I did the obligatory set up pap shots. Have calmed down a bit about Darryn and have decided that for the moment I'm probably better off as his friend than his enemy. Had pre-arranged with him for someone to come out and meet me.

Sue didn't mind in the slightest, as long as she wasn't in them! She finds it hilarious that anyone would want to see me in a bikini, and sat there taking the piss and making me laugh the entire time:

'Go on my little show pony! Earn your keep!' 'Ooh, hold that stomach in!' 'Get a real job!'

10th August 2004

Bumped into the famous flicky-haired hairdresser Nicky Clarke on the beach. He came over and started chatting and it surprised me how much I liked him.

I invited him to join me and my friends on their yacht. Had the most hilarious day. He's nothing like I expected him to be at all, he's quite self-deprecating, and funny. Sat drinking cold beers and one by one people in the group tried their hand at waterskiing off the back of the boat.

'I'll have a go at that,' Nicky offered casually.

I expected him to fall flat on his arse straight away. He didn't strike me as the type who was sporty in the slightest. But the minute he put his feet in the skis – that was it. He was off! Whizzing around the bay, practically holding the rope with one finger. At one stage I expected him to swap hands and cock one leg up in the air. Amazing. He was so good it was comical because it didn't look real. When he returned to the boat he hardly had a drop of water on him. His fabulous hair was still bone dry!

I decided to have a go and hoiked my feet into the skis. I was so busy trying to show off and laughing so much at Sue (and half-cut from all the San Miguel) that I didn't notice the boat speed off. My skis went in opposite directions and my legs were nearly torn apart.

I was walking like a cowboy with a venereal disease for the rest of the day. Later that night we all came back to our villa for a drink. Nicky and I sat up for hours putting the world to rights. We were talking about every aspect of his life, he was so candid.

I miss David.

11th August 2004

Sue and I met up with Nicky again, for lunch. As we were sitting outside the restaurant he remarked, 'I could do your hair you know.'

'Really? What should I do with it?'

'What you need is a bit more of this— ' And with that, he leant over and started whooshing my hair about at super-speed like he was in a scene from a spoof hairdressing film. He was whacking my head about from left to right and when he finally pulled back to inspect his efforts, I could feel my hair was all over the place.

Meanwhile, Sue was doubled over in stitches. She nearly couldn't breathe she was laughing so hard. 'I've got to take a picture of that,' she shrieked. Nicky didn't seem to understand what was wrong, he was completely serious, and seemed genuinely proud of his creation.

We waited until he went to the loo before I could look in the mirror.

I looked like I had a Mr Whippy on my head.

David's been texting lots since I've been here. It's so lovely to know he's thinking of me.

12th August 2004

A mate of mine, Alan Miller, has a place out here so we arranged to meet up for a drink. I know him through mutual friends and he used to go out with Claire Sweeney. It was really nice to see him again – there's never anything between us, we're just mates. Halfway through the evening, Claire walked into the bar. And it seemed from the way she was eyeing us that she still has feelings for him. She called him over and they stood chatting for a while. He told me afterwards that she'd demanded to know what he was doing with me.

Yet another one who's made assumptions. I wasn't even flirting with him. I felt sad. I hate the thought that another woman might feel threatened by me. I've been in that woman's shoes many, many times when I was with John and it's a horrible feeling. And I liked Claire, I'd met her once with John, she seemed nice. I tried to smile at her across the bar.

I went to bed and fell asleep texting David.

13th August 2004

Back in London, it was *Bo Selecta!*'s wrap party tonight. After the other day there was part of me who thought I should boycott it. But I'm starting to see the funny side, and it was fancy dress which is always good value.

You had to come as a TV character. I couldn't think of anything – but in the end I picked Farrah Fawcett in *Charlie's Angels*. Bought a shiny black cat suit with a boob-tube top and flares, added a bit of plastic seventies-style yellow jewellery and had my hair blow-dried all flicky. Got papped on the way there and wanted to shout, 'It *is* fancy dress you know!' What if people think I'm wearing it for real?

Fab party. TV people really go to town with fancy dress. The director was a Teenage Mutant Ninja Turtle but he left green hand-prints everywhere and his shell was so big he had to go through doors sideways – I laughed just looking at him. Leigh came as Popeye and his wife was Olive Oyl. Someone came as Rod Hull and Emu, with a TV aerial sticking out of his jacket and blood on his sleeve.

Met Jeremy Edwards, he's cute. A bit posh though, and that's not really my cup of tea. We chatted a bit and he asked why wasn't I in fancy dress? Oh dear God. This was a disaster.

14th August 2004

Went up to Edinburgh to meet David who was there for the festival. He's staying in an amazing boutique hotel with Rob Brydon and Jimmy Carr.

Took me hours to get there, and David opened the door eating a packet of cheese and onion crisps.

'That's so annoying! You knew I was coming to see you!'

He just laughed. And gave me a very cheesy kiss. The place is stunning; there's an enormous sitting room with a piano for people to gather round when they get back from the festival. There's a pool room, massive grounds.

I could get used to this.

Went to see Rob perform his *Keith Barrett Show* which was brilliant, and David introduced me to a guy called Russell Brand – and I liked him immediately.

He's like a ball of energy (even if he does look like he needs a bath and a decent meal). He's got a peculiar way of staring too. Some men undress you with their eyes, but with Russell it's like in one look he's already bent you over, shagged you and left.

Later, we found a bar and it was here we bumped into Jayne Middlemiss. I've never met her before and she just seemed to latch on to the group. I was thinking 'please go away', but she didn't. She came back to the hotel with us.

Everyone started singing round the piano. Jayne was batting her eyes at David – I couldn't compete with that, she's a glamorous TV presenter.

David asked her what she was up to next week and Jayne said she was filming something at the V Festival.

'Oh, Abi's going to that – will you be interviewing Abi?' David asked cheerfully.

'Er, *no*,' she said deliberately and loudly.

It was awful. I felt so small and embarrassed in front of David. An uncomfortable silence followed; no one seemed to know what to do or where to look.

I tried to pretend not to notice and muttered something stupid to Rob instead. Not long after that I went upstairs. David didn't come with me. As I walked along the landing, I overheard Jayne asking if he fancied a game of pool.

Sat in the bathroom and cried. It wasn't long before David came up. I was so upset, I just wish I felt comfortable around his friends.

I wanted to shout out, 'I'm sorry! I'm sorry I'm an embarrassment and if I didn't think so little of myself too then I probably wouldn't let someone like that make me feel so small. It's not your fault at all!'

But I didn't.

15th August 2004

Next morning I was over it. I just need to get it into perspective. It wasn't his fault. I'd be stupid to let what Jayne did cause a rift.

The *People* have run a story about me and Claire Sweeney:

'Abi Titmuss and Claire Sweeney had a furious holiday bust-up – over Claire's footballer ex. Other sunseekers were gobsmacked as the former *Brookside* star screamed at goalie Alan Miller: 'What on earth are you doing with her?'

As usual it makes me look bad. Who the hell rings them up and sells this stuff? And to cap it off, the picture they've used is of me in the sodding Farrah Fawcett, boob-tube cat-suit outfit (I knew it!) next to a lovely wholesome pic of Claire. Arghhhh!

16th August 2004

Met up with a woman called Helen Jackson at Third Space gym. Helen is a professional dancer and is going to choreograph my DVD routine. She was fantastic. Took me into the studio where she performed a routine for me. It was incredibly sexy. Not at all sleazy as I'd expected.

She thinks the DVD's a good idea. After all, most girls who have boyfriends have been asked to do a striptease at some point, and usually you feel stupid and end up tripping over your bra.

David will have to wait until I've practised before I give him a demonstration!

17th August 2004

Nuts magazine shoot. I'm editing the next edition so we did a saucy shoot with me as a kinky boss – suspenders, hair up, specs, pencil in hand and, of course, the bra showing. Had my hair tied back, which I was a bit nervous about because I don't like having hair up – it's like my security blanket. The rest of the shoot was done as if I was on a beach and it was really saucy. Some shots had me in bikinis with jewellery dripping off me, others in a soaking wet shirt leaving little to the imagination.

They wanted to have me providing readers with tips about how to pull someone like me. I loved it. Maybe it'll help some lads out there – God knows they could do with a few pointers when it comes to charming a lady.

18th August 2004

Helen really put me through my paces today. Who knew stripping was such hard work!

David's having a party for his birthday on the 21st and I'm gutted because I can't come. But I've got tickets for the V Festival and I promised the girls I'd go with them – I can't let them down for a man! He's having caterers and wine and loads of fancy trimmings. Everyone's going to be there – Jonathan Ross and Co. I'd love to be there as his girlfriend.

19th August 2004

Another standard day for the Titmuss –
12pm bikini wax.
4.30pm spray tan.
7pm questioned by police.
10pm party.

20th August 2004

Rehearsing with Helen all day. Aching all over. It's David's birthday today so I sent him off to the Sanderson where I'd treated him to a day of pampering. Then I took him for a birthday dinner at the Electric on Portobello Road. I really wish I could go to his party tomorrow night. Bloody hell.

21st August 2004

V Festival, Chelmsford.
Incredible. Had the best time EVER! Was in a right panic about what to wear though. What do you wear to a festival? What if it's muddy? My super-cool bunny Donna, who manages Ronnie Wood, just looked at me and said, with a straight face, 'Hey – it never rains backstage, honey.' We fell on the floor laughing. This is going to be the motto for every festival I ever go to from now on.

A car arrived at lunchtime to pick us up, and the driver said he'd just wait until we wanted to leave at the end of the night, whatever the time was.

Got to the festival and it was overwhelming. Everyone I passed knew who I was – people were shouting my name, wanting to meet me, running up and begging to have their picture taken. God, it was exciting. Faithless were performing – they were incredible – and I remember us all jumping up and down to the music, with our arms in the air, holding hands.

In the VIP tent it was a free bar. ALL. DAY. Got papped staggering out of a portaloo – that'll be a nice one.

Vaguely remember being interviewed by someone from the *Telegraph* later that evening. Was absolutely off my head. Christ knows what I was saying. Who cares! Love V Festival! Love my girls! Going to be sick . . .

26th August 2004

Just about recovered from V. Trained with Helen at Pineapple Dance Studios. It's hilarious in there. It's like walking on to the set of *Fame*. They actually do wear leg warmers! I was perving at the fit male dancers through the classroom windows until Helen said they were all gay.

Went straight to the gym after my dance lesson. Got to get fit again for this DVD. Why can't I maintain a constant level of fitness? It's always a mad, obsessive burst to get in shape for some event, then I achieve my goal, swear to myself I'll never be fat again and then before I know it I've got a glass of Pinot and a pizza in my hands and it's all downhill again.

Wish I was one of those girls that understand the word 'moderation', can stop at one biscuit, or one vodka and are in the gym three times a week, with no effort.

27th August 2004

9pm PA, Norwich, Riverside Time.

I feel much more comfortable doing PAs. I've learnt so much

about how to deal with crowds. There are certain delightful questions you always get asked when you're on stage, usually something like: 'Do you take it up the arse?'

Was told to say, 'Come back to me when your balls drop.'

They're silly little things, but when you're in a club situation like that it helps, because you need to be in control. I watched a Chubby Brown video recently, trying to remember all the put downs he used. I used some tonight and got a massive laugh. Felt much more in control instead of nervous. I'm like a chameleon, moulding myself to any environment. But, I'd die if anyone I knew was here!

28th August 2004

Moving house.

At last I'm finally in my new place, my first property purchase. David came over. We had a takeaway and he brought a bottle of champagne and a card. There was bugger-all furniture – all I had was a futon, and a tiny crappy cheap Argos table and two chairs.

Feel so happy.

29th August 2004

Of course happiness doesn't last long when you've got papers sniffing around at your door, trying to catch you out at every stage. The *People* have run with the headline 'ABI IN A THREE-SCRUM'.

It says that I had a bloody threesome with the rugby players I met back in June! Absolute total and utter bollocks. I went back to the house but nothing happened. Do people now have free licence to make up stuff about me?

Was really worried about what David would say, but he laughed it off.

30th August 2004

The press have already found out about my new abode. There were paps outside all night last night. Could hear them rustling in the bushes. Still can't get my head round the fact that people are out there.

31st August 2004

Moving house might be great for me, but not for my poor neighbours Tim and Noreen. They've been amazing though – I'm very lucky. Tim rings and warns me whenever there's a pap outside. But he couldn't even get in his car tonight.

'There aren't only a pack of photographers, there's a film crew,' he exclaimed down the phone.

I looked out of the window and some reporter was doing a piece to camera. What the fuck are *they* doing? Apparently making a film about the paparazzi. I was going to David's so I had no choice but to go outside, and they just pointed the camera in my face. I was a bit pissed off – I don't even know what context it's going to be used in. They didn't even ask my permission.

1st September 2004

Am a bit overwhelmed by the house. Keep looking around at the lack of furniture and how vast it is. I don't know where to start. Also feel a bit weird having bought it with the money from Television X. Somehow made it seem a bit tarnished.

Saw Helen for more training this morning. Slowly getting the hang of the routine, but there's loads to remember. My fault for wanting to do stripping really. Would be much simpler if I could just keep my clothes on and do star jumps.

Met up with a journalist called Rod Liddle this afternoon. He'd requested an interview with me for the *Sunday Times Style* magazine. Emma says he's really well respected, quite an institution in fact and it's a huge deal that he's doing the interview himself.

I liked him. We met at Century. One of the first things he did was look out of the window.

'See that restaurant over there?' he said.

'Yes.'

'My girlfriend's sitting in there because she wants to wait and make sure I come out alone.'

I thought, 'Christ! What does she think I'm going to do to him? That's not what I'm like!'

The interview seemed to go well, and I could tell he warmed to me. He tried to push me on drugs – 'So d'you do much coke, Abs?' – which I refused to talk about, but I was open about everything else. He asked what a threesome was like and I replied 'It's all right,' at which he laughed. He spoke about David as 'a nice young man' and we chatted about my background, the fact that I wanted to act but also about the fact that I was under no illusion as to why I was a 'celebrity' in the first place.

Emma says they're using images from the calendar shoot for the piece – and that it's going to be on the cover! To be on the front of the *Times Style* is one mammoth feat in itself. To have persuaded them to use one of your own pictures is quite another.

2nd September 2004

Went to Mum's today. Just to hibernate from the world and be treated to home cooked food and telly. Bliss.

3rd September 2004

Got train to Sheffield for Claire's wedding. She was a good mate from school and we hadn't met up for a couple of years. It was so great to see her. It's funny how, when you went to school with someone, they stay that age in your head. I felt like saying, 'What are you wearing that mad dress for, we've got chemistry next!'

She looked beautiful and happy. Another one bites the dust.

4th September 2004

Am in the surveillance bit of 3am in the *Mirror* – 'Spotted: Abi Titmuss, with two duvets outside Argos, New Oxford Street. Classy bird.'

Why does buying new bedding make me un-classy?

PA, Nottingham, The Works.

PA, Birmingham, The Works.

Came back from the PAs tonight feeling rubbish and pissed.

5th September 2004

David invited me to be in the audience for the filming of *Little Britain* at the BBC. I took a group of my friends. I'd been showing off all day: 'I think you'll find I'm taking you all to the BBC. To watch my boyfriend.'

It was hilarious but David had failed to mention that it was the episode where his character 'Sebastian' finally confesses his love for his boss, the Prime Minister, played by Anthony Head. As David held Anthony's face lovingly in his hands and gave him a two-minute-long, full-on snog, I baulked in horror and turned my head away, to see the row of my mates beside me all looking at me and wetting themselves with laughter.

Ruthers could barely speak. She finally composed herself.

'I think you'll find that's your boyfriend.'

6th September 2004

Tim rang this morning. 'Do know you've got at least fifteen photographers outside?'

Have had to put on a hat or shades before going to the shop these days. I used to always take the piss out of John for having so many pairs of sunglasses. Thought he was such a poser. Now I realise it's just easier. Plus, the pictures are worth less if there's no eye contact.

8th September 2004

There's a big article in the *Daily Record* about me in *Nuts*:

'This week, rather than making headlines, Abi was creating them, as she accepted the job of guest editor on lads' magazine *Nuts*. And as one of the most desired women in the country, this put her in a perfect position to give male readers tips on winning the woman of their dreams. Here, we reveal some of Abi's advice for guys looking to bag themselves a stunning date. You can see more pictures of Abi in *Nuts* magazine, on sale today.'

The pictures look fantastic. Should wear hair up more often.

2pm dance training with Helen. Really like Helen, we get on brilliantly, thank God. I'm not sure I could be learning how to strip out of a long evening dress, in high heels, elbow-length gloves and a feather boa, with someone who couldn't see the funny side.

9th September 2004

Went live on air with Johnny Vaughan and the breakfast team at Capital Radio from 7am till 9am this morning. I was nervous that he might take the piss out of me but actually he was nice. He's so quick I had to work to get a word in edgeways but I did, and even managed to get a few laughs from the team.

I was sorry when it was over, I could've stayed all day. Starting to get my confidence on the radio now and I love it. You can really be yourself.

Not sure that Johnny thought much of me when I walked in but I think he'd really warmed to me at the end. That seems to happen all the time with everyone I meet now. It's starting to bother me that it means they mustn't think very highly of me to start with.

11am Helen @ Pineapple Studios then gym.

Picked up my first ever car this afternoon! A red, convertible Mini Cooper. I've called him Alice. Alice Cooper.

10th September 2004

PA, Hull, Circus Circus.

I'm starting to drink too much. I know it. Spoke to David after the PA and was so pissed I was incoherent. I'm revelling in the celeb lifestyle, but most of the time I'm only drinking and partying because deep down I'm unhappy. I'm uncomfortable in my own skin until I've had a few drinks. I don't show that though. To everyone else, including David, I look like I'm having a great time.

12th September 2004

The *Sunday Times Style* piece is out. And it's fantastic. The picture they've used for the cover is the one from the calendar of me in underwear, lying on a glass table surrounded by money and smoking a cigar and Rod Liddle has written a really kind piece. At the start he says he couldn't believe it was me.

'While I'm sipping my wine, this pretty, cheerful, demure woman makes a quiet entrance and shakes my hand and says: "Hi, I'm Abi. How are you?" And at that moment, a million male fantasies dissolve. I mean, this girl is Abi Titmuss? This quintessentially nice girl-next-door thing? Frankly, I'm astonished. Some mistake, surely?'

Then he goes on to say that I'm 'clever . . . and delightfully self-aware.'

He does note that I talk a lot though: 'She rabbits at nineteen to the dozen. Throughout our conversation, self-justification pours from her mouth, non-stop. I tell her she has no need to justify herself to me. But then I'm not sure it is to me.'

He's very astute.

Sitting on my own I read the piece four or five times over. I can't believe I've finally been taken seriously by a journalist. A respected, intelligent journalist, not a tabloid hack. Unlike other interviews, there's very little dialogue – it's all basically prose amounting to his opinion of me. It feels very strange to read that I justify myself all the time. I couldn't pull the fish nets over Rod's eyes and get away with the 'naughty nurse' role, as I do with other interviewers. He's far too bright. I really enjoyed that interview and am so grateful for the write-up he gives me.

My eyes welled up. I wanted to call him, thank him and then tell him how bad I really felt about myself. But I didn't. His girlfriend probably wouldn't like it.

Sam and my manager called separately, raving about it.

Another set of pictures from the calendar is in the *News of the World*. The *Sunday Times* Style and the *News of the World* on the same day. From high street to high fashion on one newspaper stand. Brilliant. What an achievement really, considering where I'd come from.

13th September 2004

Training with Helen for DVD.

David came over. I mentioned that I would love to meet his friends. Privately I have wondered why it hasn't happened before but I can see there's a pressure on David. There are people around him who don't understand our relationship. I'm sorry for him that he has to deal with it. I wish they'd leave us alone.

14th September 2004

More training.

Got some copies of the calendar – it looks sensational. I can't believe it's me, and it's so imaginative, really interesting and almost arty. Bloody genius. Am so proud. Couldn't wait to give one to David.

It was an achievement for me; it meant I was going to be around for the whole of the next year! Proved I had some semblance of a career.

I wish David had shared my enthusiasm. I could see he thought they were just more shots of me in my bra and pants – again. And that hurt, because there was truth in it. I wasn't pursuing my acting dream, I was still taking my clothes off.

I suppose he was attracted to me initially because he had seen me in sexy pictures on the cover of magazines. But it felt like now we were in a relationship he didn't like it any more. I couldn't believe it.

Men.

16th September 2004

The *Daily Star* says my earnings are about to hit the million mark. Where the heck do they get all these figures from?

David called and joked that given how much I was worth these days, dinner was on me. I couldn't help laughing, I was so relieved to hear from him. We are going to see each other again.

David and Matt did an interview with the *Sun* to promote the set of *Little Britain* scripts they're releasing in book form for Series One. Apparently the paper tried probing about me, but he didn't give anything away. They never do interviews with the tabloids so it's quite a big deal for them. It'll be a double spread.

19th September 2004

News of the World has run loads more pics from the calendar – the one of me in a confessional box, and being arrested by the policeman. Not only have they given a huge plug about how to buy the calendar, they've splashed on the fact that I'm doing a fitness DVD. I'm blown away by the amount of coverage the calendar is receiving. Every publication seems to be bidding for them. It's really flattering. I'm getting a lot of feedback through Sam that people in the media think they are really terrific pictures and that's a nice feeling.

20th September 2004

Victoria Silvstedt and I spent the day together. In our knickers.

Unbelievably *FHM* wanted to put me on the cover again and to make it interesting they shot me with Victoria. My tongue fell on the floor when she turned up. She's huge! What was this stunning, Amazonian long-legged creature doing in a shoot with me? I was like a little squirt next to her. Had to stand on a copy of the Yellow Pages in one shot because she was towering over me so much!

David and Matt's interview is in the *Sun*. We were together when the paper arrived. When we opened it up, I was nearly sick. No, no, no, no, no . . .

Spread across two pages is the headline: 'ABI WAS WILD . . . BUT I TAMED HER' alongside a huge picture of me in my underwear with washing-up gloves on (one from the shoot I did before I went into *Hell's Kitchen* – so they will have had to buy it). Then, right at the end there's a small shot of him and Matt together with a plug for *Little Britain*.

Apart from that, the whole thing is about our relationship.

I tried to make a joke of it but there was a sinking feeling in the pit of my stomach. This is going to ruin us. I'd be pissed off if that was me. There's nothing we can control about our relationship any more. We're public property.

'In a rare interview, David, 32, told the *Sun* how porn TV presenter Abi now prefers cosy nights in with him to wild clubbing. He said: "We lead a pretty quiet life these days. We don't go to many places. We try to stay in and lead as normal a life as possible. In general, I prefer to be anonymous."'

Can almost sense it's the beginning of the end for us.

22nd September 2004

Am on the cover of *Zoo*. This time with a proper shoot they've bought from Money's picture agency. Really sexy images actually. They're billed as 'my steamiest pictures ever'. Hilarious – I almost work to a script now – every one I do is 'my steamiest ever'. I sound like a Turkish-bath salesman.

I do enjoy the shoots though and I have to 'get into the mood' when I'm working. That's what makes a good picture.

The interview I did is plugging the tour I'm doing with them to promote the calendar – loads of sexy talk.

God, do men really read this stuff?

David came over and before long the subject of me doing raunchy shoots again came up. I explained that acting was what I really wanted to do and that this would all change.

He didn't look convinced.

That got to me and even though it was pissing down with rain, I asked him to leave.

Feel devastated.

23rd September 2004

If you're ever going to have a row with your boyfriend, make sure you have a private jet waiting to whisk you to Monaco the following day.

As I stepped off another jet this afternoon and slipped my sunglasses on, I thought to myself that this was probably the most preposterously easy, and fabulous, 'job' that I was ever likely to do in my life.

I'd booked into an impossibly luxurious hotel, simply to be a guest at a party! It was the launch of Club 328, a company which caters to the needs of millionaires – jets, yachts, limousines, anything they wanted. I had no idea why they would want Titters there but apparently I was so newsworthy that a picture of me would guarantee press for them in England.

The party was on a staggeringly huge luxury yacht. The owner showed me around it; you could fit my house on it twice over. He had two armed guards that never left his side. Wow. Seemed like quite a price to pay for riches.

As I stood on the deck this evening in the warm Mediterranean air, the lights of Monte Carlo bay twinkling behind me, drinking chilled champagne and nibbling from the mind-boggling array of seafood, I wondered where it all went wrong. I could hear Sue's voice in my head, 'Who do you think you ARE?' and giggled to myself.

24th September 2004

I flew home this evening and David wanted to see me.

I went, but the damage has been done. Our bubble has burst. I know that if I hadn't been drowning my sorrows and partying so much I would have been a much better girlfriend.

It's over.

I held it together until I got into my car, Alice, and then sobbed and sobbed.

As I drove home Keane's 'Bedshaped' came on the radio. It will always remind me of today now.

Sam texted to tell me I'm on the cover of *Nuts* again. They've run the calendar pics in all their glory. She also said it looked like the cover with me on as guest editor sold more than any other issue they've had out so far. She said something about them normally selling 25,000 copies a week and mine sold double that. I was too sad to really take it in.

25th September 2004

Wow. Great way to cheer a girl up when she's feeling down. It says in the *Sun* that Robbie Williams fancies me!

'Randy Robbie Williams yesterday confessed he wants to bed Abi Titmuss – after hearing she had split from her funny man boyfriend.'

Bloody hell, bad news travels fast.

'. . . Robbie, on a flying visit back to Britain, spoke out on Jonathan Ross's Radio 2 show. The DJ told him ex-nurse Abi has broken up with *Little Britain* star David Walliams, 32 days after the comic spoke of their "quiet nights in".'

I guess David must've told his close friends. They probably sent him champagne to celebrate.

'Robbie told Ross: "Fantastic! I quite fancy Abi Titmuss." . . . Wossy suggested he go for a more serious girlfriend, but Robbie, 30, suggestively replied: "I don't plan to go out with her. I'm only here for a week and a half."'

So he just wants a shag. Naturally.
    Still, at least the picture they've used is one of mine, so I look good.
    Sam rang.
    'This is massive, Abi!'
    And it is.
    I'm so flattered. Especially after all the shit I've been getting from the papers.

26th September 2004

Sam rang.
    'Since Robbie's been over here – he's mentioned you in nearly every interview he's done. First the radio, now he's been talking about you on T4!'
    Amazing. I wonder if he'll try and get in touch?
    He's friends with David though. Hope he doesn't mind all this.

27th September 2004

David drove over tonight. We've been texting each other and we can't seem to quite call it a day. Had a really long chat about us. I miss him, but I know it's not going to work any more. Too much has happened. It's been three months and we both know we're not going to be marrying each other. I genuinely think we are going to stay friends though. I'm still enormously fond of him.

'I've been on a calendar but I've never been on time.'

Marilyn Monroe

2nd October 2004

Just got back from a PA in Glasgow. A load of local journalists turned up at the nightclub to interview me. The Scottish *Sun* showed me pictures of famous men in Scotland and got me to rank them out of ten for sex appeal. There were some really funny-looking ones on there and so naturally I picked them as my favourites. It was quite a laugh!

3rd October 2004

Had a huge Sunday lunch with the girls at 'our place', a lovely gastro-pub with organic food. The laid-back clientele there don't bat an eyelid at me and so I can really relax and not get stared at or have any hassle at the bar. I've become a bit of a liability for the girls when we go out now as I tend to generate a lot of attention. It's actually not fun for them as I get pulled left, right and centre by people interrupting our conversation and wanting to talk to me. Some bars are now totally out of bounds. You can forget taking me to the Pitcher and Piano.

I told them all about David and they cheered me up.

'Pick your bottom lip off the floor, you'll be shagging in the back of Robbie's tour bus next week.'

Ha, love the bunnies.

4th October 2004

Is nothing sacred? Just read yesterday's papers.

The *People* have got wind of our 'late night talks':

'A neighbour said the 6ft 2in comedian popped round to Abi's pad in his Merc last week and stayed until the early hours. A friend of the pair said: "They split because of certain issues but they care for each other a lot. David went to Abi's to talk things through."'

What neighbour?
More importantly, what friend?

5th October 2004

I was called to the police station again. This is agonising. The officer said today that it would be unusual for the CPS not to proceed now after taking so much time and calling me back so many times. I can't believe I am hearing this. WHY WHY WHY was I so bloody *stupid* that night?

Ludicrous story in the *Sun*:

'Beaming Berti Vogts yesterday admitted he's thrilled Abi Titmuss wants to bed him – telling fans: "I bet you wish you were me." Telly babe Abi, left, revealed she has the hots for the fifty-seven-year-old Scotland boss – giving him 10 out of 10 in the hunk stakes. And German Berti, pictured right yesterday, said he was delighted that he had topped her saucy league table.'

Oh Lord. It was a joke! I was in a good mood so I gave this old guy 10 out of 10 and they turned it into a massive double page spread! It did make me smile though. Sounded like I'd made his day.

8th October 2004

10am shoot for *Zoo*.
6.30pm *Glamour* interview @ Century.
The *Sun* is saying I'm changing my name to 'Nurse Tit' and am

going to be like J-Lo! Hilarious. As if I'd want to be known as Nurse bloody Tit! I'm not even a flipping nurse anymore. Honestly, that is one of the most desperate pieces of journalism I've ever seen. They will literally write anything.

9th October 2004

PA in Loughborough.

The best PA I've ever done! It was the university freshers' ball – which meant there were about 5,000 people there. It was amazing.

Everyone was in black tie. Trevor Nelson was DJing and I spent the night up in the DJ box jumping around. I thought I was Freddie Mercury. Everything I did the crowd would copy me, even the girls. It was brilliant. I brought boxes of my calendars with me and sold the lot.

Dave Read had sorted it. My agent introduced me to him a while ago and he really knows what's what. He was with me, getting equally pissed. And why not? I was getting paid to party! And there were so many gorgeous men there. Made me wish I'd gone to Loughborough Uni. Two totally lovely, quite posh young guys in their dinner jackets, propositioned me with a threesome and have to admit, I was seriously tempted.

Was only supposed to be there till 2am, but the organisers kept saying 'Stay!'

So I did.

Till six in the morning.

Problem was, I then had to travel back to London. Didn't get to my house till 9am. Had to be picked up in two hours to go live on Radio 1 . . .

Sat in the kitchen with my head in my hands. Sam picked me up in the car.

'I've only had about an hour's sleep,' I lied apologetically. But I hadn't really slept a wink. And that was not clever.

Sam said, 'You look fucking terrible.'

I had shades on. How could she see? I must've reeked of booze. Got to Radio 1 and Sam forced a coffee down me. Was desperately trying to act normal.

I was appearing on the *J.K. and Joel* show. The slot was meant to last at least an hour. I got on air, and could hardly speak. They kept asking me questions from the listeners and all I could say was 'Um . . . I dunno.' Then I made it worse.

I started laughing. About ten minutes in, Loughborough University rang and got on air – they'd told me last night they were all going to listen in the canteen.

'Whaaeey! Hello Loughborough!'

It was like I was in a football match. It wasn't long before the producer politely told me I was free to go. They didn't want me on air any more.

Got in the car and Sam looked at me sternly.

'They took you off air because you couldn't speak.'

'You're kidding me.'

I didn't realise. I was too caught up in myself. Some people would kill to be in the position I'm in, and here I am pissing it up the wall. I was feeling invincible and this has just given me the wake-up call. Now I feel embarrassed and horribly hungover. But deep down I don't really care as much as I should. I don't know why they want me on the radio anyway, why anyone wants me. At this moment I don't like what I am becoming and I want to run away and hide. I hope I feel better after a night's sleep.

Sam was not impressed.

14th October 2004

It's in the *Mirror*.

'Everyone's favourite naughty nurse was taken off air live on Radio 1 for being too hungover . . . It appears Ms Titmuss, 28, didn't have much shut-eye before appearing on the show. It was deemed too dangerous to let her continue on-air in case the adult TV presenter said something inappropriate.'

Me? Inappropriate? Never.

15th October 2004

The lawyer called.

'It's about your cocaine charge.'

My heart leapt to my mouth. This was it.

'The CPS have decided there is not a case for charging you. You are all clear.'

I can't believe it!

I put the phone down and cried. And cried. And cried.

I've been pushing this to the back of my head, drinking, partying, trying everything to forget about it. I never allowed myself to imagine what would happen if I'd been charged. But thank you.

Thank you.
Thank you.

It was over. It had cost me a huge amount of money in lawyers' fees but I didn't care. I was free. The feeling of relief was over-whelming. I don't have to carry this horrible secret fear around with me any more, gnawing at my insides. I vowed to myself never, ever to be so stupid as to touch drugs again. I sincerely hope I can keep that promise. After a few drinks I am no Mother Teresa.

The first person I texted was David. He was one of the very few people I had shared it with and I couldn't wait to tell him. He was really glad for me. I think he just hopes I behave myself from now on. So do I.

Had a PA in Newmarket tonight. Wanted to scream the place down with happiness. So utterly, absolutely and gratefully relieved. My friend Sara came with me for a giggle. We sat in the VIP area and got merry on free champagne and shots (well I had to celebrate not going to Borstal, didn't I?).

My driver came round and held the car door open for Sara and me to fall into and we left.

On the motorway home Sara realised she was going to be sick so the driver quickly pulled over and she staggered out. I was now desperate for a wee and thought I'd seize the opportunity.

So there we were, on the hard shoulder at 3am, her being sick and holding the car to keep her upright, and me crouched next to her, hanging on to her leg, having a wee. Pure class.

16th October 2004

Gym today and rehearsed with Helen for my fitness DVD. I'm shooting it next week. Holy crap! Whose stupid idea was it to do strip routines? I keep tripping over my feather boa . . . Oh hang on, it was my idea.

17th October 2004

Did my *FHM* agony aunt chat today. The journalist reads out the questions to me and I dictate my answer back. Loads of questions were about willy size; guys are worried about that most of all. They've got no idea that that's not the most important thing AT ALL for most women. It's how good they are at everything else that really makes great sex. Most of the guys I've known with big schlongs have been rubbish in bed! They think that because they're well hung that it's 'job done'. The best sex I've ever had was with a guy who had a really average-size willy but he was brilliant at all the other stuff. I need to get the message out there. It's down to me to help all the women of Britain. I'm starting Campaign Cunnilingus!

19th October 2004

11.30am DVD training.

We're filming the bloody thing in about two days and I still haven't got a clue what I'm doing. The stripping part seems OK (who'd have thought it?) but I've got to learn a script and present the thing too.

20th October 2004

DVD dress rehearsal.

21st October 2004

DVD filming.

Filming took place at the Cobden Club in West London. There were lights and cameras everywhere. Looked like a real film set. That made me even more nervous.

Gok Wan did my make-up but there was no mirror so I couldn't see what he was doing. All I could feel was him drawing a lip line that felt like it almost reached to my nose and down to my chin. What was going on? Looked at myself afterwards and saw a clown.

'You cannot be serious, Gok.'

'What's wrong?'

I started humming circus music. My lipstick was all around my mouth.

'It's for camera, you won't see it from a distance,' he protested.

The next sign that it was all going wrong emerged after we performed a whole routine to the tune of 'You Can Leave Your Hat On'. We executed it perfectly, and it felt really cool. That was until the director announced: 'We can't actually use that music because of copyright – when we edit it together, we'll use our own version.'

I asked to hear it.

It sounded like lift music. The kind of lift you wished would hurry up so you could get out of it and away from the dreadful music. We filmed from 6am until midnight. I fell asleep in the car.

22nd October 2004

Second day's filming for *Tone and Tease* – that's the title we've come up with. I had two backing dancers in stockings and suspenders. They looked much better than I did.

Filmed for fourteen hours including an interview in the back of a moving limousine. I don't know whose clever idea that was. Trying to talk to the camera with a straight face while, just out of shot, the crew were slipping all over the leather seats every time we turned a corner was not easy. Plus looking at the camera while the car was moving made me car sick. Went straight from the shoot to a PA. By the time I got to bed at 4am I'd been up for twenty-three hours and working solidly for twenty-two of them. You try doing that without a glass of wine.

1st November 2004

Zoo magazine are doing a big amnesty for my stolen sex video – they're trying to get readers to bring in their copies and burn them. Because they know it makes me upset. I am genuinely touched by them doing that. Really quite taken aback. It's like someone has actually acknowledged that I am human, not just a headline, and I have feelings about it. Bloody hell though, if they're having an 'amnesty', how many sodding people have bought it?

2nd November 2004

The *FHM* with me and Victoria Silvstedt on the cover is out – it's their December issue. Implausibly, *FHM* have told Sam that I am the only girl in their history so far to be put on the cover twice in one year. I cannot understand it. But it looks incredible if I do say so myself, really sexy. No one would ever know that I was standing on a copy of the Yellow Pages. I called a friend and he said, 'She looks like she's just posing whereas you can tell you were genuinely thinking about sex.' That's what the photographer said works, so am chuffed.

3rd November 2004

Did a shoot for *Arena*. Abi Ltd has gone gold standard. It won't run for a few months but like all monthlies they work so far ahead.

Pictures were wonderful though. Probably the most provocative yet, but because it's a high-gloss, high-brow men's mag I agreed. In fact, some of them were totally my idea. Plus, the fact that the photographer was a woman made it so much easier to go that bit further.

There's one where I'm sitting on the loo, knickers round my ankles (or as some journalists might say 'completely untroubled by clothing'), my left nipple is showing, but somehow it looks tasteful. Arty. In another I'm dribbling milk down my front with a cheeky glint in my eye. Then there's a shot that really pushes the boundaries of taste – I'm head first on the sofa, pants half-way down round my knees, as if I've been thrown there in a fit of passion. I think the photographer was quite shocked because I suggested it.

Did I go too far? I think my psyche is becoming so sexualised from doing all these shoots and being treated as a sex object, that I am starting to internalise it and therefore act it out even more. It's all I think I am good for. Although I didn't feel exploited on this shoot, or any shoot. On the contrary, on this one today I felt particularly powerful. But again, I trusted this photographer to make it look stylised and that made me feel totally liberated to go a bit crazy. Then again, maybe I *am* going a bit crazy.

Sam said: 'I'm going to try and get the cover.'

'What do you mean, try and get it?'

'Abi, you don't realise, do you? Covers are not always guaranteed.'

Then she laughed. 'Of course, you don't know any different, do you?'

My first ever taste of magazines was being on the cover of *FHM*. And since then, I've never been in a magazine and not been on the front cover. I've come to expect it now.

4th November 2004

Had my first calendar signing at HMV in Woking today. I was so scared no one would turn up but the place was mobbed. I felt like the Beatles. Well, a beetle with big boobs anyway. It was mainly guys but there were even a few girls getting the calendars for their boyfriends and they actually didn't seem to hate me. Which was a result. One of the guys came over and told me how he loved my *FHM* column and that he was getting some good tips. See, I am helping people!

Saw the rough edit of the DVD. Nothing like I imagined at all. The director said 'It's not mixed yet, so try and see beyond that.'

Beyond that? How can you look beyond me prancing around a dining room chair in high heels trying to persuade people this was 'sexy and fun'? It's hilariously awful. Had to laugh.

5th November 2004

DVD cover shoot.

Am still cringing about this bloody DVD, but have to go with it. We shot loads of extra pics to sell when I do press for the DVD. Me with majestic headdresses, killer heels, and ostentatiously long feather boas. I pointed out that they should put a disclaimer on the back of the DVD saying 'Abi doesn't advise that you work out in high heels.' Imagine if we didn't and someone broke their neck in mid-strip! We could get sued. What a farce.

8th November 2004

I did a shoot for *Heat* magazine's Christmas issue. They've got a feature called 'stars dress up' where they get certain celebs to recreate iconic images of the past year. I was transformed into Halle Berry in *Catwoman*.

Halle Berry and me? Can't get much more bloody different. Texted David to tell him. He found it most entertaining. He told me he and Matt had done something for the same issue. They're recreating the shot of Justin Timberlake and Janet Jackson when she had her nipple-baring 'wardrobe malfunction' on stage at the Super Bowl. Matt's Janet, naturally.

In the real *Catwoman*, Halle has these amazing leather trousers that must've cost a million dollars. The ones I was given were made of dodgy rubber and falling apart. And the stylist had to stuff the cat's ears so they didn't keep flopping. The Polaroid looked uncanny though. Thank the Lord.

9th November 2004

Flying to Newcastle and back for a calendar signing and to open a massive HMV store.

11th November 2004

Nuts shoot.

Felt really fat today. Kept trying to tell myself 'You're a curvy girl. Celebrate your figure. You've always had big boobs, you've never been skinny – they'll airbrush you anyway.'

At least my management controls the pictures so they can only be used once, but there's always this irksome doubt. The feeling that I shouldn't be doing all this. I'm an impostor, selling a body that I don't even really like.

Ironic that they've named me 'Woman of the Year'.

The best cure for having a fat day? Going out and getting pissed at the UK Music Hall of Fame party! One of my bunnies, Donna, got the tickets through work. I wore a short black dress with a little green fluffy shrug, a brooch and black Gucci boots. The paps went mad on the red carpet. Made me feel much better. Miranda, who'd come with me, walked straight inside and waited for me to do my bit.

When we entered there were rows and rows of celeb photos on the seats to let the cameras know who was sitting where. And mine was there – I'd been put next to Tamsin Outhwaite, two rows from the front. Poor Miranda, we came out for a girlie night on the town, but even though I have had my 'Arabiatta' moment, the cameras are still on us anyway. She glanced around nervously. 'There's no fucking way they're getting my face on camera,' she grimaced.

Robbie's playing tonight. And he said he wanted to meet me! When he appeared on stage I kept craning my head (as if he was going to bloody notice me sitting there). Somehow he didn't seem quite right though. He kept talking about the fact that he'd taken loads of painkillers because he'd hurt his wrist.

Odd thing to say to an audience, I thought. At the after party I was obsessed with looking for him. I kept asking people 'Is Robbie here?'

He wasn't.

16th November 2004

Had a meeting with Virgin Books today. My management are talking to them about me publishing an erotic novel.

It just sounds to me like more and more cheesy sex stuff. I'm going down a road that I'm not sure I want to be on and I'm getting further away from being an actress. Doing things for magazines is all very well and fun for a while but what am I now, a flipping sex writer? I don't want to just be all about sex, that's not who I am at all – there's more to me than that. I feel like things are snowballing.

However, on the plus side although it's about sex, it's aimed at the women's market, not men's, which would be good for me to tap into. Also it's only a bit of fun and another smart business move. Wouldn't it be fun to be a published 'author'?

17th November 2004

Did a Christmas-themed shoot to sell with my next lot of interviews. My management and I decided to ditch the usual Sexy Santa outfits, so instead it's me giving Santa a lap dance, riding a sleigh in my bra and pants and posing as the Virgin Mary with a pregnancy test. I certainly can't be accused of taking myself too seriously!

23rd November 2004

Another meeting with Virgin Books. If I decide to get involved in something then I want to have done it myself. At least to some degree. I've read one of their Black Lace books – remember getting mine free on the cover of *Cosmo* when I was a teenager. I've still got it somewhere. So I was interested but . . . If a job's worth doing it's worth doing well. Sitting around a table in a huge, posh boardroom with the Virgin team and my manager, I said, 'So it's basically a wank book for women?'

To the head of Virgin Books. Not sure he was very impressed.

'Look,' I told him. 'People always skip to the best bits, so we should just have a collection of, say, ten short stories.'

'Are you sure you can come up with ten scenarios?'

No problem. This is going to be fun . . .

24th November 2004

Closer magazine shoot.

25th November 2004

Had a calendar signing in Dublin and then a PA in the evening. Makes perfect sense that if I'm doing a PA somewhere I spend the afternoon there too and try to flog some copies of my calendar. Great business for Abi Titmuss Ltd.

The PA was at the opening of a bar called Brannigans. Got stupidly pissed. Someone randomly gave me a trombone which I dutifully blew on as a snapper took my picture. That should give the papers something to play with.

The *Star* have run pictures from my latest *Nuts* shoot. 'For more great pictures of Abi Titmuss check out this week's issue of *Nuts*.'

Make that, 'more fat pictures'.

27th November 2004

Bury St Edmonds. PA at a club called Brasilia. Calendar signings.

One of the papers has run the shot of me in the Dublin bar. 'She rarely misses an opportunity to blow her own trumpet, but Abi Titmuss turned her attention to the trombone as she turned up for the opening of trendy Brannigan's Bar in Dublin.' Well, I handed them that on a plate, didn't I?

28th November 2004

My agents, Money Management, have set up a deal with Shine and Channel 4 for a documentary about me. Had a meeting with the production company.

'People just see this two-dimensional image of you. This will give them the full picture – let's make them realise you are a business-woman who's in control of her own image and career.'

Still not convinced.

29th November 2004

2pm Matthew Bingham *FHM* column interview.

Am loving the *FHM* column now. Have one phone call a week and the poor journalist clears his throat nervously:

'Right, er, question one. Are you ready?'

'Go for it.'

'My girlfriend and I have recently got into a bit of bondage but we're running out of ideas, can you help us?'

'There's a whole world of sexy things out there . . . try dressing up in leather and rubber underwear, handcuffs are useful, there are some starter kits in Ann Summers that are quite sweet . . . never do up anything you can't undo and have a code word that means stop – something obscure like "green".'

Not sure where that came from.

2nd December 2004

Went to the *Loaded* LAFTA awards. Met a guy called Gavin. He says he's an ex-Calvin Klein model. Seemed a bit too short to me. He was nice, but not my type. Liked the idea of him being a model though. We were all pissed as farts by the time the party finished. Went back to my house with him and a few others. I ended up rambling to him about an ex from ages ago that I still liked. Poor guy. Then he announced that he wanted to have a shower. Thought it was a bit odd, but let him.

When he returned downstairs I continued pouring my heart out. Was completely unsexy. He just comforted me. Had to apologise for going on in the end. He left at about 3am.

3rd December 2004

Did a PA at a club in Norwich tonight as I was there for a calendar signing at HMV. The men were great. On stage, the compère made us play a game called 'What's your best chat up line?' Three blokes were brought up and sat on stools like in *Blind Date*.

1. Fancy a fuck?
2. Can I be your prince?
3. Have you got a raisin? No, why? Would you like a date?

I thought that number three was brilliant. He won.

The stuff people will do for a free T-shirt. Unbelievable.

4th December 2004

The *Star* has run a story about me and that guy called Gavin! Says I 'whisked him straight home after meeting him at the *Loaded* LAFTA-awards after party at Pangaea.

If only they knew how much I bored him to death that night. And he didn't exactly set me on fire. Hardly the behaviour of a vixen.

5th December 2004

Bloody hell. And another one.

The *Sunday Mirror* says I was playing 'tonsil tennis' with 'Kerry McFadden's former beau, Dan Corsi'. According to them it happened at Pangaea too. I must have a different boy in every corner of that club.

Absolute total rubbish. Can hardly remember talking to him. Think he came pushing forward and introduced himself to me, then I went to the bar with my mates. One of them said, 'He looks familiar – who is it?' Spoke for about twenty seconds. Nice guy, didn't fancy him.

8th December 2004

Gavin texted and asked me out. Haven't replied.

I'm so tired from all the PAs and late nights. When I get there I need one drink to perk me up so I can get on stage in front of a thousand baying clubbers, but once I've had one drink it's like a bell rings in my head. Ding ding, and we're off! It's all downhill from there. Also, I feel like I'm in a vicious circle: the worse I feel about myself the more I want to be out partying to numb it, and the more I party the more tired I am and then I feel even worse about myself. And so on.

I've stopped exercising as I'm either too hungover or tired, and started comfort-eating.

When will I learn that eating an entire packet of HobNobs will not solve your problems?

9th December 2004

In Manchester for yet another PA, the launch of a club called the Amber Lounge. Did a few calendar signings in the afternoon first of course. The men were great as usual and supplied me with all the customary jeers, but there were a handful of women there too and every time I walked past them I got shivers down my spine. Couldn't relax.

I desperately wanted them to like me. I can't bear that I'm seen as such an embodiment of evil amongst women. Wish I could prove to them that I'm just a normal girl and I'm not going to steal their husbands. Kept expecting them to chuck a bottle at me. One girl had about twenty earrings in one ear and a really tight top that said 'Prize Bitch' on it. Was convinced she was going to kill me. Why am I feeling so paranoid these days? Must be losing it.

10th December 2004

Zoo is out. 'Fifty Sexiest Girls 2004'.
The main image is 'We Wish You an Abi Christmas'.
They've used pics from our Christmas shoot too.

11th December 2004

The *Sun* has an awful picture of me with a quadruple chin.

'Looks like Abi's getting flabby. We always knew she could be cheeky – now it seems Abi Titmuss has gone all chinny too.'

I am mortified. It is so humiliating. I'm laughing in the pic, with my chin down and the photographer has also taken it from literally under my chin. I am barely recognisable.

Ate three bowls of Frosties and went to bed.

12th December 2004

News of the World has gone for the Sexy Santa pictures. Perfect.

13th December 2004

Did a cover shoot for *Maxim*. One pic was of me wearing nothing but a telephone wire! It was all strategically placed to cover the necessary bits – but still very risqué. Every time I do a shoot now I know I need to step up my game, get a different image – something that's going to make me stand out from the rest. And have to say, I've never seen anyone wear a telephone before.

It's for their April 2005 issue and the premise of the rest of the shoot was around a cinema theme (they sold it to me by saying I was the Marilyn Monroe of our time – which would be lovely to believe but I'm not that narcissistic!). One shot was like the iconic *American Beauty* image except I had popcorn covering me. There was another with me in silhouette leaning provocatively over a cinema seat clasping old fashioned binoculars. Another, in my bra and knickers, leg cocked up on a cinema seat.

Just as Marilyn used to do, ahem.

14th December 2004

When a person needs advice and help from a sympathetic and knowledgeable agony aunt, it is a prerequisite that that person also needs to see said agony aunt in thigh-high lace-up boots.

With that in mind, I did a shoot today for the pictures to go alongside my *FHM* column 'Ask Abi'.

15th December 2004

Started doing press for the DVD, *Tone and Tease*.

Spoke to my management at length about the documentary idea. We are going to do this. I do want people to see the fact that I'm treating all this as a job – that I've turned a bad situation around to my advantage, and I'm not just doing it for the sake of it. Emma says they want to film me at home, with my friends, hanging out – even going to acting classes. This could actually be a really good opportunity. The start of a new chapter.

They want to do the first lot of filming at Christmas when I go home and see Mum. Wow, I've just realised that I think I have seen my mum twice this entire year. I've been so busy it's been crazy. I feel terrible that I haven't made time for her but to be honest, with some of the stuff that's been in the papers I haven't really wanted to face my parents. It's just easier not to, all the sex stuff is embarrassing. I'm embarrassing.

16th December 2004

Ha ha, gave an exercise class to the boys at the *Nuts* office. They were all in leotards and legwarmers, smoking pipes and drinking cans of beer throughout. It was a shoot for the mag to promote my DVD. I'm not sure any of them could even lift a DVD.

17th December 2004

Was guest of honour at Vogue House for *GQ* magazine's staff Christmas lunch. Was all going well until I found out the other guest of honour was Piers Morgan.

He was editor of the *Mirror* throughout John's troubles and printed some of the most damaging things about him. When he arrived it was all I could do not to lean over and stick a fork in him.

I no longer have anything to do with John and I am not going to spend my life defending him, but to sit next to one of the men who I believe had helped to destroy him was very hard.

I completely ignored him, which drove him mad, and he eventually forced me into conversing with him. This resulted in me calmly telling him exactly what I thought of what he'd done, as the room fell into a hushed silence. I drew his attention to one particular front page he had sanctioned. The whole page was a close-up of John's face with the headline 'MONSTER'. On the basis of rumour and gossip.

He had no real answer.

Later in the evening he took me aside and apologised.

I actually felt like he meant it.

I replied, 'You should be saying that to John, not me.'

I walked off and for the first time in over a year, I texted John and told him. I felt like I'd won a tiny battle for him, although it was of course far too little, far too late.

Full of adrenaline I then got completely sloshed and ended up in one of the *GQ* offices, taped to editor Dylan Jones, from head to toe with '*GQ*' masking tape.

20th December 2004

Heat's out and my *Catwoman* shoot is in it. Looks genius! You'd never be able to tell it was me.

There's a story in one of the papers: 'Abi's party night hell' saying I got hassled in a place called the Players Bar – 'a woman launched at her and ranted abuse . . . called her a "trollop" . . . knocked her drink out of her hand . . . '

Complete rubbish. I've only ever been there once and that was with John. Still, it doesn't paint a good image. What kind of person does that make me look like?

Called Sam.

'I want to do something meaningful. It's nearly the end of December. I've worked as a nurse every Christmas until now and know its their busiest time . . . '

'What are you saying?'

'I want to go back to the hospital for a few days. I want to help the nurses.'

'Sweetheart, you can't go back and do that. It's just not a viable option . . . Can you not see that?'

'But . . . '

She was right of course. When I thought about it. Imagine me on the ward – trying to concentrate on drug calculations with people recognising me and staring. Fat lot of good I'd be to people's lives.

The conversation made me realise what a complete whirlwind my life has become. It's been non-stop PAs, photo shoots, signings . . . When I think about what's happened to me over the last eighteen months it's unbelievable. What's even more shocking is how accustomed to it I've become.

21st December 2004

A photo from my Christmas shoot has made the front cover of the *Star* – me in my bra, pants and a hooded cape. Then inside they've gone big on the one of me lap dancing for Santa on a sleigh.

I feel slightly ridiculous, but hey, it's my job.

22nd December 2004

Watched the Comedy Awards on telly tonight. Jonathan Ross made another joke about me.

'Abi Titmuss has been tied to more bedposts than David Blunkett's dog.'

I couldn't decide what to feel when he said that. My immediate reaction was, 'I don't want my family to hear, it's embarrassing.' But then I had a sudden realisation – there's the irony that Jonathan Ross is mentioning my name on television and everyone knows who he's talking about.

I'm a household name. That feels very, very strange.

24th December 2004

Back in Lincolnshire. Went out with Mum and my mates from home, to the usual pubs. But of course it wasn't usual, not any more.

All eyes were on me. Didn't help that we had a film crew following us, everyone was swarming around me. Tried to talk to Mum but people kept interrupting us all the time. It all got a bit much.

Mum got upset. People were shouting 'Abi – pictures!' then thrusting the camera in her hand like she was just a punter.

She said to me afterwards, 'Everything's changed. I wasn't expecting it to be like this.'

That made me sad. What have I become? Must make sure I spend some time with her alone.

25th December 2004

Christmas Day with Mum. Perfect, felt so blissful to be relaxed, normal, and allowed to sit in my PJs and stuff my face with mince pies without fear of anyone taking my picture.

29th December 2004

Start spreading the news, I'm leaving today, New York, Noooo Yorrrrk! Had it up to here with England, the papers and the men. Sue and I are off on a mini-break to the Big Apple. Hurrah.

The film crew are coming along with us, unfortunately, but they promise they will only film little bits and then leave me alone.

At the airport I saw I'd made the cover of the *Sun* – 'Abi's Page 3 Tease.'

Massive piece on my DVD with a nice full-page pic of me wearing the feather headdress from the extra shoot we did. Nice to leave on a slightly positive note. Although true to form, Sue of course said, 'What the hell are you wearing? A chicken?'

31st December 2004

Oh wow. We're having such a brilliant time. As the sun went down on the last day of 2004, Sue and I were ice skating in Central Park. I looked across the gleaming ice at the camera crew spying on me and it nearly took my breath away at how much had changed for me. This time last year I had just come out of the most gruelling few months of court case, accusations and darkness. We'd just filmed a programme about John's year of hell, now there's a crew filming a documentary about my life, and I've paid for myself to come to New York!

Still, I knew what I had to do. I'd prearranged to get some 'pap' shots of me ice skating as I knew it would cover the cost of the trip. So I snuck away from the camera crew for half an hour – Sue managed to deflect them.

Think they knew. Don't care. It's called being shrewd.

Walking back to the hotel it was so nice not having to wear a hat or shades. I found myself purposely staring people right in the eye to test that they didn't have a clue who I was. And I loved it. To a point.

I enjoyed it in the daytime, but I was secretly worried about the fact that I might not get noticed in bars.

The hotel we were staying in was having a massive New Year's Eve party so we bought tickets there. Balconies circled the main bar, with ornate corridors peering over on to the sea of colourful activity below.

Went to Nobu for dinner. Really expensive and a bit disappointing. Had about twenty different things and none of them were nice. My first mouthful was fish eggs and nearly made me vomit. Then came a soup with crab legs hanging out of it like something out of *Star Wars*.

Went back to the hotel. It was packed. Sue and I hadn't admitted it to each other but we both had that 'It's New Year's Eve and we have to have a great time but we're not yet' feeling. And we're in New York too . . .

Then suddenly the DJ played our song – Lionel Richie's 'All Night Long'! It's proper cheese and it's *our* cheese. That was it, just like that we were laughing and the night began.

We placed ourselves as elegantly as possible around the circular bar, trying nonchalantly to act as if we went there all the time.

Perched on the barstool, I had a bit of a panic.

'If no one looks at me . . . that means I'm not actually attractive. And it proves that the only reason people say I'm a sex symbol at home is because of my name.'

That was it. I began straining for attention. Flicking my hair about, coyly following the rim of my glass with my finger. Basically, looking like a prostitute.

After a few minutes, a guy came over. Very cute. Dark hair, tall, and oooh, that American accent was lovely. He told me he was a physiotherapist. And of course he didn't have the foggiest who I was. Which was brilliant. He was interested in me, for me.

'What do you do?' cute American asked politely.

'I'm a nurse,' I lied. Well, not entirely. Actually it was brilliant to feel like a normal nurse again for a bit and to be able to chat to him about the ward, patients, proper work. Ended the night with a snog in the corridor. He wasn't staying in the hotel and I couldn't bring him back to our room. Not yet anyway.

'I'll call you tomorrow,' he grinned. I looked at my watch. It *was* tomorrow – 6.30am!

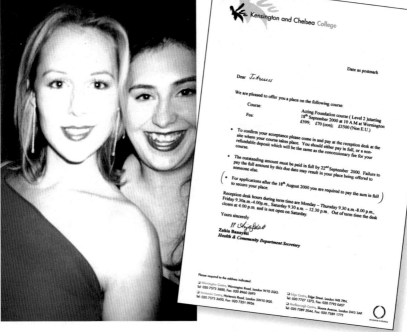

1999. Sanderson bar with Marisa. I had no idea what was coming!

Getting in to drama school. I actually jumped up and down when I got this.

The Bentham ward girls at Katie's wedding (she's in the middle).

Faced with the headlines at a magazine shoot.

2004. My first red carpet moment.

Gok Wan doing my "lips" at the filming of *Tone and Tease*.

Clearly having a terrible time on the *Loaded* shoot, Las Vegas…!

My 30th birthday party
with the Bunnies.
Shortly before
I put my face in the
cake!

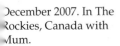

December 2007. In The
Rockies, Canada with
Mum.

February 2004. An unairbrushed Polaroid from my first *FHM* shoot.

August 2005. Backstage at V Festival with my girl Sam.

I first caught the acting bug at university.

C.U.S.U. DRAMA SOCIETY
proudly presents

Monty Python's

'THE LIFE
OF BRIAN'

THURSDAY 20TH FEBRUARY &
FRIDAY 21ST FEBRUARY 1997

JESUS/EX-LEPER/BORIS FEINBERG/
COMMANDO C/BURT/ELSIE/MR OPTIMISTIC......NOEL MOON

BIG NOSE/FRANK GOLIATH/FALSE PROPHET/
EDDIE/BOB......LEE WEINERT

WIFE OF BIG NOSE/CULPRIT 1/FRANCIS/FRANK...CARLA CAPOLUON

MR CHEEKY/HARRY/COMMANDO D......ABI TITMUSS

WIFE OF GREGORY......PRISCILLA FERNA

A.N. OTHER/OFFICIAL/COMMANDO B/ARTHUR/
GUARD/BIGGUS DICKUS......THEO SPYROU

January 2008. Taken secretly whilst on a romantic weekend away.

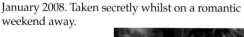

I'm very proud of this beautiful piece that Jay and I performed.

February 2008. I'd just done the jacket shoot for this book.

July 2007. Atlas Mountains, Morocco.
I feel free. And twirly.

In the shower, Morocco.
Simply stunning!!

February 2007. "Skiing" in Verbier. I'm not sunbathing, I'm stuck!

The brilliant cast of 'Fat Christ'. Clockwise from centre: director Heather Simpkin, Gavin Davis, Tim Downie, Jennifer Matter

As Susan Frobisher in 'Fat Christ'. I loved every second on that stage

Studying Latin. So engrossed I didn't know this picture was being taken.

Another shoot: A spontaneous picture taken during a lunch-break. It turned out to be one of my favourite shots.

2005

'If I'd observed all the rules I'd never have got anywhere.'
Marilyn Monroe

1st January 2005

Cute American called at about midday. Arranged to meet him and a mate of his that evening. His friend, a doctor, had the deepest Bronx accent I'd ever heard. Was hoping Sue would fancy him but no such luck. She called it a night at around 11.30pm.

It wasn't long before his mate left and we were snogging all over the place. Once I was convinced Sue was asleep we snuck into the room. I tiptoed to the fabulous white bathroom, trying not to giggle, and closed the door. I thought, 'Sod it I'm in New York! I want to have holiday sex!' and to be honest it was thrilling that this gorgeous guy liked me just for me. Everybody recognises me in the bars at home now and I'm never sure if guys are genuine.

It was mind-blowing sex. I was leaning forward on the sink of the pristine white bathroom, eyes locked on his through the mirror. It felt so sexy and exciting . . . He had an amazing body.

Then, one of my hair extensions fell out on the floor.

Shit.

I could see it lingering around by my feet. It looked like a dead raccoon. Had he seen it? I tried to kick it away as subtly as I could, without looking like I was a horse in a paddock.

'What the hell is that?' he asked.

I pushed my hair back in an effort to be sexy and hoped he wouldn't ask again. I stared at him through the mirror.

It worked. Phew. He was really very good at this . . . and what a body.

Afterwards we sat on the bathroom floor and talked for an hour.

Very romantic! It was sweet actually. He left at around 5am and I crept to bed. Then I heard Sue giggling and we both started laughing.

2nd January 2005

Woke the next morning thinking, 'Bugger, hope he calls me.'

But he did. And he was lovely. The best part about it all was that he still didn't have a clue who I was. We arranged to meet again.

'I'll book a room at the hotel,' he said. What a good idea that was.

During the daytime, Sue and I went shopping – she was cool that I'd met Cute American but there was no way I was going to abandon her for him for the entire trip. Went to Victoria's Secret to buy something for me to wear that night. Ended up buying so many pairs of pants that by the time I stood at the till to pay you could hardly see my head. I turned to Sue, 'Thank God no one knows me here!'

Then came a voice from behind the bras: 'Abi Titmuss is buying a load of knickers!'

A whole family emerged, pointing at me and waving. One of the kids came over to take my picture, undeterred by the mountain of pants between us.

Ended up spending a grand. Bought so much that the cashier made me sign a disclaimer saying I wasn't planning on selling them elsewhere!

After that we went to the Museum of Modern Art, which I adored. The documentary crew appeared while we were here. 'Great,' I thought, 'I hope they show this – me being cultured.'

Cute American joined us for drinks after dinner and the three of us had a right laugh. Sue didn't mind him being there at all; it was fun to talk to a real New Yorker, plus he had friends at the hotel who were having a party so we all went there.

At the end of the night we went to our rooms. Wore my new underwear for him tonight. He loved it.

3rd January 2005

Ground Zero was overwhelming. I stood there motionless for over half an hour. You can't help but feel moved when you see the vast emptiness where the Twin Towers once sat. It's like a vacuum that sucks you in. Almost as if you can hear the spirits of all those people, those lost lives. I was moved to tears reading all the messages people had written.

4th January 2005

Last night. Met up with Cute American for farewell drinks. Have grown quite attached to him. Typical; I meet a decent man who likes me for me and he lives on the other side of the sodding world.

Bit the bullet and told him who I was in England. When I said I'd been on the front cover of *FHM* he was in shock.

'Oh my Gad!' It wasn't so nice telling him how it had all come about in the first place though . . .

He said he'd call me when he's next in London. I know it was a holiday fling but can't help hoping he calls.

5th January 2005

Got home to see yours truly on the front cover of *Nuts* – giving the lads from the office an exercise master class. I know the *Nuts* boys so well now, it's easy to have a laugh with them. I appreciate how much they've done for me and vice versa. Like a mutual love-in.

The editor Phil Hilton told me, 'I wish we could reproduce you Abi, we'd be raking it in. Every time we put you on the cover our sales go up by fifty per cent.'

Hmm. Read the papers. Guess who's been seen out on dates with David Walliams?

Jayne Middlemiss.

He can't like her. Can he?

9th January 2005

There's a new show launching on Channel 4 called *The Friday Night Project*. Jimmy Carr is one of the hosts and it'll be live, with a few little clips on it. The producers called me in for a meeting.

'We're thinking of doing a VT like in *A Question of Sport*, where viewers have to guess who the mystery guest is. Except each week it's you and a celebrity, and people have to guess who that celeb is.'

All sounded pretty straightforward until it transpired that what they actually wanted to do, was simulate me shagging that diff celeb each week.

As funny as it is, there's no way I'm doing that. So I told them I'd try and think of something else instead. Really want to be involved, but not as a complete slapper. Please.

10th January 2005

The *Mirror* has run a story: 'Walli pines for Abi' – says David can't stop thinking about me and keeps texting.

Oh no, he's going to think I planted it. Which I didn't. But he'll know that. It made me smile. And I bet it will him.

11th January 2005

Went to premiere of *Team America: World Police* with Miranda. Arriving wasn't a problem, it was afterwards when it really hit the fan. I have never seen so many paparazzi. It was swamped and there was nowhere for me to hide. The PR for the film hadn't laid on any security – it's like they'd got what they wanted, the celebrity audience, and now we had to find our own way home. But the paps were scrambling on top of each other, it was crazy.

The Cheeky Girls were there. I watched them go outside and do their bit for the camera – they have a little routine that they do, wiggling their hips then dropping their coats. Bingo! I thought, and tried to sneak out behind them, but that was it. It was as if the street had exploded into one big flashbulb.

Instantly the paps surged forward. An elbow connected with the head of one of the Cheeky Girls and she dropped to the floor. Then, the culprit climbed over her to get to me! I couldn't see what I was doing, it was so scary. The pack swarmed round me as I tried to walk and followed me down the street.

I wanted to cry. Miranda and I tried desperately to find a pub, to get away from the scrum. Found one, crushed our way in and saw Darius Danesh, he'd been at the film too. He's surprisingly good looking. Now he's had his hair cut he doesn't look like a Spanish waiter any more. Really, really nice too. We sat next to each other and there were photographers peering through the window. I didn't have anything against him, but neither did I want to be linked with him, so I swapped places with Miranda. Still think he wanted my number though.

Everyone from the PR company that were organising it had disappeared. I just wanted to go home. They hadn't arranged for a cab which was fine, but all I wanted was some help getting one – there were so many paps out there, it was scary. I felt really vulnerable. And stuck.

People had started to gather outside – more and more of them. I felt claustrophobic and anxious. I saw a side door, and Miranda and I pretended we were going to the loo. Saw a taxi – quick! Made a run for it. Before we knew it there were photographers on the bonnet, grappling the back of the car and rocking it. As soon as we got in, some of them opened doors on the other side. Paparazzi have a pack mentality – once one of them starts crossing the line they think they all can.

Suddenly, this disgusting big guy lent over and tried to kiss me, then he grabbed me – so hard that his finger almost went up my crotch. It hurt. I froze. 'Go! Please move!' I screamed and the driver started moving away. We pushed the men out and closed the doors. Miranda and I just looked straight ahead, gripping each other's hands as blinding flashes went off all around and camera lenses banged on the windows.

'Come on,' mouthed Miranda. 'Don't cry.'

I need to get a security guard. Something. Can't cope with this.

13th January 2005

I know I shouldn't be shocked, but I am. There's a story in the bloody *Star* saying that I was a diva after the *Team America* premiere – demanding a car to take me home! 'Left a PR girl distraught after throwing a strop because she didn't have a limo to ferry her home . . .'

That's so unfair.

Filmed some of the documentary at my house. Simon, the director, asked me, 'What do you see yourself as?'

Good question.

I had to think. I really didn't know.

'A mag voted me the most pointless celebrity recently . . . I couldn't agree more.'

16th January 2005

My calendar is apparently selling like nobody's business! My management reckons it could beat even David Beckham's. It's gobsmacking when I sit and think about it.

17th January 2005

It's Radio Aid today. DJs are joining forces and the entire programming output is being broadcast across the board as one channel, all in aid of the Tsunami victims. I was a guest on the breakfast show with Davina McCall. It was such a feel-good day, everyone coming together for a cause, and Davina was lovely.

The other guest on the show with me was John Culshaw, the impressionist from *Dead Ringers*. He was so warm and friendly. He apologised for referring to me on the show so often – I told him not to worry, I thought it was hilarious. I remember one sketch he did when he was playing George Bush and waffling nonsense so instead of saying 'My fellow Americans' he said 'My fellow Abi Titmusses'. He kept saying he felt really bad, but I thought it was so flattering. While we were on air, some guy bid £4,000 for dinner with me! Are these people mad?

18th January 2005

Nuts shoot.

Darius Danesh called and asked me out. Am very tempted. He's actually really lovely.

Had another meeting with the guys from *The Friday Night Project*. I came back with the idea of doing spoofs of films where there's a couple involved. I explained that we could still get that slightly sexy element into it without me actually looking like I was shagging. I suggested *Ghost, Titanic, Nine and a Half Weeks, Indecent Proposal, The Postman Always Rings Twice*. They loved it.

Genius. My first acting role!

Also, Emma called. 'Abi, there's a multi-millionaire who's got a villa in Barbados, he's having a party and he wants to pay you to be there.'

This kind of thing only happens in films! We've arranged to meet him at the Sanderson Hotel tomorrow. Emma said she couldn't determine how old he was from his phone voice, but he sounded classy enough. She also asked him to send over details about the party, information about himself etc – I don't want him to think

I'm like one of these upper-class hookers. We'll make that very clear when we see him. Bet he's a wrinkly old perv.

19th January 2005

Got to the Sanderson with Emma. We were both amazed – he was an absolutely gorgeous. Very cute millionaire! He must only be about thirty-something and he was dressed immaculately.

He introduced himself and as soon as he turned to order drinks I mouthed to Emma, 'Oh, holy Jesus!' Very Cute Millionaire wanted to pay me to go to a party with him. I thought, 'I'll do it for free!'

Throughout the meeting Very Cute Millionaire was incredibly business-like, and by the end I was convinced he didn't fancy me at all. So why was I here? Why had he asked for me?

'We've been looking at a few options of people to come and do this job,' he explained. 'And my PA had suggested Abi.'

So he didn't even know who I was! After about thirty minutes, Very Cute Millionaire declared the meeting over. He signed the drinks bill (even his pen looked posh). I had never met anyone like that before. He oozed money and class. Plus, I was now getting fixated by the fact that he wasn't paying me any attention whatso-ever.

I was determined to get VCM to notice me. We got up to leave, Emma headed off for a meeting and VCM said the driver was bringing his car round, so I walked with him to the door. It was an Aston Martin.

I said I'd give him my number (You know, so he could call me if there was any more info he needed to pass on about the party . . . and the rest). VCM took the piece of paper I'd scribbled it on – politely folded it and put it in his pocket.

I crossed the road and got into my mini. As I drove off I clocked VCM smiling at me in the wing mirror.

Bingo.

22nd January 2005

Am chuffed to bits.

10.45am: VCM texted and asked me out! I really don't want the papers finding out about this one. We've arranged to meet secretly, out in the countryside somewhere.

Went to a party for a BBC show called *TV Moments*. Don't know what it was for – there are so many these days that they merge into one after a while. Brendan Cole, one of the cast of *Strictly Come Dancing*, was there. I'd never seen him before, but I was sat across the bar from him and, as far as I was concerned, he couldn't take his eyes off me. It was evident he hasn't been in the limelight long, I kept thinking, 'You have no idea, do you? This whole room is full of journalists and they can see you staring!' It did tickle me though. He practically had his tongue hanging out. I was wearing a gorgeous pink, black and white Missoni dress and I knew I looked good, so it made me smile to myself.

I couldn't help thinking Brendan was sexy. And there's no doubt there was real chemistry between us. I was trying not to look at him, but it was really difficult. I even moved round the other side of the bar to get away from his eyes. Besides, if anyone clocked what was going on, they'd automatically presume it was me doing the chasing.

23rd January 2005

Spoke on the phone to VCM for an hour today. He's adorable. Am really excited about our date tomorrow.

24th January 2005

VCM suggested we met at his 'town house', which was nearer to me. It's darn swanky.

He took me to a pretty little secluded restaurant for dinner. He seemed quite clued up about the fact that I wouldn't want anyone to recognise me. We went back to his house and had a bit of a kiss and cuddle. Was worried I might knock over a Ming vase or something. But not so worried it stopped me having fun.

25th January 2005

Have been asked to be on an ITV show called *Celebrity Love Island*. Spoke to my management about it and we've decided to say no. To me the premise sounds like they get a load of celebs on a sunny island and wait to see if anyone shags.

Feels wrong to me.

26th January 2005

Full page in the *Star* of me in pool sipping a cocktail on holiday from one of the shoots I did with Darryn, alongside a drop-in of my latest interview in *Nuts*. 'I love sexy older women.' God, I get worse.

Saw Very Cute Millionaire again. Things are getting a bit serious. Or he is anyway . . . not entirely sure that's a good thing. But I can't deny I like him.

27th January 2005

Recorded some scenes for *The Friday Night Project* with various celeb guests. Well, I say celeb guests – they were no Jude Law (try Richard Blackwood, Jean-Christophe Novelli and, er, . . . Keith Harris) – but it was great throwing myself into it like a proper acting job.

My favourite one was re-enacting the sexy fridge scene from *Nine and a Half Weeks* with chef Jean-Christophe. Except he had to feed me random things like potato waffles, frazzles, and chillies. Did a spoof from *Ghost* too with Bez from the Happy Mondays. It was hilarious because he had to lift me up at one point, and he's not a big man.

VCM rang and we chatted for about an hour. He's so sweet.

30th January 2005

Sunday Mirror:

'The world's cheesiest pop star Darius Danesh, 24, made a big play for Abi Titmuss, 28, in a London pub after a celebrity screening of new flick *Team America: World Police* . . . my mole says: "Darius looked gutted when Abi turned him down."'

Oops.

1st February 2005

Went over to VCM's town pad again tonight. He picked me up in a different car this time – a Porsche. Lovely!

2nd February 2005

The *Love Island* producers have been back on the phone to my management, upping the money. They're not getting me that easily. It sounds so tasteless.

4th February 2005

The Friday Night Project started tonight. Was so excited about seeing it and had the bunnies all round for the evening to watch it and eat rubbish food. The *Ghost* sketch was the first one they played, but when it went on air I was a bit miffed. Unbeknownst to me the producers had added a shot in afterwards, a close up of some hands - not mine – massaging a pottery penis on a wheel! I knew it was funny. But I didn't like it. They hadn't told me they were going to do it and I found that disrespectful. Thought about calling my management to have a moan, but knew there was no point. Too late now. Besides, the bunnies found it bloody hilarious.

5th February 2005

Had another PA this evening. This time in the glam location of Bedford at a club called Mission. The guys were crazy this evening – thought I was going to get my skirt ripped off at one point. Just as I was leaving, some guy pushed through the crowd and said really seriously, 'I love your work.'

Nice, but honestly, I mean, I ask you . . . ?

6th February 2005

Went to *An Audience with Al Murray* tonight at LWT studios. It was a great show. Al's doing so well since *Hell's Kitchen*; I'm so happy for him. We are still mates a year on.

7th February 2005

Another photo shoot with my management's picture agency. We came up with the idea of shooting me . . . with me. Double images. *Nuts* have already said they'll buy the photos. We did one where I'm standing behind 'me', holding my boobs. Another where we're standing chest to chest, another where I'm pulling my hair. There was also a really great pic, which was a copy of the film poster from *Blow Up* which had me lying down with another 'me' astride taking a picture. We used another girl as a stand in, then the photographer said he's going to morph them together afterwards. With a nice little help from Lady Airbrush if possible. The tabloids are going to love them.

VCM called again and wanted to take me to dinner. I told him I was too tired. Which I was. But I also felt like I wanted a bit of space tonight. We're both so busy it's hard to find the right time to see each other.

8th February 2005

My birthday!

Went to Nobu with the girls. Having a party on Friday night at Umbaba. Can't wait.

Got really spoilt today. VCM bought me a stunning gold necklace with a diamond crucifix. I didn't have a clue of its worth though – I'd never had any nice jewellery. It wasn't until I showed Miranda who knows exactly what diamonds look like that I realised. 'Oh my God, Abi! That will have cost him at least a grand.'

Blimey. He's perfect. I hope he's perfect . . . Oh, he could be perfect, you never know!

So . . . why oh why am I going off him?

9th February 2005

Sooo hungover. Couldn't speak or move all day.

10th February 2005

VCM has been texting about meeting up. Found myself making excuses. This is not good.

13th February 2005

Guess what? My calendar has sold over 25,000 copies. It's number two in the country, beating David Beckham, Kylie and Man United! Peter Kay's number one – but I'm happy to give him that. Ha ha. Can't believe I've beaten Becks.

14th February 2005

Oh. My. God. VCM sent me the biggest bunch of roses I have EVER seen. I almost couldn't get them through the door. If you're going to date a millionaire – make sure it coincides with Valentine's.

Shit. I didn't send him anything. Maybe I'll text him a picture of me in my bra and pants . . .

15th February 2005

Love Island called my management again. More money this time, but as far as I'm concerned, the survey still says 'Uh Uh'.

19th February 2005

Birthday party.

I put two grand behind the bar at Umbaba for my friends. God, it was fantastic to be able to do that. To say, 'You've put up with all my shit over the last year, helped me through some hellish times, and now you can get as pissed as you like all night – on me!'

The best part was seeing all my mates who'd come down from Lincolnshire. I hadn't seen them for ages. One of them got really drunk and threw up everywhere.

VCM came too of course. He only stayed for a bit then drove home. Think I might've been ignoring him. Well, I was pissed as a fart.

22nd February 2005

It was Chris Moyles' birthday, so his producers at Radio 1 had asked me if I'd mind jumping out of a cake to surprise him as his 'treat'. They kept telling me how he's always talking about me on the show, apparently he really fancies me.

Got there at 7am when he was already on air. Then they brought out a gigantic 'present' box. They moved it just outside the studio door and I had to crouch inside. Comedy Dave got him to turn around in the studio, while I scuttled in under the box and was manoeuvred in front of him. Then I had to wait until I could hear he was touching the top of the box before I could spring out.

It was brilliant. Chris was flabbergasted, and it's not very often that man is speechless. He actually seemed a little bit nervous, which I thought was hilarious. Girls Aloud trotted in as guests after me. They're much shorter than I imagined.

Bit of a jam-packed 'celeb-y' day all in all. It's the premiere for Will Smith's new film *Hitch* tonight. Because of this, the documentary crew followed me about all day – even wanted to see me having my hair washed at the hairdressers. Are people really going to want to see that? It's Sue's birthday so I took her as a treat (to the premiere, not the hairdressers).

I borrowed a gorgeous Missoni dress from her but en route I must've taken my coat on and off about ten million times because I couldn't decide what to do for the paps . . . Sue was getting infuriated – 'Does it bloody matter?' – but of course, Arabiatta knows it does matter. A great deal. The paparazzi want to see boobs and flesh, not some woolly winter coat. So off it came.

I don't know if I was imagining it but the crowd and the photographers seemed to go wilder than ever tonight. Sue nipped in ahead of me and afterwards she laughed, 'Will Smith didn't get the reception you did! Its like you're more famous than him over here.'

Then speak of the devil, just as I was standing and being snapped by more photographers in the lobby of the cinema, I heard an American voice say, 'Well, you're sure popular.'

I turned around—

It was Will Smith. Right by my side, looking in my eyes and speaking to me. I said, 'Thanks! I don't know why.'

Then he kissed me on the cheek, as the flashbulbs went off (I hoped they'd got that!) and was whisked away. I don't think he had the foggiest idea who I was. He got up on stage to introduce the film and had the crowd in stitches – he's so warm and intelligent. Such a nice normal guy considering he's an A-list star.

Can't remember much about the after party as got royally drunk. Well, it does take it out of you all that posing on the red carpet, you know.

26th February 2005

Went home to see Mum and took her, her friend Val and my old mate Cheryl out for a lovely dinner in a little local pub-restaurant. I didn't see Will out tonight, oddly enough.

27th February 2005

The stills from the *Maxim* shoot have made the papers. They're bloody raunchy.

1st March 2005

Arena is on sale this week. Sam said loads of papers are gagging for the pictures from it. That's brilliant news.

Had a *Zoo* interview at the Sanderson. Love those boys. As long as I give them a tiny bit of sexy talk they're happy.

2nd March 2005

The *Arena* shots are in the *Sun* and the *Mirror*. They look amazing too, am really proud.

Spoke to Mum. 'Saw you in that magazine – looking a bit cheeky!' Bless her.

Simon from the documentary called. He's been researching me and apparently I've been on the front of thirty-five magazines and sixty-eight national newspapers so far.

Bloody hell.

3rd March 2005

More *Arena* shots in the papers. They must love them. Sam said it's usually unheard of for tabloids to spread them across more than one day if it's basically advertising another publication.

It's so ironic that I'm getting press from all these great pictures when I know I'm no longer in my best shape. Am constantly out caning it and I'm not eating properly. I just keep relying on the fact that I know my pictures sell, and that there's always airbrushing . . . which is not really the best attitude.

How long can it last? Then again, how long do I want it to last? This is a means to an end, I want to do more with my life, to act.

4th March 2005

Had a full day filming with the documentary crew and wasn't even doing much. But I'm glad they're with me when I'm being 'normal' as well as having my picture taken. That's the side I want people to see of me.

5th March 2005

Went to Lincolnshire to see my mum. She's amazing, especially considering she's constantly batting questions about her daughter being so scandalous.

6th March 2005

Oh my God. There's a story about me and that Gavin guy in the *People*.

'A hunky male model has told how sex-bomb Abi Titmuss took him home, stripped him stark naked and begged him to "Take me now". But despite being in a position that millions of men can only fantasise about, Gavin Dixon REFUSED to go all the way with the raunchy TV presenter. The Calvin Klein model, 24, kept getting visions of a lovely girlfriend he had just split with – and in the end he turned down 28-year-old Abi's chance-of-a-lifetime offer.'

Well if that's how he remembers it, that's up to him . . .

I was droning on about *my* ex all night! But you know what, there's always a picture at the end of every tunnel. The paper had to use my image on the page, which was one of mine, so I got paid for it.

7th March 2005

Cambridge with Dad and documentary crew.

8th March 2005

This is getting silly. *Love Island* must seriously want me. They're offering ridiculous amounts now.

11th March 2005

Did a shoot for *FHM* today and then went to a club in town with the girls. A cute blonde guy came up to me.

'Hi, I'm Zac.'

'Hi Zac.'

'Do you remember meeting me about a year ago?'

I didn't.

'You lost me my girlfriend.' He was smiling though.

'What?'

'I met you at Pangaea,' he explained. 'And afterwards there was a story in the newspaper saying we snogged in a broom cupboard.'

I remembered.

He shrugged. 'My girlfriend dumped me over that.'

'John dumped me over that too,' I laughed despairingly.

12th March 2005

Went out for dinner with Darryn to talk about business. He wants to do another set of pictures soon. Think he knows I'm trying to distance myself from him a bit. Still, there's a part of me that feels like I owe him a set every now and again. He's just no longer going to have exclusive hold over what I do. He can't have the monopoly over me. It doesn't make financial sense.

It was quite a posh restaurant so I made sure I looked the part. Wore tight jeans, heels and a really expensive black and pink Diane von Furstenburg top. It had a high neck with a little hole in the cleavage to show a tiny bit of boob. We met in a posh Italian restaurant on Park Lane. As we sat down to eat I thought, 'For once, I'm actually going to turn my phone off and concentrate on the matter in hand.'

The meeting seemed to go well. It's good to keep him a bit happy otherwise he might turn on me. Hailed a black cab to go home, and switched my phone back on as we were driving up Park Lane.

Beep beep.

There was a message. It was from David Walliams.

'Where are you tonight?'

'Park Lane, just finished dinner. Why?'

'I'm with RW. He would like to meet you'

I didn't need time to work out who RW was. Robbie. Williams.

This was it.

'Whoo hoo!' Without thinking I shouted really loudly and punched the air. The cab driver looked round and smirked.

'Have you just had some good news or something?'

I laughed. 'Yeah – you could say that!'

I looked at the text again. Loving the fact that because my phone had been off, I hadn't replied straight away and it made me look cool, like I wasn't bothered.

I texted back, 'I'm on way home,' to at least TRY and play it cool.

He texted back telling me where they were. I checked myself in the wing mirror. Smart, sexy but not too try-hard. Perfectly suitable attire for meeting a world famous pop-star. My heart was in my mouth.

'Turn the cab around!'

The cab driver was laughing. 'You're going to meet someone exciting aren't you?'

'Yes!' I shrieked.

I was bursting to tell him who it was but I couldn't.

Then I thought about the irony of the fact that I'd just been to dinner with the head of a paparazzi company. If Darryn knew I was going to meet Robbie Williams and hadn't called to tip him off, he'd go berserk. Should I tell him?

What a picture that would make. Me and Robbie bloody Williams. That would show the people who hate me. Part of me wants proof that this was actually happening, but I know I can't.

It's not fair on him. And I'm not that much of a media whore, am I? Don't even answer that.

My chest was pounding as we arrived. Just be calm, Abi. You are normal. You are not meeting a superstar, he's an ordinary bloke . . . it's all fine. I plastered a smile on my face, walked through the door and there he was.

David, who was on his right, stood up, smiled and introduced Robbie.

I tried to maintain an air of nonchalance. As if I'd just happened to be passing, not that I'd nearly hyperventilated with excitement on the way here. He had a cheeky glint in his eye.

We got on really well, and as the conversation loosened, so did his eye level. I noticed him glancing at my boobs on more than one occasion. Thank God I wore this top.

Oh my God, what I'd give to send the bunnies a text telling them what I was up to! I kept glancing over at David, wondering what was going through his head.

Before we knew it, it was 12 o'clock and Robbie was asking if I'd like a lift home!

Of course I would, I wanted to spend as much time with him as I could. But should I try to play it cool?

Play it cool? Oh fuck that. He's already said he's going back to LA in a couple of days. You might never get an opportunity to hang around with Robbie Williams again, even if it is only in a car!

Go on.

'OK, then'.

David said goodbye and Robbie texted his driver.

In a matter of seconds, a blacked-out Range Rover pulled up and we climbed in – and off we went.

Robbie was in the front seat and put some of his music on the stereo. He told me he wanted to know what I thought. Luckily I genuinely liked it, but I wasn't exactly going to say it was a load of shit.

The journey passed in a flash and I was home before I knew it.

Being in a car with an international pop star was so surreal, but was that all I was feeling? I think it was – but I'd still love it if he called me. Blimey, what a night . . . !

13th March 2005

Spark or no spark, I booked an appointment at the hairdressers to get my extensions redone. Just in case Robbie called later.

He didn't.

I was kidding myself.

14th March 2005

No phone call.

15th March 2005

Still no call.

Really having to restrain myself from asking David if he's spoken to Robbie. Be cool. Can't put him in that position.

16th March 2005

Mum's birthday today. I had arranged a day of surprises for her – a trip on the London Eye, dinner at The Ivy and tickets to *The Producers*. She loved all of it.

There was a party at Umbaba so I took her out for a drink. Calum Best was there; haven't seen him for a long time. He's so cute. I'd always thought he was sexy – there's just this aura about him. No wonder he has his pick of the ladies, he's gorgeous.

17th March 2005

I didn't tell Mum to buy a hat for my wedding to Robbie.

18th March 2005

All the papers have been given the tip-off about me writing my fantasy books. They're not out until July but its great to get the PR ball rolling now. That means that every time the papers write about me they'll stick it in somewhere as 'new' information.

19th March 2005

Was a guest on T4's Honours show. Was really embarrassed about meeting the host Steve Jones though. I told *Heat* magazine I fancied him in a little interview I did for their TV pages a while ago. After that they asked Steve what he thought of me and he replied, 'Oh yes, she's a lovely girl but I wouldn't go out with her.'

I wanted to crawl under a car and die.

Steve walked past. He smiled and came over.

'Hi Abi.'

I should've just acted nonchalantly but typical me, I had to say something.

'Steve, I really never said I fancied you, you know.' It was all a bit pathetic.

'Oh, don't be silly, it's fine.' He smiled awkwardly before walking off.

Should I just shoot myself now?

20th March 2005

The *News of the World*:

'Cameras at the ready . . . Abi Titmuss and Calum Best have been caught canoodling. After working their way through London's party crowd, I guess it was only a matter of time before they hooked up together. So on Wednesday they bowed to the inevitable at London's Umbaba club. I'm told: "Abi was sat on Calum's knee and he was clearly happy. She was very attentive and kept turning to kiss him as they cuddled." As if we can't guess what happened next . . . Abi and Calum are used to having their love-lives in the spotlight – as well as in the dirty boys' video shop.'

Last Wednesday then? Hmm, and my mum would have been so proud sitting there next to me as I snogged the face off Calum.

There's something else about me in the Sundays. It's a story from a guy who I went out with when I was ten: 'Lifting the lid on her not-so raunchy past . . . '

Of course my past isn't going to be raunchy! I was ten years old! There was a ridiculous picture of him sitting there grinning. I'm guessing he must have been paid and he'd given them a picture of me from primary school that I'd never even seen before. I had a bowl haircut! At least he was nice about me.

And that's a rarity these days. It still made me feel a little sad though. All my old school friends seem to be talking to the papers about my childhood.

21st March 2005

Loaded have booked me for a shoot in Tenerife. It's for the cover of their January issue. Took Sue (promised Miranda she can come on the next one).

Got to the airport and Martin, the editor, introduced himself and all the team. He's really cool. And very tall. I could tell from his manner that we were in for a fun time. Have never done a foreign beach shoot before. Feels so glam. Like I've properly made it. Sam said this was a great opportunity for me. I must be unfailingly professional.

Just one little drinky with the team on the plane. Well, we are on holiday! Sort of.

An hour later we were singing 'Viva Espana'.

Rolled off the plane and started shooting pretty much straightaway. The beach was an expanse of glistening black sand; it was stunning.

So was the photographer, Luke. He's got dirty blonde surfers' hair, and there he was in nothing but a pair of shorts and a tan, taking my picture on the beach. Instantly we had a rapport, i.e. I fancied him. I must've been looking down the lens saying 'shag me' because the others were getting all excited about how great the shots were looking. I was in the sea, lying on the sand, and basically flirting like mad.

We finished and all went for dinner, by which point I'd got straight off a plane and spent seven hours working in the blazing sunshine. I was full of adrenaline from the shoot, excitement at fancying Luke, slight sunstroke . . . and sangria. Add to this the general holiday atmosphere and the next thing I know I'm back in my room in bed.

With Luke.

22nd March 2005

Oh BOLLOCKS.

Way to be professional Abs. Day one of my first overseas job and I've just shagged the photographer.

Woke up and Luke had gone; he'd got up at ridiculous o'clock to go surfing before the shoot began. Then I heard a noise. It was someone talking in the room next door.

The walls were like paper.

What have I done? Everyone on the shoot has heard me having sex all night! Knew I couldn't deny it though. Walked down to breakfast and everybody looked up and grinned in unison. I wanted to die.

'Morning!' They all laughed. 'Good night?' They thought it was hilarious.

Today's shoot was on a banana plantation. A mini bus was arriving at 9am to get us there. Boy, it was messy. We were all drinking 'hair of the dog' at 8.45am in the hotel bar. Had such a laugh on the bus. Luke's fab and there was no atmosphere, thank God, apart from everyone taking the piss.

We weren't laughing so much after seven hours out in the sun though.

23rd March 2005

The plane was packed on the way home. It was like a school trip – we were all sat at the back giggling and being loud. Luke and I kept joking that we were going to have sex in the loo.

I'd always wanted to join the 'mile-high club', just so I could say I'd done it. I thought, 'Sod it, why not? I might not get the chance to earn my wings again!' So I told Luke to follow me to the loo in two minutes.

It was so small and really bloody awkward, but at the same time very sexy.

When I sheepishly opened the door to creep out there was a round of applause from the frigging team and a flash. They had all been waiting and took a photo of us for posterity as we came out.

That better not make it into the mag.

24th March 2005

Arrived home exhausted but still chuckling with Sue. We agreed that it was probably the most fun trip we've ever done.

The producers of *Love Island* have increased my potential fee yet more! A lot more in fact.

Still saying no though. If it's anything like the debauched trip I've just had abroad I don't want it on camera.

25th March 2005

Went to Marks and Spencer's to buy a sandwich this afternoon. A guy came up to me while I was in the queue.

'Excuse me, are you famous?' he asked.

'Well, considering you have to ask and you don't know my name, I would have to say – clearly not.'

26th March 2005

Still no word from RW. Thinking of cancelling the church.

27th March 2005

There's a story in the *News of the World* about me behaving badly on the flight home from Tenerife. When I read it I was nearly sick with horror in case they'd found out everything – that'll improve my reputation no end – but they hadn't. Just said that I was lording it about and annoying the air stewardesses. That's not true. I hope.

29th March 2005

The *Love Island* money has been upped again.

Had a long chat with my management – I think they're starting to think that they can make it work for me.

31st March 2005

Got the first draft of my *Ten Fantasies* book from the writer. I wrote a synopsis for each of the ten stories that she then padded out. Need to fill in the gaps and tell her the bits I don't like. Have been chatting to her on the phone about what I want but she's got experience in that kind of stuff, so she knows how to put it together better than me.

Saw Luke this evening. He's a darling but it's not quite the same back in England.

1st April 2005

The May issue of *FHM* is out. There's a five-foot-long poster of me inside. It's bloody gigantic!

2nd April 2005

Went to the Money offices to talk about *Love Island*. The offer is much better. Plus it's in Fiji, so I could just think of it like being paid to go on holiday.

Did a PA tonight in Chesterfield. Had a marriage proposal from a guy who followed me into the toilets. Every girl's dream.

3rd April 2005

A guy came up to me in the street today and told me he was doing media studies at university and had written an essay about me. What is the world coming to?

4th April 2005

The *Ten Fantasies* re-drafts are coming in thick and fast.

The best thing about doing this book is the fact that I found out today I can write a dedication. I'm going to put the girls in there – my 'bunnies'. I might use their names for the characters in the stories too. Hilarious. I think Donna can be the bride I have a three-way with on their wedding night. Hee hee!

5th April 2005

What was I thinking considering doing *Love Island*? I've got to wear a bikini. And I feel fat.

In professional photos it's all about standing a certain way, arching your back, getting the right pose ... and photographers light you so you look amazing. And then of course there's airbrushing. You don't get that on telly.

7th April 2005

8am *Nuts* shoot.

The documentary crew wanted to come with me when I did a PA and I've got one in Northern Ireland tomorrow. Checked into the Malmaison in Belfast overnight – I love their hotels. Went to the bar for a few drinks before we went out and got chatting to one of the barmen.

'Oh yeah, we get loads of celebrities in here. We're known for being a really cool hotel because we're all specially trained not to bother them, so they can relax.'

I replied, 'Oh great! That's a relief.'

He passed me my drink. 'Is it OK if you come in to the kitchen for a second so we can all get pictures with you?'

8th April 2005

The PA was in Antrim, a place called The Stables. Right in the middle of nowhere. It was mental. There were coachloads of people. Apparently they come and pick people up from their homes in villages, take them to the club then bring them home again. It was such an experience.

When I arrived I could hear the hordes, the screams, the madness coming from inside the club. The guy who was hosting it sat me down and said, in a really strong accent, 'I have to warn you, they're absolute animals out there.'

He wasn't kidding.

'They'll tear you to pieces – but they love you. Don't be scared.'

Then came the killer question.

'Do you mind if I mention the video?'

What choice did I have? 'No – we've all seen it.'

He smiled. 'I'll look after you. Stick with me. Do not move from me.' He took my hand and looked back. 'Don't go too close to them.'

By now I was petrified. I walked through the door, stepped out into the club, through the crowd and they all went insane. It was terrifying, but fantastic. I couldn't believe the reaction; they were reaching out to me and the noise was incredible. It was like a riot.

'If they get a chance they'll rip your clothes off.'

Still had my clothes on at the end of it, though.

There was a police van outside the club – they'd been hired to make sure there were no stampedes. That made it sound like a rodeo. I obviously decided it was only fair to jump into their van afterwards and say thank you in person. Don't think the boys in blue were quite expecting that, but they didn't complain.

10th April 2005

It's in the *Sunday Mirror*:

' . . . And she wanted to thank the lads personally for looking after her so she left her limo behind and darted across the road. At first the policemen were worried that they'd get into trouble and refused to open the van door. But then Abi persuaded them and she got in and plonked herself on one unsuspecting cop's knee. He was asking the photographer not to take any pictures but I don't know who he was more worried about – his bosses or his wife.'

Well, a girl's got to remember her manners and it seemed the best way at the time . . .

11th April 2005

9am *Nuts* shoot. I'm doing these practically every week, it's amazing. No idea why I'm so popular.

Am going to do *Love Island*.

My management have finally made me see that the money's fine and I can double it with picture sales. Besides, the producers can't make me do anything I don't want to do.

13th April 2005

Had to be interviewed on camera for *Love Island* today. As I sat there, I still couldn't work out why the hell I was doing the show. I'd been turning it down for so long, surely there must be a reason for it. But then, what else can I do? I've become, to all intents and purposes a 'glamour model' and that's not what I want to do. I've been sucked into it all and I'm going along for the ride. When I'm going to be able to act, I don't know. This show has to open some doors, surely? (Maybe the door to the end of my career once people see what my body actually looks like.)

I just hope people will actually find me funny or like what I have to say and therefore forgive me for not being skinny enough in my bikini.

The producer asked me: 'What do you look for in a man, Abi?'

I replied, 'Someone I can take to a party and not have to worry he's in the bathroom doing drugs or having sex with someone else.'

Stunned silence. Then a big laugh. OK, so I 'borrowed' it from Susan Sarandon. But it's a great quote so who cares.

14th April 2005

I'm really not skinny enough for a bikini. At all.

16th April 2005

Called Emma in a fluster. 'When people see me on telly they'll think I'm not who they thought I was. I look fat!'

'Don't be silly, Abi. You don't. But if you are worried you've got a few weeks to train so you can stop panicking.'

Went out for Miranda's birthday tonight and soon forgot about panicking.

18th April 2005

Until this morning when I looked in the mirror.

Have scared myself into getting a personal trainer before *Love Island*. Helen who taught me for *Tone and Tease* has been trying to get me to kick ass. But I just can't seem to focus like I have in the past. I'm just not doing it properly. Am still drinking loads. The whole thing with John, everything that's happened . . . I can't explain it.

20th April 2005

The anticipation about the show is really getting to me now. Filmed my part of the title sequence, where I had to stand there flicking my hair and grinning to the camera like a twerp. I wonder who else is going to be on it? Maybe I will actually find love there. That would be a result.

Spoke to Emma afterwards and turns out we still haven't signed the contract yet. So I could still pull out if I get really scared (or fat).

Loaded party tonight for the launch of their 'new look' mag and I'm the cover! Giant blow-ups of the cover, with my arse on it, were on all the walls. Free bar!

21st April 2005

Kill me now.

Ended up partying all night and then had to go and do the shoot for the promotional pictures for *Love Island* having not slept. Why do I keep doing this?? I'm never drinking again. EVER. I'd rather die.

Hmm, forgot it's the *FHM* 100 Sexiest Women party tonight . . .

Last year, even though I made the cover, I was number ninety-five. This year I'm number seven! Sometimes I still have to pinch myself to believe this is all happening to me.

I was wearing a pink dress. My stylist Gok Wan had persuaded me to wear it. Wasn't sure about it at first because it had a really high neck yet was quite see-through, but from the moment I arrived the compliments were flowing so I was more than happy.

Won an award for being the highest climber. Jennifer Ellison was there too. And Calum. He kept looking at me across the room and I reciprocated. We were being really flirty. Ended the night perched on his knee.

I'm sure people must have been looking at us but we were too engrossed to care. We didn't need to discuss what was going to happen next. He was coming back to my house. We got on really well and I so didn't want to be another notch on his bedpost. And let's face it, Calum's bedpost must be crumbling away with the amount of bloody notches he's got. Am sure no one will believe this but we spent most of the night just talking; he seems a bit sad deep down. Like he needs a friend.

The most amazing thing is he's also been approached for *Love Island*. I feel so much better about going on the show now. We agreed that we would be friends and look out for each other when we got there. That's nice.

22nd April 2005

My figure is not getting any better. Know I should quit the drinking – but I'm off to Manchester tonight for another PA in a nightclub.

23rd April 2005

The *Sun* has got wind of me and Calum spending the night together. And a flipping picture of Calum leaving my house. Let them print what they want. They'd never believe the truth anyway. Abi Titmuss and Calum Best? And all they did was talk? Yeah, right.

24th April 2005

The *People* bought some of the shots I did when I was last abroad. One's of me on a yacht taking a shower with a quote saying 'One onlooker said: "Even when she knew she'd been spotted, she just carried on. Talk about nautical but nice."'

25th April 2005

Have been signed up as *Nuts* columnist now for a year. Again it's sex talk, but it's really not just that this time – it's advice to lads about things like where to take a girl on a first date (not up the arse, ha ha! Oops, couldn't resist) and what to wear. Quite sweet really. I got such a thrill out of doing the one for *FHM* (and loved it when blokes came up to me at PAs saying I'd actually helped them). It sounds bizarre but I'm treating it a bit like talking to patients with problems. So it feels a bit like being a nurse again.

27th April 2005

Did a PA in Portsmouth this evening – I do enjoy them (some-times!) but think I'll be glad to have a rest once *Love Island* starts. They're killing my liver. I drink to get the confidence to go on stage. Then once I'm off stage I have more drinks while I'm signing my calendar. Then I drink on the way home or back at the hotel. All in all, it's one big booze-athon.

28th April 2005

Did a set of pictures with themes that tie in with *Love Island*. Did some shots of me kneeling in the water, some of me on a beach, my management had the idea to do one of me with 'Gerrard' scrawled on my back too – because the football will be on while I'm out there. And one of me in a deckchair holding a copy of the *Sun*. Hmm, who'll buy that, I wonder? Made sure I didn't eat anything except fruit yesterday so didn't feel like such a lump today.

29th April 2005

Fly to Ireland at 12.30 for a PA tonight. Hope it's not as bonkers as the last one. I'd like to keep all my limbs for *Love Island*.

Ate well again today, must keep up my fruit intake.

30th April 2005

Ughh my head. I blame the Irish.

At least I had plenty of lemon slices in my vodkas.

'It's better to be looked over than to be over-looked.'

Mae West

1st May 2005

Went shopping to buy some bikinis and dresses for *Love Island*. Am seriously worried about how I'm going to look on the beach. I'm going to be found out. Once upon a time I was super fit and healthy, but I've let myself slide a bit. Plus, I have finished the Atkins Diet – which didn't really agree with me. There's a huge part of me wants to be who I actually am, to show other women that I've got lumps and bumps too. I am not overweight for my height at all, but I'm scared. And my image is my livelihood.

3rd May 2005

As predicted the shots of me and my 'twin' have gone down particularly well with the tabs. The *Sun* has used them with the headline 'A great pair of Titmusses' and the *Star* has gone mad too:

'TWO HOT TO HANDLE; PICTURE EXCLUSIVE: ABI TITMUSS, THE NATION'S NAUGHTIEST GIRL, GOES FOR THE DOUBLE'

'We're sure Abi would be the perfect choice for the upcoming ITV reality show, *Celebrity Love Island*. The show, which is due to hit our screens next month, will fix up a host of stars on blind dates on the exotic island of Fiji. An ITV source said: 'We want Abi by hook or by crook. Just the thought of her roaming about in her bikini is bound to get millions tuning in.'

Oh God.

6th May 2005

Love Island medical 10.30am.

We've got to have a diving medical in case they shove us overboard!

9th May 2005

Glorious sunny day with Primrose Hill written all over it. Bought some rosé and nibbles and sent a 'round robin' text to a few others: 'On the hill, lovely day, come and have a drink.' It went to Calum, and also – naïvely – to Darryn Lyons – who I thought might come as a friend.

Calum turned up and we started messing about on the grass, flirting and having a laugh.

Then we heard a noise from the bushes. Calum jumped. Immediately his demeanour changed and he accused me of setting him up. I tried to explain it was nothing to do with me, that Darryn must have sent someone after he received my text, but he was having none of it. He recognised the pap as a guy from BIG Pictures and got his agent to call Darryn's people.

Some bastard told Calum I knew about it! That's it. Calum's never going to forgive me. Or believe me.

This is awful.

10th May 2005

Am shaking. So upset.

Have just seen the edit of my documentary.

How I wish I hadn't.

I've spent all this time, all these months with the same documentary crew – one director, Simon, following my every move. He knows more about me than some of my closest friends. He came to New York with me, met my family, did PAs . . . We'd done so many long interviews. I'd broken down and told him intimate feelings about John, I'd been filmed watching a play, opening up about my childhood . . . Everything I wanted to say, in order to show the real me. I'd trusted him to put it all together; I'd left it to his discretion. And in my opinion, he's completely fucked me over.

It's all about sex and money. Me in my bra and pants, giggling at PAs . . . A plethora of snippets of people slagging me off – people who've never even met me. There's hardly anything of me on there at all. Nothing of me being funny or anything remotely warm.

Just sex and money. That, it seems, is the sum of my parts.

What was the point? There's even a tally as to how much I've earned over the last year. No one had even asked me how much I was being paid – it's just all guestimated and sensationalised.

It's awful. I hate it. My management tried to calm me down: 'Abi, its good. It's what it was designed to be. It's about the new business of sex and glamour and how you run the show.'

'It's not good.'

Then I remembered there was a blank part of the edit.

'Rewind the tape a second—'

My manager gave me the remote.

I wasn't seeing things. There was a blank space in more than one part of the documentary that read: 'sex tape to be added here.'

'Sex tape? What? They're not going to do that, are they?'

My manager looked at me. 'They want to. We think it should be in. It makes sense of the story and any way that tape is now – however unfortunately and illegally – in the public domain.'

No way. No way.

An hour later, Simon texted. 'What did you think? I sent the tape to Money's offices but haven't heard from you.'

'I hate it. What have you done?'

'I'm sorry you feel that way.'

That's it?

Couldn't stop crying. They can't add that footage in. They can't.

To top it all I had to have a bloody photo shoot with the *Observer* magazine. I had tears streaming down my face the whole time. They wanted it 'bare' so I had no make-up on. Absolutely none, not even mascara. Good job really because it would've streaked down my face. The make-up artist just put a bit of Vaseline on my lips.

'Don't worry,' the make-up assistant assured me, 'they'll airbrush your tears out.'

I felt ugly and small. I can't cope with all this any more. Seeing the tape has tipped me over the edge. I'm going to be humiliated again when it comes out. Everything is my fault.

I was really struggling to hold it together. The photographer, Hamish, was lovely and really considerate. He took me aside and talked to me quietly. He said I should just focus on him and the camera lens. The emotion behind my eyes would come through and make a great picture, but he must've thought I was mad. At the end of the shoot he gave me a Polaroid of the two of us together. He wrote on it:

'Dear Abigail, thank you for being so naturally beautiful.'

I felt like he meant it. I will treasure it.

11th May 2005

Had an interview with the journalist from the *Observer* to sit along-side yesterday's shoot. Told him I'd been in tears yesterday; not sure he liked me very much – I felt like he wanted to catch me out all the time. Am past caring to be honest. More worried about the tape.

Called Emma afterwards. 'They can't put it in. Can they?'

'They can't unless we say yes and we want to say yes. We think it's a good thing.'

The papers are also awash with who's on *Love Island* now. Not sure what to believe. Rebecca Loos is meant to be there, and Fran Cosgrave.

God, I hope Calum doesn't hate me when we arrive. Can't believe I fly out there tomorrow. All I keep thinking about is the documentary; it's airing this weekend. I can't stop crying.

Had a farewell dinner with all my friends at Momo's tonight. It was so lovely. I was emotional. It's sinking in now that I'm going to be away from everyone, on the other side of the world, with no contact for up to two months. It was hard enough being in *Hell's Kitchen* for two weeks, and that was in Shoreditch. I'll be able to receive vetted emails occasionally but not send any. I made the girls promise they would send loads.

I hope I'm going to be alright.

12th May 2005

Spoke to Emma on the way to the airport. The sex tape has been added, not once but about three or four times, with the agreement of my management. 'It's fine, Abi, it's in the context of the documentary and it's part of the story.'

I can't believe it. Everyone's going to hate me. On the plane to Fiji I couldn't stop sobbing. Feel devastated and let down. Simon's been calling but I can't face speaking to him. I just feel he's shafted me.

People who have never seen or had any desire to see my 'video' but happen to be watching prime-time TV – my family, Mum and Dad, all those girls who hate me enough already – will soon have no choice but to see it.

They'll think I'm a money-grabbing idiot, hating me even more than they do already. What am I doing a reality TV show for when people have this kind of thing to cement their already-formed opinion? I'll be the first person booted off the show.

Just before I got on the plane I had a nice text: 'Hi, it's Rebecca (Loos) looking forward to meeting you, have a great flight.'

Someone must've given her my number. Texted back and forth a few times. She seems lovely. Maybe this is just what I need after all.

Almost missed the connecting flight to Singapore, I was moping about in duty free, feeling sorry for myself. Ran across the airport so fast I nearly puked. But it was all business class, and there were palm trees in the airport . . . What's that? Am I actually starting to feel excited?

13th May 2005

I was the last person to turn up apparently and there were swarms of photographers at Fiji airport. One reporter asked if I'd brought condoms. What was this place? Had I been completely naive?

Got to the hotel and spoke to Sam on the phone. She told me there's a picture in the *Sun* of me and Calum 'romping' in the park. No one else is in the shot, so, as predicted it looks like it's just me and him. Cheers, Darryn Lyons.

Opened my suitcase . . . I've spent a fortune on clothes – Missoni bikinis, hats, kaftans – but am getting increasingly worried about what I'm going to look like. Will I people think I'm a fat lump?

Met some of the production girls and begged them to tell me what the blokes are like. They weren't meant to reveal names but most of us had seen the speculation in the papers so it seemed fruitless being secretive. Lee Sharpe was the name that caused most of a ripple among the ladies. Hmm. That surprised me, I thought it would be Calum. I've no idea who Lee is. Or what he looks like.

Texted Rebecca again – we were going to meet for a drink later but the producers found out and asked if we'd stay apart. They want it to be spontaneous and fresh when we see each other tomorrow. Probably a good thing: I'll only end up getting rat-arsed and breaking my neck in the pool.

14th May 2005

Met all the girls in the hotel lobby. Most of them seem lovely – Rebecca was by far the nicest. Really pleased that she's here. Liz McClarnon from Atomic Kitten is sweet, Judi Shekoni, the *EastEnders* actress seems funny and Isabella Hervey the I-don't-know-what-she-does-but-she's-very-well-spoken is nice but not my type of person . . . and guess who else is here?

Jayne

Middlemiss!

Do the producers know we've met before? Don't see how they can. Anyway, it was ages ago. Am a better person than that, no point being bitter. It's not like she stole David off me. She was a bit stand-offish but I thought 'I can cope with that'.

But it was impossible to be a sour puss once we set off. We were transported to the island on a massive speedboat. My fears about being the fattest girl there were now redundant – apart from Isabella, most of the girls have normal figures. No one's super-toned. Still sucked my tummy in whenever a camera came close though.

The budget must be massive – felt like we were making a feature film. A helicopter was flying above, circling us as we zoomed across the ocean, camera crew hanging off the side. A second camera unit skirted past us on this majestic yacht, capturing our stunned expressions. There was a collective intake of breath as we all took stock. This TV lark is a pretty big deal.

And Fiji is awe-inspiringly beautiful. I'm so lucky to be here. Need to buck myself up and start enjoying it. We ladies landed on the island first, then the boys emerged one by one on jet-skis. I kept hoping Jude Law might appear from the ocean and that maybe the papers had been wrong.

Wow, I can't believe how much I'd really like to meet someone special.

When Calum arrived I felt a surge of territorialism. I fancied him, so the other girls sure as hell would. But thanks to Darryn Lyons and his pap machine, things were now so weird between us. When he jumped off the jet-ski and said hi, I could sense his frostiness – he's wary of me.

Fran Cosgrave rocked up all cocksure of himself. He and Calum are mates back home so they must think their ships have come in (OK, jet-skis). He's certainly good looking but I wouldn't want to go there.

Paul Danan – the ex *Hollyoaks* actor – is mad but great. No way do I fancy him but he's such a ball of energy, he's already got people in stitches and he's only been here a few hours. The footballer Lee Sharpe arrived too. Not my type. Shame. Michael Greco – the *EastEnders* star – came flying in on a jet-ski too. No thanks. In fact, I don't fancy any of them.

Great.

I could easily fall in love with this place though – it's achingly beautiful. Once everyone was on the island and we began to comprehend that this was going to be our home for the next few weeks, we turned into little kids in a sand pit, running around the place, uprooting everything in our path. Then suddenly there'd be the abrupt awareness of the plethora of cameras zooming in on our every gasp, each furtive glance and love handle.

All day I've wavered between feeling completely spellbound and extraordinarily edgy. I clocked my bronzed elbows as I opened a drawer in the kitchen area and thought, 'My fake tan is going to come off in about a second.' It takes me ages to go brown – as soon as this disappears I'm going to be like a milk bottle. A king-size one.

The sleeping area is open plan and breathtaking. The beds (all doubles!) are laid out in sets of three. Rebecca and I had the same idea and ran straight to the one in the centre because it's the only one with a clear view of the sea and the shore. Imagine waking up to that every morning! Lee picked the bed next to mine; the rest of the lads followed, sticking to one side while the girls congregated at the other.

Then it wasn't long before the boys all put on their trunks. Well,

I say all. For some unknown reason, Michael Greco went to unpack, then materialised in his underpants. That broke the ice!

15th May 2005

It's so surreal being on the other side of the world. Keep forgetting people might be watching us. All we've done is sunbathe and eat so far — it's hardly a knock out.

The viewers will just be seeing me with my hair sticking to my head and getting whiter by the minute as my tan comes off. Calum seems to like Rebecca — he's not really disguising it. She obviously fancies him too. Not that I'm jealous or anything . . . He's my friend. I thought we were going to look out for each other.

Suddenly feel very alone.

And very sweaty.

16th May 2005

Fran called me promiscuous this evening. It really hurt. It felt like he was trying to say that because I've done sexy shoots I'm some kind of slag. Calum didn't stick up for me either. I was in a relationship with John for five years . . . that's not promiscuous! I was really upset. In the end I had to say it wasn't an issue — otherwise I'll end up as the one who looks bad.

Consoled myself with the fact that to be honest I'm not entirely sure he knows what the word means.

17th May 2005

Chatted to Lee a bit today; he's very funny. So is his headgear. He wears the most unattractive sun hats I've ever seen.

Am sure you can see the sexual tension between Calum and Rebecca from the moon.

18th May 2005

Jayne keeps darting off to the beach hut where the cameras are and coming out rubbing her eyes. I think she's really homesick. And I can't blame her; it is unsettling in this place. One minute you look at everyone and think, 'What a fab bunch,' the next you realise it's a game, you're on show as a potential love-interest and people are at home, right this second, criticising what you look like.

Lee's very funny. Don't remotely fancy him but he's a real tonic. Easy to take the piss out of and talk shit to. Which I guess he wouldn't be if I thought he was hot.

If Calum and Rebecca haven't shagged by the end of the week I'll eat my flip-flop. Or another biscuit.

19th May 2005

It's so easy to lose track of time in this place. Nevertheless, can't take my mind off the fact that my documentary is going out on Channel 4 tonight. Those who haven't already witnessed me having sex will have seen everything by the time I go to bed.

20th May 2005

Calum and I got the first day trip!

Thought it would be the perfect opportunity to clear the air. Went to a little market in town but it was all a bit tense. It was clear Calum didn't want to be there, either that or he was being too cool for school – he can't let himself go. I wanted to get a green coconut because I'd never had one before but he just seemed annoyed. The cameras were hovering expectantly, scrutinising for the chemistry that everyone thought would be so apparent. But it wasn't. And it wasn't fun.

Who am I kidding anyway? Calum fancies Rebecca. He almost galloped towards her when we got back. It was then that I became aware that things with Jayne are decidedly on edge. She's virtually living in the beach hut confessional. And she's no longer making any attempt to hide the fact that she's been crying. And it's now plainly clear it's about Lee. She was talking to Isabella for ages while we were out sunbathing, then I saw her with Rebecca in the beach house before taking Lee aside and whispering something.

Not sure what was said between them, but thank God something seems to have defrosted the tension. Shockingly, after dinner Jayne actually came over and told me she felt bad for judging me and apologised for what happened in Edinburgh.

I was so glad she did. I just want to be friends with everyone. Lee told me afterwards that he told Jayne he wasn't interested. She's obviously upset. I told Lee he shouldn't make her look bad on TV, but he genuinely hasn't got a clue he's done anything. He looked at me as if to say; 'What have I done?'

Judi (Shekoni from *EastEnders*) was the first to get the boot. We're all in shock. Think we forgot what the show was all about. We're not just here on holiday.

21st May 2005

I could be wrong but I think Michael might like me. I need to knock it on the head before people start getting ideas and voting us into the Love Shack. He's a nice guy and we get on but that's it.

22nd May 2005

Christ, now Rebecca's being flirty and suggestive with me.

Had to say something. 'I really like you, you're great, but I've come on this show to try and get away from that whole image of me playing up to the cameras and being saucy.'

I know that doing this whole lipstick lesbian thing is not going to win any women's votes and that's what I want. She obviously thinks it's all about being raunchy for the fellas.

Have to admit she's attractive though. She's sweet too. I didn't have time to get a pedicure before we came so she took pity and did my feet for me. I had toes like Shrek.

Of course Lee walked past and laughed. 'Get the angle grinder out?'

Cheeky shit. Ha ha!

23rd May 2005

Thank God for Lee. We're having a real laugh. Have started to fall into a pattern of making tea together at a certain time of the day, and just hanging out – sunbathing near each other. It's nice. Because I don't fancy him there's no pressure and it means I can be myself. It's nice to have an ally. Still don't think Jayne likes it much but she hasn't got anything to worry about. I'm more self-conscious around Calum than Lee.

24th May 2005

Calum and Rebecca have been voted into the Love Shack. Don't want to think about it otherwise my face might go green. Wonder if they'll actually shag?

I'm acting like I can't be bothered to do any exercise but the reality is that I feel too self-conscious doing it in front of the cameras and all these other people. Plus I haven't got a sports bra – and no one wants to see these babies jumping up and down!

I was serving dinner later and happened to look over at Lee who smiled, so I winked. I didn't mean anything by it – but am sure he blushed in return. Was I imagining it, or did he get flustered?

What does that mean?

26th May 2005

We were playing a game by the pool, which meant we had to dress up. I went to the bedroom and put some slap on and trotted out in high heels and my bikini. When I emerged the boys all looked like their tongues were about to drop off.

Fran shouted – 'Finally! I meet Abi Titmuss!'

I liked it. Until I realised he meant I look like shit the rest of the time.

Had amazing evening. Paul announced at dinner that we all had to get up and do something creative so I decided to recite a poem, 'The Road Less Travelled'. Think everyone was really shocked that I knew anything about poetry, let alone knew it off by heart.

After I'd done it, Lee seemed genuinely moved.

'Wow, how can you follow that?'

Paul looked at me curiously. 'You done acting before haven't you?'

I was so chuffed.

Think it pissed off a few of the others though.

27th May 2005

Rebecca's really changing now she's with Calum. We were so close before, but now she's like a different person – walking round, getting him beers and giving him massages. I don't like it. And I don't like the way he's bossing her about.

It was Lee's birthday today and we went down to the beach for a walk. I'm starting to feel closer to him now. Don't know what it is about this person but there's something special. Walked up and down, just talking. Played giant hangman in the sand with a stick. We've been joking that we're the only ones without a tan so every word we spelt out had something to do with white ... 'White Christmas' ... 'Snow White and the Seven Dwarves'.

We found it funny anyway.

It was a lovely moment, just the two of us on the other side of the world from home, on a beautiful, white, empty beach. We walked up and down a bit and started talking about where we came from, family etc. Getting to know each other. Need to remember we're not on a date though, we're on a TV show, and anyway I don't want to upset Jayne.

This evening we were given a school uniform party. Sang karaoke with Jayne and thought she might just like me, for a minute. Went to the beach hut with Lee, to talk to the camera. I watched him as he talked. He was a bit pissed and he talks so slowly but I like his calmness. It's nice to be around. He doesn't seem to fancy me though. He had a towel round his shoulders and looked like a dopey Northerner. But so sweet. Made me smile.

Then I stupidly did the one thing my manager had given me strict instructions not to do on the island – I got totally drunk. Last thing I remember is Paul and I jumping in the pool fully clothed . . . and then I kissed him. What was I thinking? Don't know why. Calum and Rebecca were somewhere and I think I thought 'I want someone to pay me attention.'

Then Paul got out and headed straight to bed.

29th May 2005

Lee and Jayne have gone. Booted off.

Can't believe it. I really miss him; it's left a massive gap knowing I might not see him again for ages. No one can get their head round it. What are they showing on TV at home? How can no one like Lee?

Paul couldn't stop crying. 'There was something really special about Lee,' he blubbed. 'He loved wearing his hat.'

30th May 2005

I had told Lee that one of my friends at home calls me 'Shabs' (short for 'Shabby') and he thought it was funny so started calling me Shabster all the time. I called him Sharpester.

God I really miss him. I guess that's it, he's gone. I'll probably never see him again, he lives in Leeds after all.

31st May 2005

Won a day trip today. Went to the world surfing championships . . . with Michael.

Suddenly this Aussie guy pulled up in a boat alongside ours and said, 'Is your name Abi Tit something?'

'Titmuss,' I laughed.

I couldn't believe that in the middle of the ocean in Fiji, some guy knew who I was! His name's Paul Fisher and he knew some friends of mine. How odd. He was cute, different, Australian . . . Cool. He gave me his number. We had a nice flirt too. Sorry Michael.

1st June 2005

Lee came back!

Couldn't believe it. Turns out the producers had only sent them on a 'make or break' boat. God, viewers must be desperate for them to get together. Lee said it was excruciating. Jayne said, 'It's fine'. I thought that meant that everything had worked out between them. But it didn't.

As soon as I saw him get off the boat I ran to meet him. I don't know why but I'm just so pleased to have him back.

2nd June 2005

Am an invalid.

The kitchen is equipped with these stupid mugs with a rounded base. The kettle had just boiled so I poured a mug of tea and knocked it flying. Boiling water went straight down my leg. There was a searing pain on my thigh. I was in shock, terrified. I was going to be scarred for life.

Lee rushed over to see what was wrong. I started crying and ran into the medical hut. My skin was starting to come away, I was in agony – and then the distress kicked in.

'Second-degree burns,' I heard the doctor say. Panic. I was a nurse once, I knew this was massive. It got so bad they had to give me morphine injections – and normally I can take some pain . . .

Lying there in the little medical hut for what seemed like hours, the doctors were palpably worried. I was screaming and wailing... They kept putting on ice and taking it off. Then there was a knock at the door and a voice said, 'Are you alright, Shabs?'

It was Lee.

He'd come to see if I was alright. No one else had. I asked the doctors to let him in but they were so busy with me they refused at first. He sounded so worried.

After about an hour the doctors sent me off, and instructed me to sleep outside in case they needed to get to me quickly. Lee was so caring, he wouldn't stop fussing. Night time came and suddenly I felt so scared. Everyone else was going to bed. Lee said, 'I'll stay outside with you.'

He didn't offer it in a leading, expectant way like others might have done. I could see he was genuinely concerned. I wanted him to stay with me so much but when we lay down on the day bed I was glaringly conscious of Jayne. I know nothing's happening with them, but I really didn't want to hurt her feelings or put it in her face. I told Lee and said we'd better at least turn around and sleep top-to-toe.

The morphine gave me nightmares. It must've been about 3am when I woke and sat bolt upright.

'Are you OK?' Lee was startled. I would have given anything right then for him to put his arm round me, to cuddle up.

Here's me, looking a right mess, so unsexy, bandages all down my legs, tear-stained face, and he still liked me.

3rd June 2005

Something had changed with Lee last night. Something special. I wasn't going to forget him staying outside with me all night and taking care of me like that. He looked knackered, he'd hardly slept.

Spent the day hanging out with Lee. He's the only one I really give a shit about here any more.

5th June 2005

New arrival today – Nikki Ziering – she was a *Playboy* model apparently. Why can't they send in a nice guy?

6th June 2005

Calum and Rebecca disappeared into the loo for about twenty minutes. And they say romance is dead.

7th June 2005

Gutted. Viewers voted Lee into the Love Shack with Nikki. The public clearly hate me. I don't want Nikki and Lee to hit it off. No one fancies me and I haven't got the best body in the world. I haven't felt less attractive in years and I am on a fucking TV show in a bikini, with a burn on my leg and a great big bandage round my thigh.

I can't sunbathe or swim, there's absolutely nothing to do. We weren't allowed books. I keep nibbling food to pass the time and comfort me. I'm fat and unattractive anyway so what's the difference? Why do I always reach for food when I'm upset? It's just an instinctive thing to do. Got to stop.

Comfort eating in a bikini? Am I mad?

Maybe the public have seen something between Lee and Nikki that I haven't. Have I misread the signs? He's going to have all that time to get to know her, and he might really fall for her.

Moped about all day, then something dramatic happened.

Rebecca FARTED by accident when she was laughing! The rest of us were at the dinner table and you could hear it so loudly there was no way she could deny it. Calum's face was a picture. It was like you could see distaste painting itself across his cheeks. He visibly recoiled from her. The poor girl, I felt SO sorry for her.

Was funny though.

8th June 2005

We were asked to write postcards to each other, and were told we could write one to Lee or Nikki. I wrote one to Nikki. I thought, 'Well, no one else will write her one, it won't be very nice for her to have none.' And I didn't know where to start with writing to Lee, besides, we all had to read them out afterwards and my message would be too personal.

Fran kept staring at me saying, 'Oh, very clever,' in a not very nice way. As if I was doing it for some sort of master plan to get popular. It made me uncomfortable. Why can no one believe I am a nice girl? Then we got our replies – one from each of them. Lee had written his to me, it was long and at the end it said,

'Not the same without you. Hope you've not talked too much. See you tomorrow Shabster, sleep tight, love the Sharpester.'

I started welling up as I read it out to the group. I really miss him – and he gets me. It's like he's supporting me. 'Not talking too much' – that was the little detail he'd noticed about me.

Later, sitting at the table I saw a reflection in the mirror behind me.

'What's that running towards us?'

It was Lee! He'd burst out of the shack and was fleeing up the beach. Without hesitation, I pelted towards him, and without even thinking I just jumped straight into his arms! I've never done that to anyone (didn't think anyone could lift me up). It was such a romantic moment. Lee spun round and hugged me. I didn't want to let him go.

Wasn't long before security rushed him back in. 'I'm alone Abi,' he mouthed as he was escorted back. It was like a sign, he wanted me to know he wasn't into Nikki.

9th June 2005

The public chose to replace Nikki with me! Am overjoyed!

Was told to go down a path and Lee would be there. Grabbed a jar of Twisters – our favourite little snack – to make him laugh, and went towards the Love Shack. So unsexy – me staggering along with the equivalent of cheesy Quavers under my arm.

But his face absolutely lit up when he saw me. 'Shabs!'

It was so cool.

Then, typical: it pissed it down for the entire day. We lay inside the door watching the rain and ordered cocktails, laughing and joking about how, out of all the couples to go into the Love Shack, we were the only ones that hadn't had sunshine. But I didn't even mind, it sort of made ours different. At one stage we both put one of his stupid hats on, then went for a walk on the beach in the rain. I looked horrible but for a refreshing change, I didn't give a shit.

Got dressed up for dinner – I felt under pressure because Rebecca told me she and Calum had put on matching outfits when they were in the Love Shack and looked 'amazing'. I kept telling Lee we had to look the part. In the end he sighed, 'OK, I get the bloody message!'

We talked and talked even though the cameras in our faces didn't make for the most romantic atmosphere.

I don't understand what I'm feeling for Lee; I'm starting to fancy him more and more yet it's not the same way that I find Calum attractive. It's more his personality. Then there was this weird voice in my head – 'You're going to be with him.'

I felt this overpowering sense that I'm going to marry him or something. Like some psychic moment. Almost like someone whispering it in my ear. I didn't repeat it out loud of course. Odd.

Afterwards, we were lying on the bed and he tried to kiss me. Suddenly I felt really uncomfortable. Awkward. And overwhelmed. The cameras were on me and people at home were watching. People who had seen my video. Didn't want this to happen on national TV. Was freaking me out. Didn't want my emotions, feelings or privacy exposed. Not again.

So I pushed him away.

10th June 2005

Back in the main house where Nikki has allegedly given Paul a blowjob in the loo. Nice.

11th June 2005

Felt really rubbish today. Feeling a bit overwhelmed with the whole experience. Sat with Lee on the bed and tried to explain it.

'Lots of things happened to me last year like stories about my sex life and the video thing. It made me feel really violated as a woman. It was really intimate stuff and when you and I were in the Love Shack together it was really, really nice just being in bed, even though we were fully dressed and just having a cuddle. It suddenly felt all wrong that we were being filmed and I couldn't stop crying.' I told him I'd felt like I let a bit of myself go again. But it was all on camera.

It made me feel really strange. I know I came on the show and everyone expected me to have sex. But I'm not like that really. He looked at me so sweetly; 'You've done nothing wrong.' I knew he was right but it was just really odd because people were watching us. Last year I didn't think I had anything left that was private.

I was worried that now Lee would think I was a nut-case but he seemed really relieved. 'I had a lovely night,' he said. 'I thought something had gone wrong suddenly. Perhaps it was too nice for the situation we are in.'

That just made me cry again.

12th June 2005

Calum was voted off tonight. We're all stunned. Everyone thought it would be Paul – including him. Rebecca ran to the toilets for a good cry. She really likes him. Although I'm not sure he feels the same after her fart.

13th June 2005

What a night.

Lee grabbed my hand and we ran off together down the beach – along a path, and we took the mics off. I crouched down, hoping the cameras wouldn't see. I was wearing a really low-cut top and he looked at me earnestly.

'You've got nice eyes.'

'I can't believe I'm standing here with my tits out and you're saying I've got nice eyes. That's a first!'

We laughed.

I didn't know what he was going to say; we were both a bit pissed. But I wasn't expecting what came next.

He started telling me that he was falling for me, that he thinks I am amazing. Oh my God. I don't know what to do. I don't know what I feel. It's all getting a bit too much for me. I don't want to start spilling my heart out on national telly. Lee's doing well, he must be really liked – I don't want to do the wrong thing or spoil it. There is something really magical there. I just want to be on my own with him to see how we feel properly, away from the cameras. Am terrified of losing control of myself.

We kissed, it was so lovely. But I still felt so self-conscious. Could people see us or not?

Afterwards I was worried. So I said to him: 'I don't want you to change. I want you to stay really cool because we're on TV. I don't know what's going to happen when we get out of here. I can't make any promises; do you know what I mean? It's not a normal situation.'

Lee agreed to wait until we got home to deal with our feelings.

Wow.

14th June 2005

Fran and Jayne were voted into the Love Shack. With her gone it made things with Lee much more relaxed. Spent most of the night whispering across our beds before sneaking off for a snog. Think we've found a spot where the cameras can't see us. It's behind the door between the bedroom and the bathroom, but finding your way back to the bedroom in the pitch dark isn't exactly straightforward. I tripped right over one of the suitcases, then Lee followed suit two minutes later and did exactly the same thing. We couldn't stop giggling after that. The others must've got really pissed off!

16th June 2005

All this food. Even Rebecca's piling on the pounds. We got weighed today and she's put on a stone – I've put on a few pounds. Liz has put weight on too. We all have – apart from the exercise freaks.

Aaaargh! I'm trying not to eat the crisps but it's hard.

Lee and I have our nightly ritual of tea and Twisters. Fran keeps saying we're like an old married couple. When we fall asleep we hold hands under the covers through the wooden slats that separate the beds. I don't think anyone can see, it's our little secret.

17th June 2005

Finally won a day trip with Lee. Fran predictably began complaining that it was a fix. Lee and I are the only couple who are genuinely together here and are gagging for a romantic interlude.

I was so relieved to get away from everyone (well, apart from the crew) when we climbed into a little boat to head off. Suddenly felt a surge of emotion – away from the throng I realised how uneasy I felt around the others. We went to two islands – the first had a little village on it with people selling trinkets. We thought if we jumped off the boat quick enough we could sneak away from the cameras for a few minutes.

In the market we decided to buy something together that no one else would know about – two matching rings – and swore to keep it a secret. At the next island the producer said we could have some time on the beach before we had to leave. I begged for a few minutes without being filmed and eventually he agreed to just film us from afar. But we had our mics on, so I knew they could still hear us.

Lee didn't care. 'Fuck it, babe, let's just ignore them and enjoy it.'

We sat looking out to sea, when suddenly out of the blue a school of dolphins started doing a remarkable dance in the sea in front of us. It was unbelievably beautiful. We both started crying – it was staggering.

The return trip was so romantic – had champagne and lobster and Lee kept trying to snog me (we hadn't actually kissed in the daylight yet) but I didn't want anyone to see. At one point it looked like we could get away with it because there wasn't anyone watching but as soon as I leant in . . . the camera miraculously appeared.

The Fijian sun was beaming down on us on the glistening white boat. Lee was grinning like the Cheshire Cat.

'Look at me, sitting here drinking champagne, on a yacht with Abi Titmuss,' he grinned. 'Where did it all go wrong, eh?'

That made me laugh!

We put our rings on and wondered if any of the others would notice. I didn't want to go back to the island. Fran and Jayne have been glaring at me for days.

Isabella Hervey and Paul Danan were the next to be booted off. It's nearly the end of our time here.

18th June 2005

I'm out. I thought I would be first off the island as soon as the show started six weeks ago. I cannot believe people have voted to keep me in right to the penultimate day. That feels brilliant.

I couldn't wait to escape but I didn't want to leave Lee. As I rushed to get my things to leave we had a brief moment to say goodbye. This incredible experience on a tiny island in the middle of the ocean, where we had met, was over. I was choked up. Lee said: 'I'll see you in a couple of days. Wait for me, won't you?'

'Of course.'

When I sat with the hosts Patrick Kielty and Kelly Brook for the eviction interview I was shown a clip of Jayne calling me a 'big fat slag'. I'd had no idea she'd said that. I'd tried so hard to be nice and I thought she'd liked me in the end. I felt stupid and gullible. Had everyone watching agreed with her? I sat there, desperately trying to fight back the tears. I just felt numb. All the good memories of this experience were suddenly washed away in one embittered tidal wave.

Before I could even process what was happening to me I was shoved on to a speedboat that propelled me round the island, halting at the psychologist's hut. I was still fighting back the tears.

'I think you'd better come straight in here,' she said.

I was so nervous. Doom was written across the psychologist's

288

face. What was she going to say? Felt sick. Does everyone hate me? What's going on?

She looked at me sympathetically. 'I've got to prepare you . . . you've had a lot of criticism about one thing in particular.'

'It's my weight, isn't it?'

She nodded and beckoned me over to a pile of newspaper cuttings. One said 'Flabby Abi'. In the *Mirror*, columnist Carole Malone had written: 'If her belly gets any bigger they're going to have to get her off Fiji on a fork-lift truck.' They just went on and on. Not only that, but there was stuff about me and Lee. Nasty comments in magazines, suggesting I've stolen him away from Jayne.

The floodgates opened. I wept. I didn't know what to think or where to look. Felt so awful about myself. What did I do wrong? I just wanted to be liked. Knew I shouldn't have come here. I've been found out, I'm a fraud. People know I'm not as skinny as they thought I was. I've let everyone down – my friends, family, and my agent. I didn't lose enough weight before I got on the plane. It's my fault. I knew this would happen. I hate my body. I might well give a lot of talk about how great I feel, but I don't and now the whole nation knows what my body's really like.

The way the psychologist spoke to me – it's like I'm some kind of monster.

19th June 2005

Am really worried about leaving Lee. He's there with Liz now. And I know she likes him. He'll probably like her more than me – she knows about football and she's much prettier than me.

Spoke to Dad on the phone. His first words were . . . 'I see the food was good then.'

Cheers Dad.

20th June 2005

Jayne and Fran won the show. Couldn't give a toss to be honest. I just want to see Lee. Sat in my hotel room, nervously waiting for him to call. Was convinced he'd come and find me straight away.

Two, three hours went by. What had happened? Was he still with the psychologist? Had he seen or read something about me that had changed his mind? Had public opinion turned him against me?

Maybe he just doesn't know what room I'm in. I decided to go and look for him. He was downstairs in the hotel bar getting pissed with Fran and Calum. I hovered at the table. I'd been waiting for him all day, I was dying to see him.

'Lee, will you come over here and talk to me a second?'

Lee made a move to stand up until Fran put his arm across to stop him.

'Fuck off, Abi, let him stay here for a bit.'

He's so bloody obnoxious. Lee looked awkward, but stood up anyway.

He apologised and said he didn't know where I'd been.

'I really want to spend some time with you,' I said.

'I know babe, me too.' We went back to the room.

The first time we've been on our own with no cameras — and it was really, really weird. It was intense.

21st June 2005

Lee was stunned when he saw the footage of everything Jayne had been saying about him — forcing the idea of them as a couple on to the public's consciousness. He's really pissed off. We all had a photo call and he walked off at the end because he couldn't face speaking to her.

Lee later told me that Liz came over and confessed she likes him! I knew it. The party was great and Lee and I just kept gazing at each other across the room.

22nd June 2005

Lee and I had talked about not going home straight away, about stopping in Singapore or going somewhere else (in fact we'd shaken on it on the island) but in the end we knew we should probably get back home and see what was happening on the work front.

As we boarded the plane I felt really anxious about what to expect when I got back and unsure about everything, even Lee, but by the end of the journey I was really falling in love with him.

We played games and did crosswords all the way and we hardly stopped kissing for the entire flight. I didn't tell him how I felt though. I needed to be back in normal circumstances and see if it is real.

23rd June 2005

Back to England. At the airport Lee went one way and I went another. This is horrible. I've been with him 24/7 for nearly two months. I need to see how I feel and if it's going to go anywhere.

24th June 2005

Lee and I had our first proper 'meeting' as civilians, not in swim-suits! I was with Sam at the Sanderson and he walked in. As soon as I saw him I just knew.

We've arranged to see each other tomorrow. He's going to book a room at the Great Eastern Hotel so we will have some privacy, as there are paps camped outside my house. It will also be romantic as I think we both know it might be our first night together and we want it to be special. We've waited long enough after all.

26th June 2005

The Sunday papers are reporting our supposed 'tryst' in the Sanderson hotel. Ha, they've got it so wrong. I love that no one knows about last night yet. It's our secret.

We are now texting each other a million times a day! We find it funny that we are 'boyfriend' and 'girlfriend' now. It's Shabster and Sharpester! We can't believe it's happening.

27th June 2005

Had a shoot and interview with *Heat* magazine. They got me dressed me as a mermaid. I looked fucking ridiculous, but at least the fish tail covered my belly up. (In reality they should have made me an entire fish suit with just my eyes showing.) Was fun though. Texted the picture to Lee who's now got it as his screen-saver.

28th June 2005

Highlights and extensions re-done today. I needed it!

Reluctantly agreed to be interviewed at home by a journalist called Jasper Gerard because it was the *Sunday Times* News Review. I protested at first but Sam insisted.

'For goodness sake,' she laughed, 'the last person he interviewed was Gorbachev! He doesn't even know who you are. Jimmy Carr does all his interviews at home. It's not like your house is sacred. It's *The Times*, Abi! Not the *Daily Star*.'

'OK, of course, of course, I'm sorry.'

So I'm here, with a strange man sitting in my house, soaking up every picture, every half empty glass, every bit of dirty washing on the floor. Halfway through the chat I needed to go to the loo. During which time I could hear him getting up and snooping around.

When I came back he was writing down the contents of my notice board, kitchen and personal things. I explained to him that I'd only just moved in so I had only unpacked a few of my many books. About ten of them were visible on the side in the sitting room – they were mostly literature and plays including Chekhov, Brecht, Greek tragedies and the *Forsyte Saga*, I also had Robbie and Jordan's books out, as they'd been sent to me by a publisher vying for me to write my story.

Was glad when he'd gone. He made me feel uneasy.

29th June 2005

Nuts shoot then interview with the *Sun*.

It's such a paradox. Here I am, having made a living out of selling my story to the tabloids and now the one thing they want me to talk about, I don't want to give them. Had a bit of a row with Sam.

'I don't want to ruin what I've got with Lee by making my feelings public. I've already had one side of my love-life played out in the papers, can't this be sacred?'

Sam was resolute. 'Abi, if you want to continue being paid for interviews and photo shoots you need to give them what they want. You don't have to pour your heart out, but you have to understand, the viewers have invested their time in watching your romance unfold and now they feel like they have a right to learn what happens in the next chapter.'

She had a point. And I need to do this interview to publicise my fantasies book. The journalist kept on about sex. This is the conversation, verbatim:

'So, Abi! You've been in Fiji for two months so you haven't had sex. Did you miss it?'

'Err . . . of course, I suppose, like anyone.'

30th June 2005

The headline in the *Sun* from the interview is:

'Abi – "I'm gagging for it!"'

I ask you.

Did the Chris Moyles show this morning, but lovely as he is I couldn't focus on anything he was saying. My mind was dedicated to one man only.

The connection between us is so strong. How many people do you sleep next to in a bed on a desert island for six weeks, are with them twenty-four hours a day, and have got to know them completely, all without having sex?

We're falling in love. And it's wonderful.

1st July 2005

Went up to Leeds with Lee. He took me out to The Room restaurant last night to meet all his friends. Everyone was staring at us, but in a respectful way. Like they were pleased to see us together. A few came over and asked for autographs and it was lovely. Feel like people are talking to me as a person now, not a sex object.

We went to watch Jools Holland live in the park, with some of Lee's friends. We sat on rugs with a picnic, drinking wine till it got dark and everyone lit candles all around us. Lee and I can't take our eyes off each other. We can't believe it. Two friends have fallen in love.

Today has been one of the happiest days of my life.

2nd July 2005

The *Sun* has splashed on our hotel liaison. 'LOVE ISLE PAIR FINALLY GET IT ON.' So Victoria Newton actually thinks there is a point to writing about Abi Titmuss now then?

Met Lee's parents. They're so sweet. Feels like our relationship is on the fast track already. I like it.

3rd July 2005

There's a hilarious story in the *Star* about a PA I'm doing in Blackpool soon – must be a PR spin from the club, Brannigans, because they've got a name check. They've listed my 'rider' as 'the poshest hotel room in town, bottles of champagne . . . ' And a close friend says: 'Abi is dying to make Blackpool Rock with Lee.'

If any of my friends came out with cheesy lines like that, I'd make them live in Blackpool for good.

Braced myself and finally went back to see my personal trainer this afternoon. After the first session he weighed me.

'Well Abi,' he said gravely, 'the good news is, according to your height you are *not* overweight.'

I shrieked – 'What? Oh thank God!'

'But you *are* over-fat.'

Had to laugh otherwise I might cry.

4th July 2005

Have started my regimen of going to the gym four times a week. So desperate to lose weight. It's going to mean sacrificing seeing Lee because I need to train in London but he seems to understand.

It's so heart-warming to know that he doesn't really care how I look though. He met me looking my absolute worst – slobbing around with everything hanging out. I can be myself with him – I'm his 'Shabs' – and I love the fact that he's fallen in love with that.

5th July 2005

Went to see Jack Dee at the Apollo. I know it might sound pointless but we didn't want to be seen together. Am really keen to avoid courting the press. Yes, we started out on a TV show, but we need to lose that tag now. Otherwise people will think they have carte blanche to follow us. So we didn't even sit next to each other. And we left separately.

6th July 2005

Had a shoot with a fashion magazine called *Pop* – and I can honestly say it was the best shoot, and one of the best days of my life. I didn't even realise what *Pop* was about until Emma explained, insisting, 'Abi, it's the coolest magazine ever!'

The editor had apparently called her and requested me personally because she thought I was 'amazing'. They'd hired in real diamonds for me to wear, and even had a bloody security guard to look after them. I felt like Marilyn Monroe. The pictures they took, and the way they treated me was like nothing I've done before. I was in awe of the whole experience.

The magazine's only tri-annual, so it's a really big deal. The photographer made me feel wonderful and he said he was only interested in my face, in capturing the essence of 'me'. For once no one cared about my body and I felt divine.

7th July 2005

Was due to do a signing for my book launch in London today. Watching breakfast telly with Lee as we waited for the car to arrive. The news was on and there seemed to be something odd happening – tubes were being disrupted, panic was in the air, no one quite knew what was wrong – but there was no doubt something was.

We were glued to the TV. There had been a bomb on one, two, maybe even three of the tubes. It was horrendous. I immediately rang my old ward.

'Acute admissions unit please.'

'Hello.'

'It's Abi Titmuss, I want to come and help?'

'Thanks, er, really, thanks – but it wouldn't really work . . . it'll be too disruptive, we really appreciate your offer, but we can't take it.'

I was really disappointed. I was watching the news, seeing the paramedics, the people helping the injured across the road. This overwhelming instinct to help had taken over my body . . . but there was nothing I could do. What was I meant to be doing that day? A book launch, for stories about sex? And look what was happening out there! All my colleagues are on the ward helping bomb victims. I felt useless.

I wanted a drink.

Spoke to Sam and told her I was going to the pub to meet some friends; I just wanted to be around the people I cared about.

'Abi, you cannot go out drinking on a day like today. Even if it's innocent and you want to be with your mates, imagine what the papers will print if you're seen out boozing when there's been a bombing. It'll look really callous.'

She told me the *Mirror* is saying Lee and I snogged our way through Jack Dee! They've even pasted a picture of us together! A) We didn't and B) what does it bloody matter on a day like today?

9th July 2005

Richard & Judy's column in the *Express*:

'In the flesh, Abi looks wholesome and pretty, like a healthy milk-maid. She looks like she belongs in the country, helping with the harvest. Since she was on *Celebrity Love Island*, she says she has put on a bit of weight.'

Hilarious.

Chubby milkman more like.

Good old Richard. Thanks guys.

10th July 2005

Wonderful day. Went to the races and got mobbed by kids, teenagers, families. It was brilliant. Lee was in his element. For him it's like in his heyday, but for me it's so lovely – I'm used to being greeted by men with raging hormones. This reception was just as I'd always hoped. What's more, looking around there were actually more women and children than men.

'Haven't you lost weight?' they were saying.

Well, no actually. It's just because TV always makes you look bigger than you actually are. But I'm happy to let them think I have. Paddy McGuinness – Peter Kay's sidekick Paddy in *Phoenix Nights* and *Max and Paddy* – came over and had a chat; he's really funny and sweet.

The organisers asked me to start a race but I didn't want to (too embarrassed) so Lee went instead. Then we stood on the balcony to watch the horses and I could see the paps taking our picture. We'd had more than a few drinks by then, so I was far from camera shy. In fact I was virtually sending out emergency flares to get them to notice us.

Lee and I are so happy together. We sat on a big table with his family and friends and hardly stopped giggling all day. At one point we were gazing into each other's eyes so much that when we stopped and looked around everyone was staring at us! 'Awww, you look so good together,' said one of his mates.

11th July 2005

Have started the book tour now. It still feels a bit wrong with everything that's going on around the bombings but I know life must go on. We've been going round the country doing signings; it was Manchester and Birmingham today.

Got a call from the publisher saying that *Ten Fantasies* sold 15,000 in the first few days! That's good for erotic fiction apparently. The best thing is that there are so many couples buying them. Not just pervy men.

Saw a copy of the *Sunday Times* News Review interview that came out yesterday. The journalist wrote:

'Her library comprises a dozen volumes (*Bridget Jones's Diary*, a tribute to Robbie Williams). Her infamous John Leslie video of threesome sex is not visible, but there is one of Richard & Judy and another called *Dumb & Dumber*.'

After all my books and plays! He's just totally created a scene that is how he wants it to look. He really laid into me.

What hurt most was the fact that he dismissed my hopes of acting too. 'She twitters about plans to act and present and "move on" from sex. But that would take a public relations campaign as audacious as a plan to re-brand Pete Doherty as a saint; she might have to lump the image she has.'

I knew I shouldn't have done it. Even Sam said sorry for making me let him into my house. I feel violated again. I can trust no one.

13th July 2005

I was 9st 9lb on the island. Am back in the gym four times a week. But still too scared to weigh myself.

14th July 2005

Lee's been in Ireland all week for a sporting quiz thing. He wanted me to join him for a romantic weekend, and texted me on his way to meet me at the airport: 'Will you run and jump into my arms like you did on the beach?' He's so sweet to remember that. He says he loved it so much when I did it. We're staying in the most beautiful place – Killashee House in Naas, Co. Kildare – in a really plush suite with a jacuzzi and super king-size bed. Went for a stroll in the grounds in the afternoon and spotted a pap lurking in the bushes. Begged him not to take my picture. He didn't take any notice.

Did an interview with the *Sunday Mirror*. All the usual stuff, but this time I was asked about more than just sex. The reporter focused a lot on my body image and we even spoke about my ambitions to act. Feels like I'm moving away from the sex tape. At last.

19th July 2005

Nuts shoot. Well, I've got to pay the mortgage!

20th July 2005

Went out last night. Hammered. I'm sure Lee wasn't impressed. I got back really late then slept in so I hadn't texted him for ages. Am I drinking too much?

31st July 2005

Another piece in today's papers that really cheered me up as I ate my cornflakes: *Sunday Mirror*. Carole Malone writes:

'A friend of mine was interviewing Abi Titmuss recently and it appears she takes what I say about her very much to heart. So much so that her fugged-up little brain has concluded that the reason I write nasty things about her is because I'm jealous that she earns more money than me. Abi luv – just for the record – I'd rather eat horse manure than earn money the way you do. People might call me a lot of things – but cheap, trollopy porn star sure isn't one of them.'

Oh, fuck off you moose.

3rd August 2005

Have been partying on and off for the last month. Not sure my liver can take much more.

5th August 2005

PA, Romford, Brannigans.

I'm starting to notice a difference in the way other women are seeing me. I honestly think it's because I ate so much on *Love Island*. Getting fat has never been so good for my self-esteem! Went to the shop today and a girl came up to me and said I made her laugh.

Now that wouldn't have happened six months ago.

6th August 2005

PA, Newport, Brannigans.

Lee's been staying at mine for weeks, but I know it's not fair on him. He keeps wanting me to go to Leeds; he can't understand why I want to go out to London bars.

I love Lee but I love my lifestyle too. And I've started working with a personal trainer again down here and I have to go all the time. I'm desperate to lose weight. Lee doesn't like the paparazzi down here – he's a simple bloke, a normal Leeds man who just wants to go to the pub with his pals, no fuss.

Am secretly terrified it's going to cause a problem between us.

I'm never going to want to move to Leeds. Maybe we want different things?

I can't think about that.

7th August 2005

Emma from my agents called.

'A director called Mike Miller has been on the phone. He taught you drama at Kensington and Chelsea College apparently, and says he wants you to read for a play he's putting on in London. He says he's never forgotten about you.'

OH MY GOD!

I couldn't get to the phone quick enough.

He's putting on an Arthur Miller play called *Two Way Mirror*. It's beautiful. There's only two people in it! And its about 'complicated relationships' and is meant to have been inspired by Miller's real-life marriage with Marilyn Monroe. I remember telling Rebecca on *Love Island* that my dream come true would be to play Marilyn Monroe and Mike said he saw that. He thinks I'm made for the part.

Am ecstatic.

It's like it's meant to be.

8th August 2005

We're shooting pics for my 2006 calendar over the next two days and this time it's all about big hair, fishnets, corsets and sexy poses and me with various different look-alikes of screen idols. So there's Marilyn Monroe doing up my dress, me playing cards with Jack Nicholson . . . In one of the shots there was a guy dressed up as

Elvis. By the time he arrived (in full costume, I may add) I was in all my gear too – bra and pants, killer heels, feather headdress, loads of make-up. I turned to him and beamed: 'Hi Elvis! Thanks for coming, you look great!'

He drawled back in an American accent 'Hi I'm Clayton. And you are . . . ?'

'Er, I'm Abi.'

'Well, that's my wife over there,' he said pointing to a very stern looking woman.

12th August 2005

PA in Blackpool, then had to fly to Ireland for another one tomorrow. Got so pissed afterwards I managed to miss every single connection. Total of four trains and two flights.

13th August 2005

Lee was a guest on *Soccer AM* this morning.

He was introduced by Tim Lovejoy and Helen Chamberlain as 'Mr Abi Titmuss'.

I laughed at first, until I realised how fucking demeaning it was. In fact, it's awful. He used to be a star in his own right – what's happened?

Started getting the fear that it would be like with David and Lee would get hacked off, but thankfully, on the phone afterwards he laughed. He's so laid-back he'd hardly noticed.

Wish I was with him tonight and not in some club in Ulster doing a shitty PA.

15th August 2005

Met Mike and read for the play. Was really nervous because I wanted it so much.

He told me straight away I had the part. In fact he said I had it anyway, he just wanted to make sure I still had the acting bug in me. Too fucking right I have.

Am going to be an actress – AT LAST!

16th August 2005

Drinking too much. And am really starting to struggle. When Lee's in Leeds all I do is party then drag myself to the gym and I know he worries about me as a result. But I also know he loves me – and that means I can carry on.

19th August 2005

There's a whole spread about me in the *Star* from a shoot I've done recently.

Headline is: 'LUSCIOUS AB LOOKS SO FAB . . . she shows off her new slim and trim figure.'

The gym is slowly starting to pay off, thank the Lord.

Lee's staying at mine for a few days, then he's back in Leeds. The distance is starting to take its toll though. I really miss him.

20th August 2005

Went to the V Festival with Lee, his friend and my bunnies. It's a traditional girls' day so it felt a bit funny having a boyfriend there. I was happy though, with my two fave things – V and Lee! I did my usual thing of getting merry at the free bar and then wandering off, talking to everyone I know there. I happen to have quite a few male friends and when I'd had a few I was dancing around having a brilliant time with a bunch of them, oblivious to the world.

I don't think Lee liked it. We ended up having our first row. It was horrible falling out with him.

22nd August 2005

Had a shoot and interview with *OK* magazine today. And they actually had me wearing clothes! I still felt fat and ugly though.

The interview was supposed to be all about my 'post-*Love Island* weight-loss' but I haven't lost that much weight yet. All these 'dramatic weight-loss' features are a bit of a farce really.

26th August 2005

PA, Southampton, Jumpin' Jaks.

27th August 2005

Went to the Leeds Festival with Lee and his mates Ted and Sandra. We made up after V and I'm so in love with him now it's ridiculous. Sometimes I catch myself with my jaw open and a dazed expression when I'm listening to him because I am completely gaga. It is a truly terrifying feeling when you realise that someone has your heart in the palm of their hand, and there's absolutely nothing you can do about it, except pray that they don't drop it and kill you.

What an amazing night though. We got absolutely mobbed. It was so crazy – people were coming up every five seconds asking for our autographs. In the end it was so bad that the security guard had to usher us into a tent – 'I'm afraid we've got no alternative but to take you both backstage,' he grunted.

Oh no! Not backstage! Lee and I gave each other a wide-eyed look as if to say 'Oh my Godddd! Stay cool!'

Before we knew it we'd been escorted up some steps and suddenly found ourselves on the *actual* stage! Then The Killers came on and we were right there, within touching distance. It was the most incredible experience. A drumstick went flying past my head and I caught it (God knows what I need that for, but never mind).

Afterwards, we saw Kasabian drive past – 'Lee, we love you!' they shouted before pulling over. The lead singer gave me his sweaty towel. And for some reason I kept that too. One drumstick and one towel = one fab night.

We all went on from there to Lee's favourite bar. At one point Lee and I got up on the bar and were dancing together, laughing and holding hands while everyone in the bar was on their feet cheering and dancing too. We had so much fun together.

28th August 2005

Lee and I woke up late. About lunchtime. Switched on my phone – there were about a hundred messages. That's odd, I thought. I opened them . . . Miranda, Sue, Donna all my friends plus people I haven't heard from or spoken to for ages. David, even John, everyone I've ever known . . . all saying the same thing: 'So sorry Abi, hope it's not true – really hope you're OK.'

Immediately I knew it was the newspapers.

I felt sick to the stomach. My gut literally twisted. I knew this feeling, I'd been here before so many times. It must be really bad for so many people to have texted me, especially John Leslie and David Walliams.

Oh God, what is it now? What is it now?

Not one of them had said what it was. My first thought was 'It's another story about me – Lee's going to dump me.'

Lee was still in bed, so I nipped out into the hallway and called Sam.

'Sam?'

'Abi . . . It's Lee.'

I was looking at him across the room while she spoke.

He walked over to me and stood right in front of me, holding my hand, gazing into my eyes with a caring, worried expression. I was looking directly into his eyes, with the phone to my ear as I heard Sam's voice say, 'It's front page. The headline is: "SHARPE CHEATS ON ABI WITH A SHOP GIRL!" Some promotions girl called Kathryn . . . reckons she's known him for twelve years and it's been going on for months.'

My heart was pumping so fast. I had to steady my legs to stop them from collapsing under me. My bottom lip was trembling. I hung up the phone and Lee stared at me, asking what was wrong.

I asked if he knew anyone called Kathryn and, without flinching, he said no.

'We have to get the papers,' I stumbled.

He offered to go, hugging me before he went and reassuring me that whatever they were saying were lies. He pulled his jeans on and went to the shop. I called Sam. I wanted her to help me believe it wasn't true.

'He doesn't know that name.'

'But it says they've got text messages,' she said reluctantly. Oh God, I couldn't take it in.

'OK, but hang on, er, is it possible to cheat them? Could the girl have fudged it afterwards? You know, changed the text message to look real?'

I was desperately trying to think of a way to prove it was made up. Anything, anything, help me out Sam, please! Lee? Cheating? Can he, would he, really have done that? It absolutely floored me.

When he returned I could hardly look him in the eye. Yet his attitude was unfaltering. He read the story, and immediately looked up and told me it wasn't true.

I don't want to believe it, I so bloody don't want to.

I feel like I'm being physically torn in half. I have my boyfriend looking me straight in the eye, telling me he loves me and totally denying it. And in my hand I have the front page of a national paper with a woman looking out at me swearing he has slept with her.

Also, part of me feels that with all the shit that I have had written about me in the press, I should know better than to take the word of a tabloid rag over the man I love. I feel guilty for even doubting him. On the other hand, would I be insane to ignore the evidence that is staring me in the face?

If only they didn't have text messages then maybe I could believe it was fantasy. How can he explain those? Please, please explain those to me? I wanted to scream and shout and beg him to convince me but I didn't. I think I was in shock.

I held it together. It hadn't totally sunk in yet. I'll wake up in a minute. When he wasn't looking I actually pinched myself really hard. How sad is that? I was that desperate for it to be a dream.

But I can't help thinking that there's no smoke without fire.

We sat at the kitchen table and stared the paper. It was horrendous.

'Lee, 34 . . . had steamy car sex with promotions girl Kathryn Shaw just TEN DAYS AGO. Then he drove back to a passionate reunion with Abi, 29, at last Saturday's V festival at Chelmsford, Essex.'

What?
No.
Really?
Could he?
It got worse.

'Ex-model Kathryn, 31 . . . Revealed how the former Manchester United and Leeds footballer . . . SECRETLY ROMPED with her on and off for TWELVE YEARS even though he had other girlfriends. LIKES to meet her at a bridge near the M62 halfway between Leeds and Manchester for his illicit nookie. BOMBARDED her with saucy texts for three hours after their latest romp even though he was with Abi at the festival. LAUGHS when he reads stories about him planning to marry Abi. Kathryn is convinced the two timing star is feeding off her fame as a TV presenter and glamour model.'

Lee kept begging me to put it away, repeating that it wasn't true.

I sat there, numbly, waiting for him to explain. To make me believe it was lies. But he just didn't say anything. He's not a big talker at the best of times, but now it was clear he didn't know what to say. He just kept telling me it wasn't true.

We were meant to be going to Manchester for a party this evening. It's for his mate who'd been ill recently. Lee started getting a bag together.

'How can we go there?' I cried. 'What? And just carry on as if nothing's happened?'

He tried to reason that nothing *had* happened, and as this was his mate, we couldn't let him down. Part of me wanted to walk out of the door and never come back, but the other needed to be with him. Needed it to be OK. Lee drove.

I sat in the passenger seat and the tears came. Each minute that passed I could feel it sinking in deeper and becoming more and more real. Imploring him in my mind to say something to help me believe it wasn't true.

I just sobbed throughout the entire journey.

I looked at him. This is my Lee. We're soul mates. He's my friend. My Sharpester. He can't do this. Can he?

Got to the hotel, The Lowry, and walked up to the room in silence. Lee closed the door, and then all of a sudden, the floodgates opened and we both realised how hard this had hit us.

I just couldn't handle it and told Lee to go to the party on his own. I could see he was upset, but it was the only way I could deal with it all.

He stood there helplessly, clueless about what to do next. I turned my back until I heard the door slam behind him. The minute he'd gone, I panicked. I couldn't be on my own.

I stared at the phone for about ten minutes before texting him, 'I'm coming out.'

Deep breaths. Pull yourself together, Abi. It'll be OK.

I reached the bar and through the window I saw him laughing and chatting away to his mates as if everything was fine.

My whole world is torn apart. And he looks like he doesn't give a toss – that's what it seems like to me, anyway. I opened the door and walked across to where he was standing. I forced a smile and said hi to the two mates he was talking to, but I just couldn't look him in the eye.

People kept coming over – 'How's it going?' It took all my efforts to stop me breaking down and sobbing into their laps. The only answer was to drink . . . and drink. It seemed to ease the pain. We both got back to the hotel and passed out.

29th August 2005

As soon as I woke up I wanted to leave. I had to get out. I got dressed and asked Lee to drive me to the station. He obliged. As soon as we pulled up outside the ticket office, I shut the car door, walked away and didn't look back.

As soon as I sat on the train I broke down. I didn't even care if anyone saw me.

When I closed the front door of my house behind me, I sank to the floor gasping for breath. I wanted to be sick. Crawled towards the sofa and cried and cried. When I stopped I realised it was night time.

30th August 2005

Am in the pit of despair. Lee's texted a few times but what's a text? He's not exactly beating my door down.

Sue and I had booked to go to Champneys in Forest Mere a while back. It was meant to be a lovely break. Now it's just going to be an escape. But I have to leave this house, it's got too many memories. I don't ever want to come home and face reality again. Feel so stupid, humiliated. And so, so confused. What if I've made a huge mistake and it's not true?

Should I know better?

31st August 2005

Still in Champneys. Can't eat, can't sleep.

2nd September 2005

PA, Chester.

God it was so hard getting up on stage and pretending to be happy. I was scared shitless someone would say something about Lee. So of course, I drank my way through it. It's the only thing that helps me forget.

3rd September 2005

Have been ignoring Lee's calls. Can't face him. Just want to hide from the world. Rang David and I blubbed for over an hour. He's such a shoulder to cry on, he's been a rock over the last couple of days.

4th September 2005

Lee's been texting and phoning.

After about the seventh message I buckled and answered the phone. He kept saying that it wasn't true and that I had to believe him. But I don't. And he knows it. Of course I still want it to work between us – I feel like I can't function without him. But I just can't bring myself to trust him.

He wants to meet up. But there's no way, not yet.

5th September 2005

All I keep thinking is that people must be laughing at me, it's like I've got a stamp on my head saying, 'I'm not good enough.'

He wouldn't have done it otherwise. It feels to me like Lee is saying to the whole world 'I didn't really love her.'

6th September 2005

Had a shoot for Marks and Spencer today for their autumn/winter lingerie range. It's linked with a breast cancer charity and in spite of my flat mood, the whole experience was really uplifting. The fact that I've been asked to model underwear that's specifically aimed at women is something I've only dreamt of until now. For once these are shots of me in my bra and pants that are not designed with the whole purpose of turning men on.

Went to the Mercury Music Awards this evening. Sam encouraged me. She said I should go out and hold my head up. Plus, I'd been invited by Stuart Murphy – the head of BBC3 – so she thought I should make the effort.

It was a huge bash in the ballroom of the Dorchester, hundreds of music industry people. Stuart was lovely, so much fun; he cheered me up a bit. Then as we got to our table and I sat down, I looked up and of all the bars in all the world, and all the tables in this giant room, who was sitting at the next one and directly in my eye-line?

Lee.

I thanked my lucky stars that the first time I bumped into him I was all dressed up, and on a table with a group of men. It was such a bizarre coincidence. And of course we couldn't stop looking. After about twenty minutes of eyes flicking back and forth, he smiled and came over.

Two hours later we're leaving arm in arm.

7th September 2005

Why did I do that?

I woke and realised that nothing's changed. Nothing's been resolved.

The pain of it all has somehow hit me twice as hard.

10 September 2005

It's happened again.

A reporter from the *News of the World* called at midday and said they had another story about Lee supposedly cheating, they were running it tomorrow and would I like to comment?

I don't know what to think now. Feel a bit numb. What the hell is going on?

I rang Donna who immediately said, 'You're not going to do this alone,' and ordered me round to her house. We stayed up all night trying to distract ourselves with booze, DVDs. Then, in the early hours we headed straight out to the garage for the first edition of the papers.

'The *News of the World* EXCLUSIVE: He's caught cheating for SECOND time . . . the lewd love rat romped with model Louise Redpath (pictured with Lee, above) while the couple watched a porn movie with pals in an LA hotel room.'

Am absolutely destroyed. This can't be. How can I possibly go back now? Donna was so lovely. She sat with me and we talked . . . then got very, very pissed until we passed out. Lee texted, telling me that he had already spoken to his lawyers, that he was going to take it to court. That I had to believe him when he said it was completely untrue.

Well I don't. And I can't help it.

13th September 2005

Had to do a set of pictures to show off my new 'weight'. I'd organised it ages ago so there was no getting out of it. Tried to call Emma this morning and bail but she told me in no uncertain terms I had to do it. It's my job, the way I earn a living, and I shouldn't let Lee ruin that for me as well.

Feel like absolute shit. Was on automatic pilot all day. Barely said a word to anyone.

Still staying at Donna's. She's such a rock.

Lee has been texting all day denying the story. Can't even reply now. What's the point? How do I know what to believe any more?

14th September 2005

Lee didn't text today. That says it all. Was our whole relationship a lie? All those feelings?

He's given up already.

Going to New York tomorrow to see the Rolling Stones with the girls. Right now, the only rolling I want to do is off a cliff.

15th September 2005

Went out partying all night, and boarded the plane to New York having had no sleep and emptied a couple of drawers into a suitcase at the last minute, so I have no idea what I have packed.

16th September 2005

Being mates with Ronnie Wood's manager certainly has its perks. Donna got us great tickets to see the show. The girls did their utmost to put a smile on my face. Getting away from my flat and all the memories it conjures up is probably the best thing I could do. Besides, the Stones were awesome. Thanks to Donna we were part of their cavalry – I ended up watching the gig standing in the VIP area next to Christy Turlington and Ed Burns, Bob Geldof and Mick Jagger's ridiculously tall girlfriend! Wow. We left the stadium in a blacked-out limousine, as part of the entourage, and were accompanied through New York by a police escort!

We all went to dinner afterwards. I was seated bang opposite Bob Geldof. He didn't really say a lot to me though. Probably didn't know who I was either.

Tyrone, Ronnie's son was there. 'You're twenty-nine?' he gasped. 'Wow, you look good for your age.'

I turned round to face him. 'Don't ever say that again to any woman under thirty.'

We all ended up back in Ronnie's suite in the Waldorf Astoria. He'd hired out a whole floor. Got so drunk and was talking absolute shit in Ronnie's ear. It was a night to remember and I felt privileged to be there.

And guess who was the last person to go to bed?

17th September 2005

Went to an exhibition of Ronnie's paintings. They all looked a bit weird to me, but I had to check I wasn't being clueless. I asked one of the bunnies what they thought.

'Bloody awful,' came the reply.

Two hours later we were all at dinner together. I was placed opposite Ronnie.

I looked across. 'Ronnie, your paintings are amazing!', gushed the bunny and me.

'Thank you so much,' he grinned.

It was funny at first but on reflection it made me think. It's no wonder celebrities get messed up, when people only tell them what they want to hear is it? How many people have done that to me?

Then it was on to Naomi Campbell's party – which, on paper, sounds like it would be the best night ever. But in reality it wasn't at all. These people honestly live in a different world. Me and the girls spent the whole evening feeling like hangers-on. I'd rather be in our nice old pub at home.

19th September 2005

Woke up feeling miserable. Can't stop thinking about Lee. I'm in New York and yet I'm in such a dark place. It's like nothing I've ever felt before.

20th September 2005

Back home, and back to reality.

At the airport, noticed that the new pictures are in the *Star* already. 'ABI IS FEELING SO FIT; EXCLUSIVE: HOW LOVE ISLAND BEAUTY IS GETTING OVER HER HEARTACHE.'

Couldn't be further from the truth but at least I look nice. One benefit of heartache is losing weight. Maybe Lee will see the paper . . .

The first thing I saw when I got through my front door was Lee's trainers by the mat. Burst into tears. He's still got so much of his stuff here. How can I possibly move on? And deep down I don't want to. I want my dream back. My wonderful Fijian sunshine love-story. I actually wish we were back on the island. I want our time back. I want my friend back.

23rd September 2005

Am hosting an event for *Nuts* at the Excel Centre for three days. Not really functioning straight, but I know it's good for me to have a focus. It's a full-on live show called 'Abi's Glamour School'. There are dancers and I have to coach photo shoots for people in the audience along with a Q&A session. Scary, but I enjoyed it.

No word from Lee.

I texted him – 'Can you come and pick up your stuff please?'

24th September 2005

Thanks to my break-up, pictures of me are selling like hot cakes at the moment. The *Mirror* has bought up some old shots of me in Majorca: 'Cool at the Pool; She's Abi to be Single Again'.

It doesn't matter to them that they were taken ages ago.

Have got front cover of the *Sun* too – it's the Marks and Spencer underwear shoot. I should be really chuffed, but it's plonked right next to an exclusive interview with the wife of one of the 7/7 bombers, and my piece is bigger.

What kind of world is this?

Onstage at the Excel Centre I interviewed one of the girl's who'd won a competition to take part in the show and said she wanted advice on doing modelling shoots like me.

I said, 'So you want to be a glamour model. You must be quite an exhibitionist then?' I held the microphone to her lips,

She stared at me blankly. 'I don't know what that means.'

30th September 2005

It was Sam's leaving party tonight. She's going off travelling in a few days, she says she wants to leave the world of PR for good. Don't know what I'm going to do without her. She's been everything to me and suffered everything with me. No one else is going to know me as well as she does. I can be difficult at times – mainly because I'm struggling to cope with it all – but she always understood that.

'I'd hate to be a teetotaller. Imagine getting up in the morning and knowing that's as good as you're going to feel all day.'

Dean Martin

1st October 2005

Went back to Lincoln to see my old mates from home. Bought everyone champagne but tried not to wave it around too much as didn't want people around us thinking I was showing off. So nice to be back at home. Makes me feel safe.

2nd October 2005

The *People*:

'*Love Island* star Lee Sharpe proved he's got over his split from Abi Titmuss by entertaining a string of beauties on Friday night...'

God I feel sick.

4th October 2005

Was due on a shoot for Debenhams today. I cancelled it.

Am struggling to drag myself out of bed for anything these days. It's not so bad when I'm away from London and the flat, but when I'm back here I can't stop thinking about Lee. Can't cope.

7th October 2005

My best friend from my nursing days, Marisa, and her boyfriend have come to visit from Australia and I was really excited about treating them to a really expensive meal at the Sanderson, where we always used to go together with ten quid in our pocket.

Ordered lobster, champagne, the works. The funny thing was that all Marisa and her boyfriend wanted to know about was my mad life, while I just kept grilling them about the hospitals over there – I wanted to know all about the wards and the patients because it took me back to when I was a nurse. I have so much admiration for them.

13th October 2005

1pm *Nuts* shoot at Holborn Studios.
7pm Bar opening.

Went to the first night of a new place in Clapham called Grafton House and true to form I got completely hammered.

Some journalist kept sidling up to me and asking about my weight loss. 'It's called "the heartbreak diet",' I told her and walked off.

14th October 2005

9am *Closer* magazine shoot.

I'm losing it.

Didn't want to go, I was in such a state from last night. I'd only just got to bed when the cab arrived, and I hid under the duvet, desperately hoping it would leave.

Thirty minutes later, my manager called.

'Where are you? The car's outside.'

'I'm not going, I can't. I'm a mess.'

An hour later, she was knocking on my door along with my new PR, Roberta (talk about a baptism of fire for her!)

'Go away! I don't want to do it.'

The article's meant to be all about how healthy I am and how good I look. I look like shit and I feel FAT. Feel a fraud. Just want to hide in the house.

They kept knocking and knocking.

'You have to come out now, you can't do this to a magazine Abi – it's not professional.'

'I'm sure they're not that bothered about me, just cancel it, I don't want to do it. They won't mind.'

Don't want to face anyone. There will be a whole team of hair and make-up people . . . I don't know them, I don't want a bunch of strangers seeing me like this, let alone a journalist. Am in no state to have my picture taken. I'll be crying all the time.

'You have to do it. This is really, really bad for you if you don't.'

In the end I had no choice.

Got there. Cried. They made me up. I cried. They put on some more make-up. I cried again. But they were all being so nice, I knew they were trying their best to make me feel better.

I still had to make up a load of rubbish about my 'health plan' though. What I really should've said was, 'Listen to this *Closer* readers, I don't eat Friday, Saturday or Sunday because I'm out drinking – that's your bloody diet!'

16th October 2005

The *People*: 'SAD ABI IS ON DIET OF HEARTACHE'.

17th October 2005

How things can change, eh?

What a day. I've now got a part in a film and am buying my second house.

Have been asked to be in a film called *Goal 2*. It's only one scene, and I'm playing myself. But it's a proper movie AND David Beckham's in it. I'm playing 'Abi Titmuss' in a Hollywood film. Now that's surreal.

And the house I've put an offer on is lovely. And huge. Hopefully moving in a few weeks. David called and made me laugh. He really knows how to cheer me up. Today's events and my talk with David served to give me the confidence to ring Lee. I tried to be cheery and carefree. We had a nice chat. Maybe we can be friends . . .

18th – 24th October 2005

Madrid for *Goal 2*!

Got to Madrid and headed straight to the film set. There's a trailer with my name on it! More ridiculously, right next door to the sign that reads 'Abi Titmuss' is another door that says 'Real Madrid'. I've nearly got a bigger room than the whole football team!

Am so excited. Introduced myself to one of the film's bigwigs (Film Guy) as soon as I could, he seems really nice. I just want to soak it all up – learn as much as I can. Snuck on to the set when I wasn't meant to be there, so fascinating to watch the actors though. Was in my element.

The film guy (FG) invited me out to dinner; I think he fancies me. He's lovely but don't like him in that way. Seeing as I was meant to be making a good impact I, of course, ended up getting absolutely pissed. After the meal FG invited me back to his house – which culminated in us sitting on the street at 8am, watching the sun come up, red wine in hand. FG kept saying he was going to change my flight so I could stay longer.

God what was I doing?

At one point I ended up reciting poetry to him. I wanted to charm him so he'd give me more work. But typically I went overboard and he thinks I fancy him. Am now in the position of having to either go with him or reject him. Neither of which I want to do.

All I want to do is see Lee . . .

19th October 2005

My big scene today. It was awe-inspiring – a huge set, cameras, rigs, people everywhere. The set-up featured me being interviewed on a TV show about the Beckhams and I had to talk about what a phenomenon they were. OK, so it's not exactly Shakespeare, but it's a start. I had to improvise, no problem. And I loved it anyway.

Afterwards FG took me to see the team play at the Real Madrid stadium. I never thought I'd be one for football, but it was such an overpowering place – the stands were so high, the crowd were so vociferous, it was truly staggering.

Then all the players went for dinner. David didn't come, sadly, but I was next to Jonathan Woodgate. Seeing him in action on the pitch had really done something to me too – I probably wouldn't have taken any notice if I'd bumped into him on the street – but now I realised he was an amazing athlete.

FG was sitting the other side of me. But of course I was more interested in talking to Jonathan. He was nearer my age and we were having a right laugh. He was much brighter than I imagined (well, he spoke a bit of Spanish anyway), and incredibly funny.

As soon as the meal was over, FG, having become increasingly fidgety all evening, announced, 'Abi, I'm leaving now, you coming?'

I soooo didn't want to go with him. Jonathan looked at me. 'Me and the others were going to a club – come with us Abi!'

This was a real dilemma. I was faced with the option of getting in one of two cars – the hot-shot Film Guy of this massive Hollywood film who could possibly help forge the kind of career I want (wasn't Marilyn Monroe supposed to have done a bit of that after all?) or . . . a footballer I quite fancy?

Guess which one I chose.

Yep, the wrong one.

As we were driving away, I saw FG's disapproving face looking back at me. Was I was making a massive mistake?

I didn't have to ponder long. There, in all his glory, was Sir David of the Beckham. He was standing casually propped up against a pillar in the VIP area, a beanie hat pulled over his head. And he looked great. I've never seen why women fancied him before – he was always a bit too pretty for my tastes. But boy, oh boy, up close, he's magnetic.

David motioned for us to come over – I was slightly ahead of the rest and as I went to walk through, a security guard stuck his hand out to block me. David immediately got up and waved me in.

He leant over and kissed me on the cheek. He knew who I was!

He smiled as he asked if I was still with Lee.

I'd forgotten they used to be roommates.

'Sadly not,' I replied before laughing resentfully. 'I guess you don't look at the papers?'

He rolled his eyes. Arghh, what did I say that for? Twat. Then he looked at me, waiting for an explanation.

'Well, the papers reckon he cheated on me . . .' and I rambled on for a minute. Just like that I forgot he was David Beckham. He was one of my ex's mates and my crazy love-sick brain wanted his opinion on the situation. It didn't matter that he hadn't seen him for years. D'oh.

He shrugged.

Why didn't I just leave it as 'we've broken up'? Why did I have to go into the drama of it all? I guess I wanted him to say 'his loss', but he wasn't exactly going to do that.

Eventually left the club at about 6am. Jonathan and I had been having fun flirting all night, but he seemed to think Lee was some kind of deity too. Pah, men.

20th October 2005

Back in the UK.

Oh for GOD'S SAKE.

Saw yesterday's papers – and there's a story in the *Star* about me and David Beckham. 'Abi Scores with Becks'.

It's about the night I met him in the club but says we were getting flirty together and it was obvious something was going on. Unadulterated bollocks. David was a gentleman and I rambled about Lee.

FG rang. 'The Beckhams are really upset. Victoria's going mad about the newspaper report.'

This is way out of my control! David hadn't done anything untoward with me, or me with him. Now they think I've done the story – I can't win.

FG was suddenly talking as if the Beckhams didn't want me in the film anymore, like they thought I'd calculated this whole thing. I was furious. Got off the phone and couldn't stop crying.

Half an hour later, I texted him back.

'Will you have some backbone? You know me now; you know I wouldn't do something like that on purpose. Stick up for me please!' Not entirely sure I should be talking to a Hollywood film guy like that but, hey. I've got to fight this.

Am gutted. I know how it looks. Everyone's going to think I've done it. David will think so. I'd think exactly the same if it was me. Am devastated and I can't do anything about it. And –

Victoria? This is her husband! I hate that she thinks I've set it all up.

Is this what people think I am? Called my new PR Roberta in tears. 'I want to speak to a newspaper so I can deny it. I need to make people see it wasn't true.'

'There's nothing you can do, Abi. You just have to leave it, and wait for it to blow over.'

She's nice, and I know she's right – but she's not Sam.

21st October 2005

FG texted to say sorry. He feels guilty for not believing me.

22nd October 2005

FG called. He's got me another scene! Seems the Beckhams have forgiven me after all. I'm flying back out in two days. Not entirely sure if FG really does think I'm a good actress or just wants to shag me though . . .

24th October 2005

7am pick up, flight at 9.30am.

Booked into Hotel Urban, one of the coolest hotels in Madrid.

Shot the second scene. Felt like a proper actress. Am loving this!

FG keeps asking me what I'm doing this evening. Jonathan's already asked me out to dinner, so told FG I wanted a rest and an early night.

He seemed to buy it. Jonathan took me to a Chinese restaurant and kept asking me to go to his. At first I said no. Two drinks later it was a different story . . .

'OK, I'll at least come and see your ridiculous Footballer's house. Just take me back to my hotel so I can change these shoes.'

He drove me over in his big whopper of a Range Rover and I hurried upstairs. Thank God I did.

Opened the door and the bed was strewn with flowers, wine, food, chocolates . . . everything. I picked up the accompanying note.

'Enjoy your early night x.' It was all from FG.

Oh, for crying out loud! What am I going to do?

Snuck back out of the hotel, got in Jonathan's car and we drove to his place.

10.30pm. A text from FG.

'How are you?'

'Fine, thanks so much for the food, having a nice restful night.'

Liar, liar, pants on fire. Only I could manage to embroil myself in a love triangle with two men I have only met twice, in a foreign country.

27th October 2005

Back in dreary London.

Jonathan's been texting over the last two days. It all seemed so exciting when I was in Madrid, but now I'm back I can't stop thinking of Lee.

28th October 2005

A shot from my DVD pictures has made half the cover of the *Star*. The bottom half has a picture of Calum looking upset with the headline: 'Dad, don't die.' George Best is on his last legs and it's so incredibly sad. What a waste.

29th October 2005

Went to a restaurant called Cocoon with my friend Nadine. I got chatted up by Craig David! He's surprisingly good looking in the flesh. A bit young though. Still, he seemed so nice that when he asked for my number I was flattered so I gave it to him. Not exactly sure why he asked though, he goes out with proper models.

30th October 2005

Had a PA in Ireland – got pissed on the way there, during, and en route home. Well I wouldn't want to offend them by refusing the hospitality.

31st October 2005

It says in the *Star* that Orlando Bloom has a crush on me! He did an interview for his movie *Elizabethtown* and the reporter asked him what he thought of me.

'She would be great in LA. I know she's interested in acting so maybe we'll work together someday . . . '

And he's not taking the piss. Wow, that feels nice.

Abigail Bloom has a nice ring to it . . .

1st November 2005

Did another PA, this time in Belfast. Have stayed in Ireland for the last two days, which is nice.

Loaded magazine called my management – they're taking me away for another cover shoot in two days' time.

To LAS VEGAS, BABY!

Vegas! I'm punching the air. Tenerife was debauched enough, this is going to be mental. And because Sue came last time it's Miranda's turn.

Sue's NOT happy.

3rd November 2005

Got to Vegas. The hotel rooms are awesome; I've got a jacuzzi set into the floor!

4th November 2005

The shoot took place in a casino. I ended up virtually naked, sprawled across a craps table and everyone was still gambling around us. I guess anything goes in Vegas. Another shot had me in a glass elevator going up the side of the building in just my pants.

When I looked at the pictures on the computer afterwards they were so close up you couldn't see any of Vegas and I might as well have been in my bedroom at home. Not that I'm complaining. This place is something else.

5th November 2005

Miranda and I are supposed to be flying back tomorrow, but Daubs the editor has other ideas.

'Me and Brooksie are driving through the Nevada desert to LA – we're going to shoot Carmen Electra and Jennifer Ellison. Why don't you come?'

Hmmm let me think about that for a minute . . .

So we've changed our flight.

6th November 2005

Thank God Brooksie had some sleep last night because he was driving. The rest of us on the other hand were up boozing until the moment we had to leave. I think I've actually broken poor Daubs. When I got in the car this morning, his head was in his hands.

Then he looked up at me with a frightened face: 'What's that you're carrying?'

I was brandishing a pillowcase brimming with booze from the mini bar.

I laughed. 'ONE for the frog?' (I meant road . . .)

9th November 2005

God knows what happened over the last few days. It's one big haze. I've succeeded in electrocuting myself, blowing a grand in a slot machine and having zero sleep.

But it officially goes down in history as the best trip I've ever had.

AND I didn't even sleep with anyone!

11th November 2005

Had a meeting about possible TV formats for me with a couple of producers. Really want to do something with a bit of substance. But have had so many of these meetings and nothing ever happens in the end that I can't get my hopes up. I just have to take it with a pinch of salt.

9pm PA, Hereford . . . Yawn.

13th November 2005

Agreed to go for a drink with Craig David tonight, but in the end I couldn't go through with it. All I could think about was his Avid Merrion character and Kez. 'Craaaig David. Can't I get a reeeewind?'

16th November 2005

Met a midget dressed as Elvis tonight at the UK Music Hall of Fame Awards. He was great; said he gets paid to go to showbiz events. I said if I ever have a party I want him there. I wonder what his rates are?

20th November 2005

Had brunch with bunnies in Primrose Hill. We talked about everything that'd happened with Lee and how upset I was. They helped in their own, unique ways:

Sue – 'Pull yourself together, the man's a flake.'
Donna – 'You're old, fat and losing it Titmuss. Get over it and get your mojo back.'
Miranda – 'I love you, bun.'

I love them. Men come and go but your girls never let you down.

24th November 2005

9am *Heat* Xmas shoot.
11pm PA, Amber Lounge, Manchester.

Had a shoot for the double issue of *Heat* – this year they had me dressed up as Jessica Simpson from *Dukes Of Hazzard*. Hotpants and heels – loved it. Straight to Manchester after that – had arranged to see McGuinness's show before my PA. He was hilarious. Even funnier than he was in *Phoenix Nights*. There were loads of girls from *Hollyoaks* there, at least I think that's who they were – they all look the same to me.

Paddy came back to hotel for a quick drink afterwards, then my car picked me up for the PA. I say car, it was actually a stretch Hummer. Which is a really sensible way of getting round the back-streets of Manchester. Not.

Am staying at The Lowry. Weird coming back here tonight. The last time I was here was that heartbreaking weekend with Lee.

25th November 2005

The *News of the World* is saying I'm dating Paddy. Wondered when that one would materialise.

There's also a story about a Christmas banner of me that's been nicked from outside a club. It's the same place I'm doing a PA tomorrow. Funny that. The club has got a name check, which smacks of a PR story. But a clever one all the same. All sounds a bit *Phoenix Nights* actually!

27th November 2005

It was Stuart Murphy's leaving do – he's the chap who took me to the Mercury Music Awards when I met Lee again. He's the head of a BBC channel, so this was a big deal for me. Time to impress the bigwigs then. I noticed Stuart was dressed in a black and white suit, then I started knocking back the Bellini's.

Ended up doing several stellar performances on the karaoke then calling him a liquorice all-sort over the microphone.

It didn't go down very well.

5th December 2005

Met up at the rehearsal centre to audition actors to co-star with me in *Two Way Mirror*. It's only a two-hander so it's imperative we gel.

On paper, all my potential leading men appeared to be about forty-five, but as they filed through the doors, every single one was at least ten years older than their picture. Some were plain doddery. I nearly got a fit of the giggles it was that bad. When we said, 'Thanks, we'll be in touch,' I kept expecting them to say, 'I don't belieeeeve it!' à la Victor Meldrew.

One guy stood out though – Jay Benedict. He had a lovely handsome, charismatic face, he was a great actor and as a result he got the part. I love him already.

6th December 2005

PA, Liverpool.

8th December 2005

I've had a moment. Call it an epiphany.

I woke up at about 10am and went to the garage to get some juice. As I walked up to the glass door I noticed the display of newspapers shouting at me from behind their plastic covering. I've seen it a thousand times, so I don't know why today seemed so different. But it did. It was the *Daily Star* that leapt out. I was on the cover in my bra and knickers. Nothing new there. It was like a voice in my head shouted,

'What are you doing with your life?'

It was so vivid. I've had millions of pictures out there, I've been on the cover of *FHM* and the tabloids virtually on a daily basis but this time it just hit me. Wham. That's me, in my bra and pants. On the cover of a national newspaper. And that's all I do in life.

Honestly. What the fuck am I doing?

I stood there for a minute staring blankly. People must've thought I was obsessed with myself. (If they don't already think that). As I stood in the queue I suddenly felt overwhelmingly self-conscious. I couldn't look at anyone. Kept thinking to myself, 'Do you realise this is your whole life now? It's not just a bit of fun anymore. This is the sum of your parts. You in no clothes. That's it.' That's not what I ever wanted for myself. There's got to be something more to me.

When I got home I was in a massive panic. Couldn't sit still. Kept pacing around my lounge. This is not what I'd planned. This is not what I ever wanted. I called my manager, Emma: 'I'm having a crisis. I can't do this kind of thing anymore.'

She must love me. I'm sure she had far better things to do than listen to me moaning on about how I didn't want to do the one thing that made me a bankable commodity, but I can't help it. I've always been acutely aware of the dichotomy between what I'm doing and how I feel as a person but I've just gone along with it. And there always seemed to be that element of excitement about what was going to happen next. Meanwhile, of course, I was busy drinking myself into an early grave at another free bar.

I thought it would have stopped by now and I'd just go back to being Abi. But somehow it's become normal. And it really shouldn't have gone this far. My brain is crying out for some intellectual stimulation, that's why I drink half the time – boredom and to quiet my mind. I want to study again, to learn something, to take up Latin again (I always loved it). Modelling has numbed my neurons. Thank God I'm making money but thank God for the play.

9th December 2005

Went to Dubai with a new agency called Cruise. Beach shoots always sell well at Christmas – God knows why, it must just make people feel rubbish that they're at home full of turkey and mince pies. The *People* are already interested in the shots and I haven't even done any yet. They're the best payers, while the *News of the World* has a better circulation. I've often had to choose between getting more money or a bigger spread of readers.

Business, business.

10th December 2005

Spent the whole day shooting with silly props and poses. Then caught up with my aunt and uncle who happen to live out here. Went to bed with a book.

11th December 2005

Another day of pics. Back home tomorrow.

15th December 2005

Had my first training session with a voice coach for the play. Can't believe I'm actually going to be in a play! It's a mixture of sheer terror and absolute joy.

Mike suggested I dye my hair. In the first part I look like Marilyn Monroe and need to wear a blonde wig, but the second character I portray is a chic brunette, an Audrey Hepburn-type.

But that's exactly the problem as far as my management are concerned. They have serious worries and said I need to think about this properly. 'The blonde bombshell' image is how I earn my living. Getting rid of that image might mean 'bye bye career'. And bye bye 'Abi Titmuss'.

The thing is, that's a big part of why it's appealing to me. It would be so empowering, effectively 'resigning' from my position as head of Abi Ltd. Stripping off the blonde 'wig', with all its past and connotations and starting again. It makes me want to shave my head just thinking about it.

Best not mention that to Emma.

16th December 2005

Have to see the voice coach nearly every day now until rehearsals. Mike says it's important to strength the vocal cords for articulation in the theatre. Plus I am working on my American accent for the part.

Pictures from my Dubai trip are in some of the papers. Every time I see that an image has sold, I'm grateful now. Can't take it for granted like I used to. It's also a wake-up call that I need to have a long hard think about my future.

18th December 2005

I've made full page in the *People* and they've used another one of my pictures. It reads: 'Have an Abi Xmas'.

Brilliant. Have heard that Lee accepted damages from the *News of the World* over the Louise Redpath story. Am so glad.

21st December 2005

Lee rang. He's coming tomorrow to get his stuff once and for all.

I really hope he means it this time. Don't even care that he's collecting his belongings. Just want to see him again.

22nd December 2005

Moved house today! Yay! The removal men were ace, and I was in within hours. And I'm trying to pretend I'm not bothered but who am I kidding – I cannot wait to see Lee again. He's definitely coming tonight. I'm going to get ready. Need to be looking fabulous enough for him to want to chew his own arm off and beg me to take him back, but not so fabulous that it looks like I've made any effort whatsoever, for him.

Hmmmm, what to wear? I've got butterflies.

Before I knew it the clock read 10pm.

11pm.

11.30pm. I was getting close to tears. By the time I rang him, I was shaking.
    'Where are you?'
    He said he was coming straight over.
    Called Sue. Immediately. She's so good in a crisis.
    'Abi – prepare yourself – he's going to take his things and he's going to go. You've got to be ready for that. Be strong. Don't open yourself up to getting hurt.'

The doorbell rang.

I nearly bit myself trying to stop my lip quivering. Was convinced I'd cry the moment I clapped eyes on him, but at the same time couldn't wait to see his face. As soon as I opened the door he was begging me to believe that all the stuff in the papers wasn't true, that they'd been lying . . . Gradually he began convincing me. I knew my inability to believe him wasn't helping us to resurrect what we'd had.

And what he was saying was everything I wanted to hear.

He stayed for ages, but getting back what we had wasn't going to be easy.

'I'll call you.'

24th December 2005

Went home to Lincolnshire with a big smile on my face. Couldn't have asked for a better Christmas present.

26th December 2005

The shots from me in Dubai are in the *Sun* and the *Star*, one double page and one cover. Oh how I love a slow news week.

27th December 2005

4–9pm lesson with voice coach.
    Had a heart-to-heart with Lee this evening. He says he had no idea how bad I felt when we split up. Says he thought I wasn't arsed, that while we were together I'd often go off and leave him and have nights out. That my partying seemed more important.
    And maybe I was pushing him away – showing him my worst

behaviour just to see how much he could take. Challenging him to leave me. And in a way, he did.

28th December 2005

Had a session with the voice coach all day. This is hard work! And it's going to be relentless until the play starts.

Lee wants to make it up to me.

'I need time,' I warned him. Can't give him the upper hand again, not yet . . .

29th December 2005

Having a massive New Year's Eve party. I'm going to town – I might not ever be able to afford it again, so while I can I'm going to have the party I've always wanted. I'm calling it 'Abigail's Party', naturally!

My manager texted me today: 'I can't believe you've got me Googling "hire a midget".'

Not sure whether to invite Lee. I want to be in control of our relationship this time, which means not worrying about us all night.

30th December 2005

I love him. Of course Lee should come.

31st December 2005

Didn't invite him.

And had the best New Year's Eve EVER. Must've spent about four grand on getting the house ready. Paid for all the drinks, hired waiters, men on the door for security, light rigging, sound-system, a DJ – the lot. All I wanted was to give my friends the most brilliant time. It was fancy dress. And the theme was . . .

'Abi Titmuss.'

Genius! Miranda's idea, not mine. 'Inspired!' I laughed when a sea of blonde wigs, nurses' outfits and false tits started spilling through the door. That was the men. All my girls just came as tarts, which didn't go unnoticed.

It was still rocking at 9am. My poor neighbours.

2006

'Everyone's just laughing at me; I hate it. Big breasts, big ass, big deal. Can't I be anything else? Gee, how long can you be sexy?'

Marilyn Monroe

2nd January 2006

Lee didn't call today. I am panicking already and that has made me realise that, despite his show of emotion, I have been so deeply hurt that I no longer trust his love, so if he doesn't ring I'm more worried than I would normally be. I hope he can convince me.

3rd January 2006

There's a half page in the *Sun*, along with a drop-in of my *Loaded* Las Vegas cover. Me, half-naked, sprawled on the casino table. The news story beside my piece reads: 'Official: today is the worst day of the year'.

Not for me it isn't.

14th January 2006

So glad I've got this play. Gives me a sense of purpose at last.

20th January 2006

It's in all the papers. And the *Sun*'s Victoria Newton can't resist a dig:

'Abi Titmuss is to make her West-End stage debut, in *Two Way Mirror*, by Arthur Miller. The glamour girl will be playing a prostitute – at least she has already done the research.'

Ha Ha Ha Haaaaaaaaaaaaaaaaaaa.

25th January 2006

So not sure what to do about the hair. Emma has made it clear she's not keen on me being brunette, but says it's up to me.

Have been umming and ahhing about it for days. Lee says I should go for it.

26th January 2006

Finally plucked up the courage. Booked a hair appointment. Eeek. Two days to go.

28th January 2006

It took hours. All my extensions are gone, no more blonde bombshell. I'm now the proud owner of a short brown, shiny bob. I look like a newsreader.

Lee went to the pub over the road while he waited. He was pissed as a newt by the time it was finished.

'I love it!' he gushed.

Wasn't sure if it was the drink talking, but didn't care; it's what I needed to hear.

Got home and stared at myself in the mirror for ages. It's like I'm a totally different person. But I think I can get used to it. Yep, it actually looks nice.

29th January 2006

I hate it.

Walked to the shops and no one looked at me. Not one person. Even my oldest friends don't recognise me. Walked into a bar and Miranda and Donna looked right past me. I had to put my face in front of theirs and grin like a madman before there was any flicker of recognition.

'Oh, I didn't realise it was you!' Miranda laughed.

Came out of the bar and passed a couple of paparazzi. Not one flashbulb went off.

This is what my management said would happen – 'You won't be "Abi Titmuss" any more.' Is that what I want?

Well, yes. I think.

1st–4th February 2006

Rehearsals with voice coach.

5th February 2006

Ridiculous story in the *People* about me and Lee Ryan. Apparently we were 'all over each other' at some hotel in Liverpool. Purlease. Another man I've never met. Never even been in the same room as him. And he's so not my type.

6th February 2006

Lee's on a golf trip with one of his mates who has just proposed to his girlfriend. As I got into bed I couldn't stop the question 'What would you do if Lee actually proposed?'

And deep down I know I wouldn't accept and I have to ask myself why?

Because you can't let yourself trust him.

10th February 2006

Should I have been a bit more modest about buying this house? How am I possibly going to fill five bedrooms? I've bought it as an investment though, to be honest. Don't see myself staying here for years. Make hay while 'the *Sun*' shines!

It's set in a little mews in Islington with a massive plush kitchen on the ground floor as you walk in, and the lounge is upstairs with a balcony at the front and bedrooms up another floor. I feel like a real lady of the manor. Lady Titters of North London. Baroness von Tittentrap.

12th February 2006

There's a colour spread in the *People* – I'm in my Missoni bikini. it's one of the set-ups I did in Dubai before Christmas.

'Ahoy Pair Abi!

One tourist who spotted Abi, 30, in her skimpy bikini said: "Talk about a head-turner – we thought it couldn't get any hotter until she arrived on the sand."'

The cheese they come out with is astounding sometimes. 'One tourist', my arse. One journalist on the graveyard shift, more like.

6th–13th February 2006

Rehearsals. Soooo don't feel ready for this. Am shitting myself. What if I forget my words? What if I freeze? People are going to be willing me to fail.

Ten days till preview night. Aaaargh!

20th February 2006

The *Star* are very naughty sometimes. There's an old shot of me on the cover wrapped in nothing but a feather boa with the promise inside of pictures of 'Abi as you've never seen her before – her most shocking pics inside'. Turn a few pages in and it's a picture of me in a smart suit we took to promote the play before I turned brunette – 'Abi with clothes on!'

24th February 2006

There's a 'holiday' pic of me in the *Star*. They're making out I've been in Spain during a break from rehearsals. Thing is, my hair's blonde in the photo, which makes this an old picture. Besides, as if I've actually got time to sit on a beach! I need every second I can to practise this before the press piranhas come to eat me alive.

The *Daily Sport* has also run a beach shot. And again, it's from ages ago. Hmm.

28th February 2006

Preview night.

I warned the director, Mike, there would be press here this evening. But he wouldn't listen. Oh no. 'It's just for friends and family,' he insisted. 'We don't get sneaky tabloids in the theatre, they only come to press nights when they're invited.'

He made feel like I was being presumptuous, full of myself. He doesn't know what they are like though so I can't blame him. He's just doing his best; we are all terrified. This play would be a huge undertaking for any experienced actor, let alone me. This is Arthur MILLER. A TWO-HANDER.

I knew the media will be dying to see me fuck it all up.

They were.

Every single one of the papers had turned out for my first preview. The first time I had stepped out on stage in nine years, since a university production of *Life of Brian*. We hadn't even had a full dress rehearsal. But I still went out there and gave it all I had.

As I was speaking my heart felt like it was going to leap out of my chest, it was beating so hard. I was acutely aware of the front row consisting entirely of journalists with notebooks on their laps, scribbling notes every time I opened my mouth.

Then the unthinkable, worst-case scenario for any actor happened. The nerves and pressure got to me and I dried on one line.

You could hear everyone in the theatre holding their breath, and smiling. This is what they wanted, but I didn't go to pieces, Jay totally saved me, I picked it straight up and somehow we carried on fine.

The second half went much better. But of course all I could think about when it was over was that fluff. Berating myself remorselessly. Jay was so wonderful, I feel so dreadfully guilty that I had let him down, I have to conquer that stage fright somehow.

Lee hardly noticed though, he seemed shell-shocked afterwards. It was like he was blown away seeing me up there, seeing what I could do. My friends and family were too, my mum was in tears.

I am exhausted.

Now I just have to do it all again tomorrow night. And six nights a week for the next month. And get it RIGHT.

2nd March 2006

The *Sun*:

'Jittery Abi Titmuss had an audience in stitches as she made her West-End stage debut – and forgot her lines. The busty ex-nurse – famous for appearing in a home-made sex video with fallen TV star John Leslie, 41 – had to have the words whispered to her. One witness said, "She looked extremely uncomfortable and out of her depth, really wooden. Her American accent was all over the place."'

And thank God for my friends at the *Daily Star*:

'Sex bomb Abi Titmuss exploded on to the West-End stage doing what she does best – flashing the flesh in a sexy nightie . . . there's no hiding the star quality of gorgeous Abi, 30. She proved she's more than just a pretty face . . . There were a few first-night nerves . . . and she occasionally missed a cue. But it was an accomplished performance – and the skimpy costumes won't disappoint fans.'

Tonight was the official press night. I'd just been slated and here I was, expected to try and act my way through even more analysis.

'Ignore the tabloids,' said Mike. 'This evening is about the critics that really matter – we've got theatrical publications like *The Stage* and the *Fringe Report* coming to see you. This is your chance to shine.'

No pressure then.

I was petrified but I did it (isn't that the definition of bravery?). And I got through it. Remembered all my lines, was fluid and completely immersed myself in the emotions of the characters. Still absolutely nowhere near good enough in my book though.

My PR Roberta afterwards, 'Fuck me Abi, no one can say you haven't got balls.'

3rd March 2006

It was the real opening night tonight, for the public. Was terrified again but the audience were incredible. And after having had to wince my way through the night with all the hacks, this was a joy.

Lee and my parents couldn't stop gushing afterwards – 'We're so proud of you!'

You know what? I'm proud of me too. It has been an exceptionally trying time for everyone involved in the play but we are all doing so well. I will be forever grateful to Mike and the producer, Sue Scott-Davidson for believing in me and giving me the chance to perform this wonderful piece.

5th March 2006

Lee's been to see the play nearly every night, bless him.

Not that he gets much in the way of reward. I'm exhausted when I get home. Then all I do is lie in bed and worry. Here I am, doing what I've wanted for so long, and all I can think about is that I should be better, and what's going to happen to me when it's all over?

7th March 2006

Was on *Richard and Judy* this afternoon. They're always so warm and welcoming. Judy kept raving about my new hair. It's surreal being perched on their sofa and thinking about what I've been through since I first sat there doing my screen test.

11th March 2006

They've written about me in their newspaper column.

'Abi Titmuss came on our show the other day and I hardly recognised her. Instead of the usual glamour-model coiffure of platinum-blonde waist-length hair extensions she was sporting a shoulder-length dark brown cut that made her look chic and stylish. I didn't even notice her bosom.'

Genius. I love them.

13th March 2006

I've got a good review! Actually I've got three! No one had let me see them when they first came out, but tonight I got into my dressing room and Sue, the producer, had had blown up and laminated copies of the *Metro*, *The Stage* and the *Fringe Report* and stuck them by my mirror. Bless her! It was such an amazing feeling. These were the reviews that mattered to me. Forget the tabloids. These were the real critics.

The *Fringe Report* said the play proved I could act, that I had

'grace and elegance of movement, a perceptive and effective stage presence, and the intangible quality of letting the audience want to watch her. Like any other performer on their first professional outing, there are technical items that can be tightened up and evolved – actors spend their lives doing that. But the quality is there now.'

I burst into tears and then started laughing. I'd done it!

The Stage said, 'Abi Titmuss proves she is not just a celebrity and magazine cover-girl but an actress of genuine promise. Playing two very different roles, she not only demonstrates her versatility but delivers her lines with attractive warmth and conviction, holding the stage even in moments of repose.'

The *Metro* said I'd nailed the accent – well, they said it was passable which is the same thing as far as I'm concerned. Am so relieved. And happy.

But then of course I started picking holes. The *Metro* had also said I occasionally sounded like I didn't understand what I was saying and that we talked over each other – but the talking over was deliberate, it's what the director wanted!

I pored over every word of the other reviews again, trying to find fault. But ultimately they were bloody good.

15th March 2006

I'm in a constant state of anxiety. Despite the good reviews, all I can think about is how the audience is reacting. My life has become the play and it can't be good for Lee. But I don't have room in my head for anything else. And although I have wholly put an end to partying now I am focused on the play, at the end of the night, I'm so stressed that all I want to do is come home and have a quiet drink.

16th March 2006

Lee came to watch me again tonight but I didn't want him to sit in the audience – I asked him to wait for me in the dressing room, just so I could have the comfort of his face as soon as I came off stage.

17th March 2006

The stress is getting too much. Am hardly sleeping. What's wrong with me? This is what I wanted!

18th March 2006

Had another fitful night. This morning Lee started telling me about how when he was at Manchester United they had a psychologist who taught them how to cope under pressure. We tried some of the techniques and it really helped.

Sometimes that man really surprises me. He's a laid-back Northern bloke and it's not often he offers much in the way of emotional insight, but he was being really intelligent and supportive. At that moment it occurred to me what a big deal it must have been for him to go out and play football in front of all those people. I'd never considered that before. I'd just been thinking about me.

As always.

26th March 2006

Sometimes I wish I could stop myself reading the newspapers. In the *Mirror* today there's a picture of me and Lilo Lil from the eighties comedy *Bread* saying 'Separated at birth . . . Abi Titmuss, 30, looked the spit of drunken tart Lilo Lil (Eileen Pollock) with her new dark brown hair.'

I laughed at first. And then got paranoid.

'Hang on, I don't look like her . . . do I?'

Must've harped on about it to Lee for about three hours this evening, poor bugger.

He told me he loved my new hair and that I looked gorgeous. He reckons I could do anything to my barnet and he'd still love me.

2nd April 2006

Last night of *Two Way Mirror*.

Mike warned me it would be like this, but I didn't anticipate the anti-climax would hit me so hard. Instead of feeling elated by what I've achieved over the last few weeks, I'm crushed. What if I never get to experience this again? This has been my dream. I don't want it to end.

Lee tried to cheer me up by pointing out that it meant we got to spend quality time together.

Perhaps that's what I'm worried about. Whether we're really solid enough to stay together when there's nothing to stop me thinking about the past . . .

5th April 2006

If people ask what I do, I can now finally tell them I'm an actress. It's so liberating. For once I don't need to reference underwear, sex or my ex-boyfriend.

This is where I want to be.

6th April 2006

Went to the gym and when I came out there was an anonymous note on my car saying 'I like your arse.' Flattering but slightly spooky. I looked at my arse in the wing mirror. Well, he's only human. Hee hee.

7th April 2006

Flew to Dubai to meet Lee. He went out a couple of days ago because of some football thing. Boy, I need some sunshine! Still feeling a bit deflated that the play is over, but it's glorious to get away from dreary old London. Have arranged some set-up shots with one of the pap agencies of us on the beach. Lee's not keen, but have managed to twist his arm. I explained that if I don't do it some greasy pap will and I'll be looking over my shoulder the whole time instead of relaxing, so I play the game.

Also, I need to pay the mortgage on 'Titmuss Towers' and I'm not daft – these shots offer a lot of money. We're staying in an amazing apartment – it's about ten storeys high with floor to ceiling windows – but as soon as I got in there I felt dizzy, as if I had vertigo. I've never experienced that before. And weirdly, it felt like a sign that something's not right in me, emotionally.

I didn't mention it to Lee though.

8th April 2006

Had some snaps of me and Lee done on the beach – best to get them out of the way early.

Keep having waves of uncertainty about us. Every time I see him talking to another girl – even if it's a pretty waitress in a restaurant – it puts my hackles up. Of course if I say anything, he bristles and I can feel it's pushing him away.

9th April 2006

Spent the day on the beach then had dinner with my aunt and uncle who live here. I immediately started picking at Lee during the meal, and didn't even realise until he went to the loo when my uncle said, 'Abi, be nice to him! What's going on?'

What is going on?

I think I'm still so unhappy and full of doubt about the past that I'm letting it show in unrelated ways: having a go at him for his table manners or for his shirt not being tucked in. In actual fact, I'm just frustrated with everything that happened and I can't bring myself to trust him.

I was embarrassed nonetheless; I shouldn't have done it in front of my aunt and uncle.

10th April 2006

Went to a club with a few of Lee's football mates. Got completely hammered and Lee had to carry me home. Apparently I was unconscious. That's actually frightened me a bit.

14th April 2006

Back home and feel really flat. I thought I'd be inundated with offers of work but when I called my management they said there's been nothing right so far.

Why? I had some good reviews, didn't I? I thought this was it, that the whole world would open up for me.

Oh no.

What the fuck have I done? I've cut all my hair off, dyed it brown – I don't look like Abi Titmuss any more, nobody recognises me. God, have I made a catastrophic mistake?

15th April 2006

Saw Mum today. She told me there had been death threats against me while I was in the play. Some nutter had sent them directly to the theatre, knowing that I was there.

WHAT THE HELL?

It had apparently been decided by everyone that she should be the one to break the news to me. My poor mum, having to do that.

Everyone knew except me – my management, my family, the theatre . . . They'd taken the decision not to tell me because I would've been in too much of a state.

Now I know why there was always such a fuss about getting me out of the stage door and into a car – there was always a security guard with me. And here was me just thinking it was because I was so 'famous'.

Death threats?

Do people hate me that much?

16th April 2006

The *Sunday Mirror* has bought the snaps from Dubai.

'I'M SO ABI; EXCLUSIVE SLIMLINE BEAUTY ALL LOVED UP ON HOL WITH FOOTIE ACE LEE'.

Lee was actually quite chuffed when he saw them.

17th April 2006

The *Mirror* has used even more of the shots today as well. Double whammy! This time they've got quotes from Lee's mum Gail to back it up. At least it's all nice things.

'LEE'S SO ABI, SAYS HIS MUM'.

Sometimes I wonder what they'd do for headlines if my name were something like Bridget.

'Lovesick Lee Sharpe has whisked Abi Titmuss away for a romantic break to Dubai after confessing to his mum how much he missed her. Gail said yesterday: "I would be delighted if he married Abi. It would be fantastic to see him settle down. And I would be thrilled if Abi became my daughter-in-law."'

And I'm so thrilled she said that. If she actually did say that, of course. It's not just the negative stuff that they 'embellish'.

Who cares, though, it's lovely. Maybe someone would want me as their 'wife, mother or daughter' after all.

20th April 2006

Have been exercising like a demon. Not a day's gone by since the play finished when I haven't donned the Lycra in some form or other. I can tell it's starting to piss Lee off. He thinks I care more about how I look than being with him. He's gone back to Leeds for a few days and really wanted me to go with him but I said I couldn't – I had to see my personal trainer.

Maybe he has a point. I never do what he wants.

But I can't get fat again. I need something to make me feel good about myself. Besides, if I'm thin he will want me even more. And he'll be much less likely to want to stray.

Hmmm, having just re-read that I can't help wondering if that is an entirely healthy attitude towards one's relationship. And body.

23rd April 2006

Did an interview with the *News of the World* magazine a couple of weeks ago. It's out today.

The headline is: 'Lee would never cheat on me. Abi Titmuss on why she's back in love with Lee Sharpe.'

As I flicked through the paper I realised that the more time I've had to think, the less sure I am. Did I get back together with Lee for the right reasons? I don't think I did. I was weak, and I wanted to believe him.

It's not right. We're not right. I've been pushing him away so much recently I'm pretty sure he's had enough anyway. It's so sad. What's happened to our island love-story?

3rd May 2006

I feel fat and ugly. I know I've been to the gym, but every time I look in the mirror I feel shit. Have become really insecure again. Lee and I are hardly speaking. Every time he talks to another woman I get jealous. Then I just drink to numb my feelings. I'm driving him away.

I'm so confused.

4th May 2006

Lee and I were sitting on the sofa staring at the TV all night. Then Sue rang and for some reason I immediately went into 'I'm so happy' mode. I even found myself giggling at nothing just to show Lee how fun I could be if I wanted to.

That was the final straw.

It was over.

He left. I told him I didn't want him to go but I didn't make a scene, like I would've done when I was younger. I wanted to scream and cry and hit him and kiss him and hold him. But I didn't. I held it all in. He said his manager was in London so he'd stay with him.

I dialled Sue but by the time she answered I was crying so much I couldn't speak.

5th May 2006

So sad.

We've been texting but there's not much to say except 'Are you OK?' and neither of us are.
I'm so sad and angry at us both for not making it work.
I blame myself. If only I had been thinner, prettier, smarter, more together, drank less, been a better girlfriend.

Hang on. Haven't I been here before?

6th May 2006

Am devastated. Also am suddenly terrified that I genuinely don't know how to have a successful relationship.
This was a fairytale love-story, a dream come true, we met on a beach, at a place called LOVE ISLAND for fuck's sake, it was on a plate for me, he *loved me*. How can I have messed THAT up?

7th May 2006

When you know it's the right thing to do, why does it still seem so hard? Lee texted again. I told him to stop. We have to.

28th May 2006

News of the World:

'Abi Titmuss and Lee Sharpe have split AGAIN – this time for keeps, the *News of the World* can reveal.'

Well, now it's finally official.

8th June 2006

Oh my Christ. I have never been so terrified in my entire life. I came home from the supermarket at about 10.30pm and started unloading the shopping in the kitchen. I noticed there was a light on upstairs and thought, 'That's weird, I thought I'd turned them all off. Maybe it was the cleaner?' Then I carried on. All of a sudden I heard a noise . . . a door closing upstairs.

Shit, what was it?

I walked towards the stairs and my first (and stupid) instinct was to go up to the lounge where the light was coming from, then I heard a smash and I froze. It was the most chilling feeling.

Someone was in the house.

I ran outside and looked up towards the balcony – there was a guy standing there, and he was starting to climb down the wall with a bag on his back.

A bag full of my belongings!

In seconds, the fear dissipated and all I felt was anger.
     'What the FUCK are you doing in my house?' I screamed.
     'Oh sorry,' he mumbled but I realised he was still climbing down the wall towards me. And there was no one else in sight.
     Shit, I didn't know what to do next so I legged it back inside and shut the front door. I've had death threats – who says they're not from him?
     I grabbed the phone to dial 999 but my fingers wouldn't work, I was shaking all over the place and kept missing the keys. I looked out of the window – had he gone? Oh my God – there could be more people upstairs! I opened the front door and went back outside, Two of my neighbours had come out – they'd heard me shouting.
     'Are you OK?' they asked, then offered to call the police and

took me into their house. I couldn't stop trembling. I was so frightened. The police arrived in twenty minutes. Good job I wasn't being attacked, then.

They asked me to describe him and then they said the forensics would be in to dust everything for fingerprints. I immediately had to text Lee. Didn't even think about it. I felt so scared. I needed him.

'I've just had a break in. The police are here.'

Minutes later he called in a panic to see if I was OK.
He'd been in a nightclub but came straight out to call me.

He does still care.

After that I called Donna and she drove straight round to get me. I can't stay at home. Feel like I can never go back there again.

9th June 2006

Didn't want to go back to the house but had to let the forensics in. There is now black dust over everything. I can see his prints all over the light switch, my drawers, table, surfaces, walls . . . it makes me never want to touch those things again.

Went back to Donna's. She says I can stay as long as I like.

Lee's been on the phone seeing how I am. I know we've made the break but I cannot deny it feels so good to be in touch with him again.

10th June 2006

Went back to the house with Sue to see what was missing. He took a load of my photos, and knickers. I feel sick.

I'm scared to go upstairs in my own home now, even in the

daytime; it's ridiculous. My heart starts pounding and I start shaking as I go up. I'm terrified he will come back. He broke in through my bedroom on the top floor so I can't even contemplate sleeping there. I brought my quilt down and I am on the sofa every night.

Cannot believe what an impact the break-in has had on my psyche. I've heard about this happening when people are burgled but to be honest I thought they were exaggerating. Add to this that I have had death threats this year and it makes it a hundred times worse. Every little noise makes me jump.

With everything that has happened in the last two years and with Lee recently, I feel like I'm being pushed further and further towards the edge of a cliff and this could be the feather that knocks me off. I'm trying desperately to keep my balance.

I'm so frightened.

11th June 2006

The stolen pictures aren't even rude ones (I don't do those any more) – but they're special to me, and to think he's gawping at images of me and my friends sends shivers down my spine.

12th June 2006

There's a story about the burglary in the *Sun*:

'Abi Titmuss is reportedly distraught after photos of her were stolen in a burglary. In the shots she's fully clothed and she's worried they'll be published on the internet. It could ruin her reputation.'

Oh, my sides are splitting.

12th July 2006

Have spent the last two weeks in training every day; it's like the gym is my new boyfriend, I've seen it so much. Since splitting up with Lee this has been my raison d'être. I've still got my dark hair, but have extensions again – they make me feel more of a woman. Am shooting a cover for *Zoo* magazine in a few weeks to hail my return. The coverline is going to be 'Abi's back!' I need this. It's giving me something to work towards. And sad as it is, there's a part of me that wants Lee to see it on the shelf in the newsagents and think, 'Look what I've lost'.

24th August 2006

Zoo shoot went amazingly today. I've worked so hard on myself and it shows. No airbrushing necessary, to quote the photographer. I'm finally getting my confidence back, for the umpteenth time.

I enjoyed myself but gnawing at my insides is the sadness that I haven't even had so much as an audition for another acting job since the play.

I think about it every day. I thought I'd 'proved myself'. Was an Arthur Miller two-hander not enough? Clearly not. Yes, I've had a few meetings with producers and scripts sent to me, but they're either no good (opening scene, my clothes fall off) or they never seem to come to fruition. It's so frustrating. I've told my manager that I just want to get into some repertory theatre or something and earn my stripes, but they think I should stay strong and bide my time.

At this rate I'll be playing the grandmother.

4th September 2006

Am in the best shape I've been for years. And I need to be. In eight days it's the shoot for my 2007 calendar and it's the first time I've done it as a brunette. As much as I hate it, appearance is everything in this business (especially for a woman, grrrr. Don't get me started) and I have a lot to prove. And that's what I'm going to do.

I console myself with the knowledge that Marilyn Monroe did a scandalous nude calendar.

Willy Camden's photographing it so I know it'll be perfect. We've got two days. One of the days we'll shoot in a big old Victorian house. The other is in the penthouse suite of the Soho Hotel. Willy called me tonight to say I can have the penthouse for the night afterwards. That means I can invite someone.

Let's think about this:

I don't want to stay there on my own.
I do want someone I care about to get to share it.
I do want a bloke.

Oh, who am I kidding, the first person I thought of was Lee.

11th September 2006

I took a deep breath and texted Lee to tell him that I've got a penthouse for the night after my calendar shoot. I asked him if he wanted to come down and share the mini bar and have a laugh?

Thank God he said yes.

12th September 2006

The shoot was going brilliantly – Willy was raving about the shots and I felt great because I knew he was genuinely excited. I was dying for Lee to arrive.

I couldn't have timed it better either. When he walked in the door he was confronted with the sight of yours truly sprawled naked on the bed, with Willy Camden standing over me taking pictures and shouting 'Yeah! Come on, baby! You're gorgeous!' I looked over at Lee standing open-mouthed by the door and winked.

But after the shoot, as we sat on our own in the enormous, plush penthouse I knew deep down we were sitting there for very different reasons. I hoped he might want me back. The problem is I still love him, and it's hard for me to switch that off.

To someone looking on, it would probably seem crazy – here I am in a penthouse, many men's fantasy, physically at my peak and have just shot a fantastic, unbelievably sexy calendar, and yet I'm just as insecure and vulnerable as the next girl.

20th September 2006

I had a PA in Belfast and David Walliams called to say that the *Little Britain* tour was in Dublin. We keep in touch and he'd asked me to come and see the show many times. I'd said, if it coincides with a PA that would be perfect and now it did.

I got the train from Belfast to Dublin to see him. He paid for me to stay in the hotel with him and all the crew, which was so sweet.

He always seems to get in touch when I'm feeling low, as if he has a sixth sense. I had no hesitation in going to see them.

And it was a brilliant night. At one point on stage Matt Lucas started teasing him about being gay – and David smirked, 'I think you'll find Abi Titmuss is in the audience and she can vouch for me.' Then the whole audience turned round to gawp. It was hilarious.

Afterwards we went to Lillie's Bordello and had a couple of cocktails, but I didn't even get tiddly, for once. I told David about the fact that I was thinking of writing a book, my diaries, but was worried. He reckons that he expects a whole chapter devoted to him!

We called it a night at around 1am and then went to his room and had a long chat while he packed his things for the next stop tomorrow. And I went back to my hotel room alone.

3rd October 2006

Have started drinking again. Am going out all the time. The weeks are all rolling into one another. Can't be bothered to write diary any more. There's no point. There's nothing to say.

My life is empty.

'Get over yourself, Abi.'

Sue

3rd November 2006

Sue called me today and gave me a right talking to. She said I needed to pull myself together, stop going out so much and stop being so self-absorbed. She actually said, 'Get over yourself.' I laughed, but she was serious. And I deserved it. I've been a crap friend lately, I know that. But I can't give anyone anything. I can just about focus on myself these days.

The only way I can describe how I feel is that it's like there's a gaping void inside me that I have to fill. I've discovered there are various means of doing this: food, drink and men. But the high is transient and I am always left feeling worse than when I started. I'm in that vicious circle again.

Deeply, deeply unhappy.

There must be more to life than this?

2nd January 2007

OK, so I've known deep-down I've been depressed and unhappy. But Christmas was rock bottom. Went out the night before Christmas Eve on a massive two-day bender. I was supposed to be driving home to see Mum for Christmas, but when I got back to my house it was 4pm and I couldn't even speak, let alone drive. I texted her and made some excuse that I was feeling ill.

I woke up eighteen hours later on the sofa (that's normal, it's been months since the intruder but I'm still too scared to sleep in my own bed), still wearing the same clothes I'd been partying in. I'd completely missed Christmas Day. I was on my own, in a big house, and I had no food apart from porridge. I was a mess.

I somehow pulled myself together by Boxing Day, but as I was driving back to Mum's I felt lower than I've ever felt in my life. I hate my life and I hate myself. Something has to give. Am so depressed. Saw Mum and burst into tears.

'First I took a drink, and then the drink took me . . .'

A friend

9th February 2007

Last night was my thirty-first birthday. At least I think it was. I had ten of my friends round to my house for drinks, then we went for dinner, then to a private karaoke bar, then back to mine for a party.

I don't even remember leaving the house. Right now, I don't even know where my toothbrush is. That's because I moved house this morning. I purposely booked the move for today thinking, 'That'll keep me on the straight and narrow.'

I hadn't been to bed when the removal men arrived. Nor had I packed one single thing. I sat on the step and said, 'Please just do it,' and then it was as if time stood still for me as I sat there while they were on speeded-up film all around me, packing, wrapping and carrying.

When they drove away from my new house I was left with everything I possess in boxes in the sitting room, with no labels on.

10th February 2007

I have come to the conclusion that I am no longer doing a marvellous job of running my life (no shit, Sherlock).

I need some help.

I called my long-suffering mum. She called my management for me. They're going to help me find a therapist.

I feel sorry for him or her already.

'I knew how third rate I was. I could actually feel my lack of discernible talent, as if it were cheap clothes I was wearing inside. But my God how I wanted to learn.'

Marilyn Monroe

Epilogue

For some time I had been living day-to-day in a constant state of pain over my past, and fear of the future. My self-esteem had been low for a few years and my confidence had gone too. I had no idea who or what 'Abi Titmuss' was and I felt worthless and lost. So much for fame and fortune.

I was aware that to some people I represented some form of success that they even wanted to emulate. I was horrified when girls asked me how I 'did it'. 'Put your education first, please don't try and copy me. You can do better with your life!' I shouted into the ear of many a girl in a provincial nightclub, before I stepped on to the stage to greet the swaying crowd.

Although I was of course unendingly grateful for the money I had made, I could place no real value on any work I had done. Deep down I agreed with anyone who criticised me. 'Who can blame them?' I would think. The one huge exception to this was the Arthur Miller play. Oh, how deeply proud I am of that.

I was in a cycle of self-obsession, self-loathing and self-pity. My head was wrapped in darkness. How could I ever redeem myself when so many of the things that caused this pain had been public, and were now on record in files forever? How do you cope with that? Which of your friends can relate to that and help you? No one.

I felt hopeless and trapped. I used drink, drugs, sex, food, shopping . . . anything I could to numb the pain and fill the void inside me. I was spiritually bankrupt. No one saw just how badly I was doing of course; I would either be acting the clown and glamour girl or isolating myself at home for days with my phone switched off. There was no middle ground.

'If I could wave a magic wand, what would you want?' said my therapist Robert at our first meeting. Did I say I wanted to be happy? Have a great job? Be in love? No.

'To be someone else,' I replied, absolutely truthfully, through my tears. How awful to have reached the point where I was sitting on a therapist's couch, I thought. How self-indulgent of me. And how very clichéd for a celebrity.

I had no idea then that this was to be one of the biggest turning points of my life so far.

As well as his wonderful warmth, his time and his skill as a therapist, one of the greatest things that Robert did for me was to give me a book called *The Power of Now* by Eckhart Tolle. It took me a few months to pick it up and I finally opened it and began to read when I went on holiday on my own to Majorca.

I couldn't put it down and even burnt my back one day, lying by the pool in the sun, because I was so engrossed. The book gave me answers I had been looking for for a very long time and I felt an indescribable sense of relief, as if someone had emptied a few of the sandbags I'd been accumulating for years and carrying on my back in a giant, invisible rucksack.

I began, slowly, to realise how much of life I had been missing, and how 'small and insignificant' I am in the great scheme of things, the universe and all that nonsense. It was time to forgive myself, accept what is and start being grateful for everything life had to offer me. I knew I was at the start of a journey and that it wasn't going to be easy, but my God . . . how I wanted to learn.

'The journey of a thousand miles begins with a single "oy".'
David M. Bader, from *Zen Judaism*

Therapy was the best thing I've ever done. It enveloped me, enlightened me and changed my life. At the beginning I would go three days a week, gradually moving down to twice, then once or twice a month. Now, although I know it's a phone call away, I don't need to visit at all.

One of the first things I knew I must do to maintain my path to a better self was stop or at least cut right down on my drinking. Some people can have a couple of drinks and go home to bed. I, it seems, cannot.

So what have I been doing since my epiphany in February 2007?

Shortly after starting therapy I had a phone call from Emma at my agency one day.

'Right, missus, I've got some news that's going to cheer you up.'
I wasn't very hopeful.
'What is it, a personal appearance in Croydon?' I said, rather ungratefully, from my foetal position in front of *Frasier*.
'You've won an award!'
'Uhh,' I grunted. '"Caner of the Year"?'
'Noooo.' She savoured the surprise. 'It's for the play.'
I jumped up, biscuit crumbs flying everywhere.
'What did you say?'
'Best West-End Debut. From the *Fringe Report*.'

'What?' I couldn't take it in. 'Are you winding me up? PLEASE say you're not winding me up?'

'Their critic loved you in the play, Abi.'

I burst into tears.

'Do you have any idea how much this means to me?'

She did.

Then in April I took part in a show for ITV2 called *Deadline* in which I had to take on the role of both paparazzi and journalist.

I met a lovely friend on that show – Imogen Lloyd Webber. She's a theatre producer and at the time we first met we were both single – she'd just written a book called *The Single Girl's Guide* which I thought was brilliant. She asked me to audition for a one-woman show about it in Edinburgh. I wasn't right for that part in the end but I was happy just to have a chance. I finally feel I'm at the stage in my life when I can do something like that and I'm confident enough in my ability to act.

I spent a lot of the rest of last year seeing Robert and just living a normal, healthy, happier life.

I hadn't travelled on public transport for five years, not because I thought I was above it, simply because I felt vulnerable. Well would you want to be squashed in a tube carriage with men that had probably watched you have sex? Getting on a train again was a bit strange at first. Great though, and I love my Oyster card!

Other little things improved my quality of life too. I no longer felt my heart pounding every time I stepped out of the house because there were men on the doorstep with cameras, or worse, hiding or following me.

I could go to Sainsbury's without a hat and scarf on and people whispering and pointing and staring at what I had in my basket every time.

I could have coffee with my friends without people trying to get pictures of me on their phones when I wasn't looking. Crazy as it sounds though, I'm still nervous about eating outside at cafes or near the window, in case someone gets a picture of me shovelling food in and calls me fat.

More importantly, I put effort into all my relationships – not just whichever bloke was around at that time, or the people who were buying me drinks – but my friends and family. Miranda and Donna once wrote in a birthday card to me: 'This is your day, it's all about YOU' as a joke, because it was ALWAYS all about me. I was so self-absorbed. Hopefully not so much now.

I've already got over the hurdle of my second play, and being employed as 'an actress' again. At the start of 2008 I finished a month's run of a comedy by Gavin Davis, called *Fat Christ*, performed at the famous old King's Head Theatre in Islington.

From the first day of rehearsals to the tear-jerking last night, working on this production was an unmitigated joy for me. Heather, the director, was patient and supportive with me, as were the rest of the cast and I learned so much. We all laughed every night, from the minute we arrived for a show to the minute we left, and luckily so did the audience (most days!).

I was even excited about having my name up outside the theatre. As my co-star Tim put it, 'Ah yes, haven't you just always wanted to see your name up in . . . chalk?'

'You're far better off without all that fake tan. Orange isn't the one, Abs.'

My mate Miranda

I've removed all my hair extensions and gone back to my 'natural' blonde. All the bunnies prefer it and so do I. I love what Dolly Parton said when asked if she minded being called a dumb blonde: 'No, because I'm not a real blonde.'

The fake nails are gone and I've finally beaten my fake tan 'addiction'. Yes, shock horror, I now have pure white, creamy, natural skin ('much better. Orange isn't the one Abs'– thanks Miranda). Most men actually hate fake tan and on the plus side my sheets don't look like the Turin Shroud in the morning.

My bunnies are still very much part of my life and our love for each other grows every day. Also, these days they no longer need worry when we go out for cocktails that we'll wake up the next morning in a ploughed field in Hampshire. (Yes, that did happen.)

To anyone dreaming of becoming famous, I would say this. Firstly, that it has brought me both good times and bad. 'Celebrity' is like a runaway rollercoaster: once you are on, it's almost impossible to get off, and you can't always control how fast it goes. I've had, and continue to have, some truly amazing experiences but I don't believe that the pursuit of fame, as a goal in itself, will bring you happiness (although it might get you a bigger house).

Secondly: having read my story – are you insane?!

As far as the future goes, I have absolutely no idea what will happen next week, let alone next year. But I'm going to enjoy every second of the journey.

As Tom O'Toole said to me, as 'Angie', in *Two Way Mirror*: 'You're a soap opera, kid, I keep waiting for the next instalment!'

Acknowledgements

Massive thanks to Lucie Cave for drawing this story out of me – I am really grateful for your patience and skill.

To my constant supporters: Mum, Dad, Alison, Ian and Al.

To my management company and second family – heartfelt thanks to Francis Ridley, Emma Rouse, Daniel Bee and all at Money.

Over at Headline I would like to thank my editor, Carly Cook – what can I say, we got there in the end! Also everyone else, who has shown such enthusiasm for the book, including: Emma Tait, Georgina Moore and Josh Ireland.

At William Morris Literary Agency, I would like to thank Rowan Lawton and Eugenie Furniss.

Massive thanks to Marisa Murray, Katie Perryman-Ford, Suzanne Egleton, Miranda, Donna Worling, Becki Houlston, Claire Rutherford, Kevyn Rowlands, Nadine Wilkie, Jonothan Sothcott – for putting up with my dramas, making me laugh and always supporting me through fat and thin.

Thanks to Andy Colley at Purus for giving me back my body confidence.

Also – Robert Batt, Genevieve Lyons, Naomi Palmer.

And finally thanks to Chubs – our secret.